WHISPERS

from the

WOODS

About the Author

Sandra Kynes describes herself as an explorer of Celtic history, myth, and magic. Her curiosity has taken her to live in New York City, Europe, England, Massachusetts, and back to the New York area. Spiritually, her inquisitiveness has led her to investigate the roots of Pagan belief and study ancient texts such as *The Mabinogion*. She is a member of the England-based Order of Bards, Ovates & Druids. In addition to leading rituals and healing circles, Sandra is a certified and registered yoga instructor as well as a Reiki practitioner.

Sandra created the nontraditional approach to feng shui using gemstones and crystals, which resulted in her first book, *Gemstone Feng Shui,* published by Llewellyn in 2002. Her second book, *A Year of Ritual*, was published by Llewellyn in 2004. Her writing has also been featured in Llewellyn's *Magical Almanac, Witches' Spell-a-Day Almanac,* and *Witches' Calendar* under the name Sedwyn.

WHISPERS

from the

WOODS

THE LORE & MAGIC OF TREES

SANDRA KYNES

Llewellyn Publications
Woodbury, Minnesota

First Edition
First Printing, 2006

Author photo by Lyle Koehnlein
Book design and layout by Joanna Willis
Cover images © 2005 by DigitalStock and PhotoDisc
Cover design by Ellen L. Dahl
Illustrations in part 2 by Melissa Gay; all other illustrations by Llewellyn art department

Llewellyn is a registered trademark of Llewellyn Worldwide, Ltd.

Library of Congress Cataloging-in-Publication Data
Kynes, Sandra, 1950–
    Whispers from the woods : the lore and magic of trees / Sandra Kynes.— 1st. ed.
        p.   cm.
    Includes bibliographical references and index.
    ISBN-13: 978-0-7387-0781-5
    ISBN-10: 0-7387-0781-3
        1. Spiritual life. 2. Trees—Psychic aspects. 3. Trees—Religious aspects. 4. Trees—Miscellanea.
    5. Trees—Folklore. 6. Trees—Mythology. I. Title.

BL624.K96 2006
202'.12—dc22
                                                                                                    2005051047

Llewellyn Worldwide does not participate in, endorse, or have any authority or responsibility concerning private business transactions between our authors and the public.
    All mail addressed to the author is forwarded but the publisher cannot, unless specifically instructed by the author, give out an address or phone number.
    Any Internet references contained in this work are current at publication time, but the publisher cannot guarantee that a specific location will continue to be maintained. Please refer to the publisher's website for links to authors' websites and other sources.

Llewellyn Publications
A Division of Llewellyn Worldwide, Ltd.
2143 Wooddale Drive, Dept. 0-7387-0781-3
Woodbury, MN 55125-2989, U.S.A.
www.llewellyn.com

Printed in the United States of America

Information comes softly from the natural world.
The seeker must listen carefully to hear the many voices that call.
Listen for whispers from the woods, and wisdom will come.

Also by Sandra Kynes

Gemstone Feng Shui

A Year of Ritual

Contents

PART TWO

Introduction

MODERN PAGANS HAVE CONTINUALLY SOUGHT ways to honor the natural world and live more closely with the rhythms and spirit of the land. Many find that drawing close to nature allows them to access different levels of energy and awareness, which can bring deeper meaning and spiritual satisfaction. Trees can function as a gateway to these different levels of being as they provide us with a better understanding of ourselves and our ancestors. A walk in the woods makes it easy to understand the awe and reverence our ancestors had for trees. However, the human-tree relationship had its beginnings long before people trod upon the earth.

Millions of years ago, trees evolved into giants of the planet, and became the most successful form of plant life in the competition for sunlight and other resources. While they created advantages for themselves, they were also steadfast providers for certain members of the animal kingdom. Small creatures sought protection from predators in the aerial arms of trees, and finding a convenient bounty of food aloft, they stayed and made their homes among the welcoming branches.

Establishing a symbiotic association with the trees, these creatures provided additional means for dispersing pollen and seeds. Some of these animals, classified as prosimians, developed their distinctive characteristics, such as both eyes in the front of the head, and evolved into the simians that eventually came down from the trees. Darwin explained the rest.

With these prosimians in mind, it could be said that if it were not for the trees we would not be here. Biologically speaking, it can also be said that we could not remain here if it weren't for the trees, as they are largely responsible for creating and maintaining Earth's atmosphere.

It was the "big blue marble" view of Earth and its atmosphere that sparked scientist James Lovelock's Gaia theory (Earth as a living, self-regulating entity). Lovelock said that when he saw pictures of Earth taken from outer space, he had an epiphany of the atmosphere burning like a blue flame.[1] He realized how crucial the cycles of the elements were for life, and how humans are part of the environment, not separate from it. As we breathe, we take oxygen into our bodies and it becomes part of us. Trees produce the oxygen we take in. We breathe out carbon dioxide and trees take that in. Because of this basic biology, we still have a symbiotic association with the trees. However, a great deal has transpired in this relationship since the time of the prosimians.

Biology aside, our civilization could not have developed without trees. After humans first attached sharpened stones to the ends of sticks to extend their reach as hunters, and kindled fires for warmth and cooking, there was no going back, because trees had taken on a new importance in human life. Providing the basics was just the beginning. The more we learned to use our brains and make plans, the more we relied on trees for shelter, furniture, and tools for almost everything. Wood for wagons, ships, and bridges to get us from here to there allowed people to spread out and travel farther. We humans also developed the peculiar activities of writing and music, which relied on wood—and the forests continued to fall under the axe.

Long before this great rush to consume wood, people viewed trees as something more than a source of food, shelter, and raw material. Perhaps it was the biological connection through breathing that allowed people to sense the spark of life that we hold in common with the trees. Trees became part of human spiritual and cultural traditions as well as one of the most powerful symbols that embody life. Trees served as vivid reminders of the cycle of life, death, and rebirth, and they seemed imbued with magic because they simultaneously dwelled in the three realms of heaven, earth, and underworld. Ancestors, other spirits, and even the Divine could be found amongst the trees of the woods. The forest was a place of beautiful mystery and deep transformation. People could sense the subtle energy that moved through the trees because it also moved through them. The connection between humans and the green world was real and central to everyday life, but somewhere along the way we lost this sense of connection.

We lost our way through the woods and forgot that we, too, are part of the natural world. We continued to use more that the trees had to offer, such as gums, oils, rubber, turpentine, pitch, cork, as well as charcoal for smelting ore. Without trees, metal crafts could not have been developed. We continued to use more of everything, and the forests dwindled.

Then came the so-called age of reason. Since the time of Newton, scientists viewed the world as a machine instead of a living system—trees were just fuel for man's engine. In the excitement of scientific discovery, reverence for nature was trampled. Religious leaders of the time were also caught up in the stampede to place humans above everything else. According to the church fathers, nature represented chaos and the wild, Pagan, female side of things that were classified as evil and beneath the dignity of "man." In their minds, nature had to be subdued and controlled. As technologies advanced, a false sense of power expanded, and the momentum that moved us farther from the natural world increased. Now, "virtual reality" separates us even more from the world that was once revered as sacred.

While it seems that we have traded material wealth for spiritual poverty, quite possibly the pendulum has swung to its full extent and is now circling back. Greater numbers of people are openly turning to Paganism for spiritual fulfillment, and are consciously making everyday choices that are in line with their beliefs. Even the scientific community is beginning to acknowledge how incredibly complex and beautiful life on earth is, and some are bold enough to say that we humans are amateurs—even though we know a lot, we actually know very little.[2] The gap between science and spirituality is not the chasm it once was. There is an acknowledgement of the wisdom that comes from within—within ourselves and within nature.

As part of this change, Pagan and non-Pagan people are rediscovering the majesty of trees and are appreciating with wonder these magnificent giants. In the woods, you can't help but feel part of the natural world. With that feeling comes the self-realization of returning to Source, to the Divine. Canadian environmentalist David Suzuki noted that the forest is helping people to realize that nature is not "out there" and separate. He said,

"How you see the world is how you live in it."[3] For Pagans this translates to intention and manifestation. We know that the integrity of our spiritual lives is intimately bound to the integrity of the natural world.

Trees provide a gateway into a wider world of spirit and magic. This book is intended to help you explore your place in the "web of life"[4] and its timeless mysteries. Trees provide multiple pathways to tap into this web for magical and spiritual purposes, as well as to simply embrace and enhance life. Like music, trees speak to something deep and primal within us. They can help us open our souls to the power and spirit of Earth's rhythms. They can help us harvest the fruit of our spiritual journey and find the seeds of our future.

---

1. David Suzuki, *The Sacred Balance*. A four-part video series. (Toronto: Kensington Communications, 2003).

2. Ibid.

3. Ibid.

4. Ibid. I find it wonderful that scientists use this phrase now, too.

P A R T
ONE

Part 1 of this book contains a brief overview of trees and their biological importance as well as a survey of various beliefs from a range of cultures. It also provides an introduction to several methods of working with tree energy to help you bring the wisdom of trees into your everyday world and spiritual life.

Threefold wisdom of the tree:
Leaf wisdom—of change, ever releasing;
Branch wisdom—of growth, ever reaching;
Root wisdom—of endurance, ever deepening.

JEN DELYTH
A Celtic Journal

Living Entities; Living History

IF WE TAKE AN ENVIRONMENTAL look at trees, we find that they help to moderate the climate. They give off water and oxygen, they cool their surrounding area during the day, and the soil around them radiates heat at night. Trees protect rivers and streams and conserve water by reducing run-off, securing the ground from erosion. They offer protection from the sun, rain, snow, hail, and wind for animals and human homes.

For city dwellers, trees are especially important because they act as filters, absorbing pollutants from the air, including carbon dioxide, carbon monoxide, sulfur dioxide, and ozone. In a study on urban trees in 1994, the U.S. Forest Service estimated that the trees in New York City removed approximately 1,821 metric tons of pollutants from the air annually.[1] It is estimated that a large tree can produce five pounds of oxygen a day and provide the cooling equivalent of ten room air conditioners.[2] You can experience this cooling effect as soon as you enter a forest on a hot summer day.

While some trees are impressive in size, all trees are remarkable because they seem to defy gravity. A tree trunk can seem rather precarious to hold such a heavy load of branches and leaves. For this reason alone it is no wonder that ancient people considered them with great awe.

A tree trunk consists of three separate concentric sections. At the center of the trunk is the heartwood, which is not living wood. Its purpose is to give the tree support. However, it is not unusual to find an old tree that is hollow. This does not affect the tree because the heartwood that is gone was not part of the living system. Older trees that have become hollow have generally developed enough girth and heavy bark to assume the load-bearing role.

The heartwood is surrounded by sapwood through which water and nutrients flow up to the branches and leaves. This area of sapwood consists of the most recent annual rings.

The third section of trunk is the bark, which functions like a protective skin. As the tree grows, the bark stretches. In older trees, it is common for the bark to crack and form fissures when it can no longer stretch. The bark provides insulation against heat and cold. In addition to protection from the climate, some trees, such as blackthorn and honey locust, have prickly spines to keep animals from climbing them. Others contain their own insect repellent to guard against destructive pests.

While we tend to associate trees such as willows and birches with flexibility, all trees have enough "give" to move with the wind and not be blown down under normal weather conditions. The leaves also shift in such a way to present as little surface area to the wind as possible. The next time you have an opportunity to watch a tree during a storm, observe how it moves.

We think of spring and summer as times of growth, and they are for a tree's trunk, branches, flowers, leaves—everything above ground. When all this activity subsides in the autumn, the roots have their turn until the hard frosts arrive. There are exceptions, such as blackthorn and gorse. Of course, in climates that do not have a wide range in temperatures, tree cycles differ, but generally above and below ground growth occurs at different times.

Trees seem to hold some kind of mystery and fascination for everyone, mathematicians and numerologists included. In order to take in as much sunlight as possible, some trees have limbs that grow in spirals around the trunk to maximize positioning. In addition, many types of trees have leaves that spiral around the branches. Pine needle bundles also spiral, as do pinecone scales around the seeds.

Scientists have studied the spiral effect of branches and have found some interesting patterns. Spiral characteristics differ according to the type of tree. For example, beech trees have a 1/3 spiral, which means that if you placed a string at the base of a branch you would have to wind it around the trunk once and pass over the base of three other branches before you get to one directly above the starting branch. Oaks have 2/5 spirals, which means you would pass the string two times around the trunk and pass five branches until you get to one that is directly in line with the branch where you started the string.[3]

Spiral types are 1/2, 1/3, 2/5, 3/8, 5/13, 8/21, 13/34 and so on. As the numbers increase, the spirals get tighter. Nature loves mathematics: if you add two consecutive numbers (numerators and denominators separately), you will get the next spiral number.

Tree Rings

The ancient Greeks discovered that tree rings correspond to annual growth. Over the two millennia since then, dendrochronology has become an important scientific tool that has aided other disciplines by helping to correct flaws in radiocarbon dating, which proved to be off by as much as a thousand years in some cases.

Tree ring "signatures" are shared by all trees living at the same time, no matter what type of tree or their location. Matching and overlapping these signatures has allowed dendrochronologists to compile an unbroken record of approximately 7,500 years. In this way, trees provide a time capsule that preserves "snapshots" of the environment.

For archaeologists and historians, this record has provided insight into understanding the human historical record. For example, beginning in 1159 BCE disastrous climatic conditions affected most of the world. For eighteen years, trees experienced little or no growth during a drought that lasted almost one hundred years. In the human record, at around 1200 BCE there was a major shift to a warrior society model of civilization, with an increase in weaponry and massive hilltop forts. During times of food shortages, the strongest or most well-armed people survive.

Similarly, there were catastrophic conditions in the sixth century CE that made the tree rings go haywire worldwide. From 536 to 541, trees exhibited drastically reduced summer growth due to the cold. In Ireland and elsewhere there is evidence of increased fortification of cities and towns.

Dendrochronology has also helped scientists map sunspot cycles (11.5 and 500-year cycles) as well as predict some long-term climatic changes.

One cannot discuss tree rings without mentioning the bristlecone pines. These "immortals made of wood" grow in one of the harshest climates on earth, at ten thousand feet or more above sea level where the air is thin, the wind incessant, and the growing season only about forty-five days, most notably in the Inyo National Forest in the highest part of the White Mountains between the Sierra Nevada mountain range and Death Valley. In addition to being incredible symbols of perseverance, these trees were major contributors to extending the record back in time. They have been described as looking more dead than alive because as the trunk dies, side branches take over to support the weight. When a tree is completely dead it may continue to stand for a thousand years.

Carrying on the research that University of Arizona scientist Edmund Schulman began in the 1950s, one of his students was horrified when he had counted over 4,600 rings in a tree trunk and realized that he had probably killed the oldest living thing on the planet in order to study it. Schulman's assistants have found an older bristlecone that has become known as Methuselah. Its location is being kept secret in order to protect it.

Impact on Human Consciousness

Many types of trees live five hundred years or more. One of the nearest rivals in age to the bristlecones is the yew, which can live over two thousand years. It is no wonder that early people perceived trees as immortal.

Like mythological heroes, trees are larger than life. Their beauty evokes wonder, and so it is no surprise that they have had a central place in folklore, myth, and religion. Their grandeur serves as a symbol of life, hope, and perseverance. It is common to see new branches sprouting from the remains of an old tree, providing a vivid illustration of the cycle of life, death, and rebirth.

In early civilizations, the tree symbolized a two-fold identity: the World Tree, which connected the realms of existence, and the Tree of Life, which represented the source of life and abundance. In many instances these were aspects of the same sacred tree.

One of the best known of World Trees is the ash of Norse mythology called Yggdrasil. It was upon this tree that Odin suspended himself and from which he was able to perceive the runes. (More on this later.) While many cultures believed in the existence of three realms (heaven, earth, and the underworld), Norse legend tells of nine realms existing on three levels.[4] These realms were said to be connected by the nine roots of Yggdrasil.

In Finland, the Tree of Life also served as the cosmic sky pole that held the heavens aloft. It was believed to extend from the North/Pole Star through the center of the earth. Some sources define this tree as an oak, others as a pine.

Germanic tribes had a practice of erecting pillars, which were made from whole tree trunks, on hilltops to represent their tree of the universe. Known as *Irmensul,* some of these pillars were said to have existed into the eighth century.

Similarly, the Tree of Life in ancient Egypt was usually portrayed atop a sacred mound. As the *Axis Munde,* its branches reached to the stars and its roots extended deep into the netherworld. Osiris, the god of the dead, was sometimes represented as this World Tree. In legend, he was imprisoned in a wooden chest around which a tamarisk tree (*Tamarix africana*) grew. A great pillar containing Osiris was fashioned from the tree's trunk. He was eventually rescued and resurrected by his wife, Iris.

The Mesopotamian Tree of Life was associated with the supreme god Enlil. This tree was a symbol of cosmic order and was thought to have been either a date palm (*Phoenix dactylifera*) or a pomegranate (*Punica granatum*). In India, the sal or salwa tree (*Shorea robusta*) represented the cosmic World Tree. It was sacred to Shiva who is part of the triad of major Hindu gods. In some legends, four of these great trees supported the world and represented the cardinal directions.

The lote tree (*Ziziphus spina-christi*) was believed to exist between the realms of people and the Divine. It was both a connection and a boundary. Ancient Arabs sometimes planted lote trees to mark the end of a road. In the story of Muhammad's ascent, a lote tree marked the point beyond which no one but Allah knew what existed. The lote tree was used to represent the manifestation of Allah, as well as to symbolize the spiritual aspect of the human self.

In the spirit landscape of the shaman, it is the symbol of the Axis Munde that provides the means to traverse the realms. Tree roots provide access to the otherworld. Stretching deep into the underworld where many traditions believe departed spirits dwell, roots draw up the wisdom of those who have gone before on the earthly plane. When the gods need to be consulted, it is the branches reaching to the heavens that provide access to their airy realm. Odin is portrayed as a shaman using Yggdrasil to access knowledge.

Creation Myths and Beyond

Trees are central in the creation stories of diverse cultures including the Celts, Greeks, Indonesians, Scandinavians, Siberians, and Japanese. Peter Berresford Ellis provides a beautiful interpretation of a Celtic creation myth in which an oak tree represents Bíle, the consort of the Great Mother Goddess Danu.[5] Her divine water as rain and his seed produce the Dagda and the other De Danann gods and goddesses. In Japan, the sakaki tree (*Cleyera japonica*) is featured in creation myths as an evergreen. It also fulfills the role of World Tree and is represented in Shinto shrines as a central post. The sakaki trees near a shrine symbolize the power of the shrine's goddess.

Archaeologists in England have found numerous Neolithic sites that have come to be known as woodhenges. These structures consisted of circles of posts surrounded by a ditch with a break in the northeast sector—similar to the layout at Stonehenge. A type of woodhenge may have existed at Tara in Ireland where there is evidence of approximately three hundred postholes under the sacred mound. There is some speculation that these structures may also have been roofed. One, located on the Salisbury Plain not far from Stonehenge, consisted of 168 huge poles in six concentric oval rings. If it had a roof, walking through the dimly lit interior with all its columns may have been evocative of strolling through a thick forest. It has been theorized that cathedrals, such as Chartres in Paris, were designed to elicit the same feeling with rows of trunk-like columns and leaf and branch motifs in the stonework.

Druids are perhaps best known for worshipping in sacred groves, but they were not the only people to do so. The earliest sanctuaries of the Germanic tribes were also in forests. These tribes became known as Teutonic tribes, from the word *Teutons*, the name that the Celts applied to them which meant "the people."

Lithuanians designated certain areas as holy groves where they sought information from tree oracles. This is similar to the ancient Greek practice in the sacred groves at Dodona, which were dedicated to Zeus. Priests would interpret signs divined from the rustling of oak and plane tree leaves. A sacred grove also existed at Epidaurus around the sanctuary of Aesculapius, the god of healing. Ash groves were dedicated to Apollo, and myrtle trees were believed to be sacred to Aphrodite. In addition, several Greek myths feature people transforming into trees as a means of escape.

In ancient Rome, holy groves occupied the hills around the city and the sacred fig tree (*Ficus carica*) of Romulus, founder of Rome, was located within the forum. Diana's temples were located in sacred woods—appropriate for the goddess of wild beasts and hunting. In the temple of Vesta, the eternal flame was fuelled exclusively with oak wood.

Twin sycamores flanked the gates of the Egyptian heaven where the sun god, Ra, appeared each morning. Isis, Hathor, and Nut were believed to manifest in sycamores. The sycamore of Egypt (*Ficus sycomorus*) is a type of fig and not related to the American sycamore (*Platanus occidentalia*) or the London plane tree (*Platanus acerifolic*). Another type of fig, the pipal tree (*Ficus religiosa)*, which is also called a bo or bodhi tree, is sacred to Buddhists. Siddhartha Gautama is said to have meditated under this type of tree until he achieved enlightenment, at which time he became Buddha. The fourth direct descendant of this historic tree stands beside the Mahabodhi temple in Bodhgaya, India.

Canaanites revered their mother goddess Asherah who was represented in temples with a wooden pillar. Some believe that at one time her name may have meant "grove of trees." Trees also serve as religious symbols for Christians and are mentioned throughout the Bible. A discussion of them could fill an entire volume on its own, and so only a few will be mentioned here.

Of the trees in the Garden of Eden—the Tree of Life and the Tree of Knowledge of Good and Evil—the latter is probably the most famous. Eve, following the advice of the serpent (symbol of the Goddess), partakes of an apple and gets blamed for all the ills of the world. However, it is a palm tree that is most symbolic in Christianity for strength and longevity. The palm is a symbol of the garden of paradise and Christ's triumph over death. This dual notion is not far from Pagan concepts of the Tree of Life providing sustenance, and trees in general representing the turning Wheel of the Year and the soul's immortality through rebirth.

If one had to choose two trees most associated with the Celts, they would have to be the yew and the oak. Being an evergreen and able to live for over two thousand years, yews represented the immortality of the soul. Because stories were handed down from generation to generation and certain trees continually mentioned for centuries, one can begin to feel awe for anything that can survive so long. It is no wonder that Christians picked up on this theme and made the yew tree a seemingly requisite feature of graveyards.

The other great tree of the Celts, the oak, is mentioned throughout their legends. Druids are rarely discussed without talk of their oak groves. Although it is popularly believed that the name Druid is based on the Greek *drus*, meaning "oak," Peter

Berresford Ellis takes issue with this, and he questions why the Celts would look to the Greek language when their own root word *dru*, meaning "immersed," would seem to make more sense.[6] Combined with *uid*, "to know," a Dru-uid is someone "immersed in knowledge" or someone with great knowledge. Ellis speculates that this meaning could date back to pre-Celtic culture and have a connection to survival in the dense oak forests that were abundant at that time.[7] To the early people of Ireland and Gaul—the hunter-gatherer clans, circa 4000 BCE—a person who possessed great knowledge or wisdom of the woods was someone who knew how to survive. Clan members would look to such a person for leadership.

The oak was also important to other cultures, especially as it related to powerful thunder gods. These include the Norse Thor, the Lithuanian Perkunas (also called Perkuns), the Slavic Perun and the Teutonic Donar (or Thunar).

Trees also served as symbols for communities and events. In Celtic lands, most tribes had a particular local tree that functioned as their own sacred tree (*crann beatha*) or community talisman. It was a place to gather for important occasions. As a way to demoralize a rival tribe, one group would destroy the other's tree.

Trees that served as community symbols in Colonial America were called liberty trees, and they functioned as meeting points in each of the thirteen colonies. The first one was located in Boston and came into use in August of 1765. The Liberty Elm, as it became known, was cut down by British soldiers in 1775 because it had become a strong symbol for rebellion. Maryland's liberty tree was a tulip poplar and was the last to remain standing. It finally came down in 1999.

Sacred Trees and Holy Springs

As previously mentioned, water symbolizes the power of the Divine Mother/the Great Goddess and her gift of life and sustenance. Wells and springs were also thought to hold the power of local deities. Many pre-Christian and pre-Roman sites in Europe have been places of pilgrimage for physical healing as well as spiritual communion and cleansing. In addition to the water source, these locations frequently included a tree or grove. As part of the pilgrimage ritual, one would usually drink, bathe in, or be anointed with the water, and then he or she would leave an offering. If the site included a tree, it was common to tie a piece of cloth on a branch of the tree. The theory was that by the time the cloth disintegrated, the request would materialize. It was also symbolic of leaving a burden behind. In the British Isles, these are sometimes called "clootie trees"; in Gaelic, *clootie* is a name for the devil. It could be assumed, at least in the Christian era, that one would symbolically dump his or her burden or illness on the devil.

A similar practice of leaving offerings with a tree was described by Thomas Pennant in his *Tour of Scotland and a Voyage to the Hebrides,* published in 1771. Pennant mentions an oak tree on Inis Maree with nails and coins hammered into the bark. During the eighteenth century, the offerings were made to St. Maree, but at that particular location the practice may have dated back to the Celtic solar deity called Magh Ruith (Mow-rih). This tradition continues to the present day in other locations, such as Fore in County Westmeath, and Clonenagh, County Laois.[8]

In Cornish legend, St. Keyne is said to have planted four symbolic trees of oak, ash, elm, and withy (willow) beside the well that now carries her name. One legend about the well says that all four trees grew from one trunk. At any rate, they or it was destroyed in a storm in 1703. St. Keyne is believed to have been a daughter of the sixth century King Broccan.

The legendary thorn tree associated with the Chalice Well (although not located with it) is one of Glastonbury, England's relics. According to legend, the tree grew from the staff of Joseph of Arimathea when he stopped to rest. Because it bloomed at Christmas rather than early spring, many people took it as proof that Arimathea had come to England in 63 CE and established the first Christian church. The present tree, as the story goes, was taken as a cutting from the original.

We finally return to Odin. At the roots of Yggdrasil, a spring bubbled up from deep within the earth. As Odin hung suspended upside down, he was eventually able to stretch far enough to take a sip of water. It was then that he began to receive information. Some versions of the legend say that he saw the rune characters on the surface of the water. Perhaps the combined magic of water and tree—the reflection of branches— produced the images as his shamanic state of mind perceived related information.

Also linked with wisdom, the most important sacred spring in Celtic legend is the one inhabited by the salmon of knowledge. These salmon swam in a pool shaded by nine hazel trees. Containing the wisdom of the world, the hazelnuts dropped into the water from overhanging branches and the salmon fed on them and gained knowledge. In legend, the wisdom was transferred to a person who ate one of these salmon, or even just the roasted juices, as in the case of Fionn Mac Cumhail.

Just as the Celtic salmon and trees are linked in ancient legend, they also have an intertwined relationship in northwest British Columbia. According to Canadian environmentalist David Suzuki, as salmon return upriver to spawn, they bring incredible amounts of nutrients to the forest.[9] This happens when animals catch the fish and take them into the woods to get away from thieving competitors, and parts of the carcasses are left to decay on the forest floor. Three percent of the salmon's body is nitrogen, which trees need. A direct correlation has been detected between the size of the tree rings and the size of the annual salmon runs.[10]

The Green Man

Folklore is filled with heroes who go off into the woods and encounter tree spirits—some friendly, and some not so friendly. One demon was characterized in England as a walking tree long before J. R. R. Tolkien wrote about Ents. This story proliferated into the late seventeenth century in tales of the "Man of the Oak."

In India, the Brahma Daitya are spirits of the Brahmans who inhabit banyan trees (*Ficus benghalensis*). These spirits are more like ghosts and are sometimes referred to as demons. Other legends of tree spirits are mentioned with their respective trees in part 2 of this book.

The Green Man is a symbol that has appeared at the edge of human consciousness for well over a millennium. He embodied the vitality of nature and male sexuality as the son and consort to the Goddess/Mother Nature. He was the epitome of the Pagan god who symbolized the Wheel of the Year—he died in the autumn and was reborn in the spring. As son, the tree/plant life emerges from the womb of Mother Earth. It grows, matures, and releases seeds to fertilize the mother, becoming her consort. Fulfilling the role of Green Man in Egypt, Osiris was portrayed as a tree spirit and god of vegetation.

As the plague swept through Europe in the mid-fourteenth century, the Green Man (under Christian influence) came to represent the decay of the flesh and death rather than the spark of life and rebirth. However, he managed to survive those dark years as well as the negativity to have his image carved onto tombs throughout the Renaissance period, bridging the gap from death to life in the transformation of rebirth. As a result, the Green Man's likeness proliferates throughout mighty European cathedrals over doorways, in ceiling bosses, and choir misericords. He can also be found on the Victorian-era gates of the Royal Botanical Gardens at Kew in London.

The Green Man has come full circle as the growing Pagan community has brought him from the edge of human consciousness to center stage. He is again a strong symbol of the rising sap, the life force, and divine spirit that shares fertility with the Mother.

1. David J. Nowak, "Tree Species Selection, Design, and Management to Improve Air Quality," included in the Annual Meeting Proceedings (Washington, DC: American Society of Landscape Architects, 2000), 23.

2. *The National Arbor Day Foundation*, http://www.arborday.org/trees/index.cfm.

3. Ross E. Hutchins, *This Is a Tree* (New York: Dodd, Mead & Company, 1964), 38–39.

4. The upper level of realms consists of Asgard, domain of the gods known as the Aesir; Vanaheim, domain of the gods known as the Vanir; and Alfheim, the land of the Light Elves. The middle level holds Midgard, the world of humans; Jotunheim, the land of the giants; and Nidavellir, the land of the dwarfs. The lower level includes Svartalfheim, the domain of the Dark Elves; Niflheim, the land of ice and mist with few inhabitants; and Helheim, the domain of the dead and the goddess Hel. Arthur Cotterell & Rachel Storm, *The Ultimate Encyclopedia of Mythology* (New York: Hermes House, 1999), 180–253.

5. Peter Berresford Ellis, *The Chronicles of the Celts* (New York: Carrol & Graf Publishers, Inc., 1999), 21.

6. Ellis, *The Druids* (New York: Carrol & Graf Publishers, Inc., 2002), 38.

7. Ellis, *The Chronicles of the Celts*, 7.

8. A similar custom called "drawing the nail" was practiced in the British Isles. A vow was symbolically sealed by driving a nail into a tree. It could be reversed only by removing the nail if all parties and a witness were present. Tom MacIntyre, "Mind the Trees," *Ireland of the Welcomes Magazine*, Jan./Feb. 1990, 31–32.

9. Suzuki, *The Sacred Balance*.

10. Ibid.; Dana Codding, "Tree Ring Research Yields Clues to Pacific Climate Change," *The Ring The University of Victoria's Community Newspaper* (February 18, 2000). Available at online archive, http://ring.uvic.ca/00feb18/treering.html.

Up Close and Personal

W<small>E ONLY NEED TO LOOK</small> around us to see how trees are an integral part of our everyday lives. As material for furniture or other uses in the home, wood brings warmth and beauty and can be sensuous to the touch. Outside the home, as living entities, we plant trees in memory of loved ones and we use them to give shape to the landscape. They provide a sense of place and bring communities together by making streets pleasant to walk along and parks comfortable places in which to gather. Trees can define a neighborhood as fresh and new or older and established.

On a personal level, trees can serve as wonderful reminders of the places you have lived and events that occurred in each place. Sometimes, it's not particular events that are remembered, but certain moods and sensations. Take a few minutes to think of the places where you have lived and make a list of the houses. What tree or trees come to mind? My list is illustrated in table 2.1.

As you create your list, think of how the trees influence your recollections of each house. If you are like me, it probably brings back a number of pleasant memories. The first home I remember as a child had a huge maple in the front yard. My bedroom, on the second floor, looked out onto the branches of this massive tree that was

HOUSES BY LOCATION	TREE(S)
Jackson Street	Maple
Rose Avenue	Juniper
Forrest Green	Birch
Henry Arnaud Strasse	Cherry
Tingrith	Holly and Hawthorn
Waverly Road	Willow
Wycoff Way	Willow and Maple

Table 2.1: The author's house and tree list

taller than the house. I can remember how snow looked clinging to it, which was something I checked for first thing in the morning if it had been forecasted. Above all, it was the summers I remember and sitting under this tree to eat ice cream because it was a nice, cool place. Being right by the sidewalk, its roots played havoc with the pavement and made roller skating a challenge.

The junipers around the house where I lived as a teenager bring memories of sitting up late at night writing poetry and gazing at the moon. (I was a young romantic.) A multi-trunked birch graced the tiny backyard of the first house I owned. It was visible through the sliding glass door in my living room and seemed to be a part of the indoor environment. In spring, after dinner on the terrace of my house in Germany, my friends and I would enjoy dessert of juicy cherries as well as the fun of picking them. In England, I lived in the country and had many types of trees surrounding my house, but it was the holly and hawthorn that are most vivid in my mind. In New England, and now back in a New York suburb, it is willows and maples that shape the landscape of my memories.

This exercise of remembering trees has a two-fold purpose. One is to see where trees (currently and over time) fit at the edge or within your life, and the memories that can be evoked when recalling them. The second purpose is to begin to slow down in preparation for working with tree energy.

Our society moves so fast that events and our lives can become a blur. We must ask ourselves if this is how we want to exist. Is this how we want to live, in a blur of activity? If we are to find meaning in our lives, then we have to make time to slow down

Figure 2.1: Yoga tree posture

and open ourselves, body and soul, to the pulse of earth energy in order to find where we truly live. It is possible to go through life and be quite happy and never have an urge to do this, but for many of us this is not an option.

The depths of the soul can be reached only through quiet, soft moments. By exploring this depth, we learn about ourselves and where we fit within the web of existence that is life. As our spiritual energy moves inward, it also moves outward, providing balance. Trees can be our companions and guides in this exploration. They embody the spirit of balance because they extend in two directions; one towards the dark and the other towards the light.

The yoga posture called "the tree" (*vrikshasana*)[1] is about balance, and not just in a physical sense. I find that I have difficulty doing this pose if my energy is out of whack. When this occurs, I concentrate on calming myself first before trying the posture again because it aids in bringing me into balance. Because it requires physical balance, you have to put part of your mind to this function. Yoga is about the union of body, mind, and spirit, and so to truly find balance in the tree pose, you have to reach inside yourself and bring your body, mind, and spirit into alignment.

The tree posture is also a good way to begin preparing yourself for working with tree energy. Give it a try. Wear loose-fitting, comfortable clothing. Take a few moments to quiet your breath and mind as you would for meditation.

Stand up straight, but do not lock your knees, and keep the energy in your legs engaged. Place your hands on your hips and shift your weight onto one foot. Think of your connection with the earth flowing through this foot as though you had roots. Bring the other foot up, with knee pointing to the side, to rest the sole on the inner thigh of the grounded leg. Let it rest there and not push the leg outward or move your hips out of alignment. Breathe slowly and steadily. When you feel ready, bring your palms together in front of your chest, keeping your back straight and your body aligned. If you are comfortable with this, you can take the posture to its full extent by raising your hands above your head.

Keep your gaze soft, or if you are comfortable, close your eyes. Become aware of the solid strength of your body and your connection to the ground. Imagine your energy roots extending down into Mother Earth and drawing nourishment from her. Feel the movement of life flowing up through your body, and then focus on your head and/or raised arms. Feel your energy move outward to the sky. When you feel in balance, lower your arms and then your foot. Shift your weight back to both feet. Take a moment to note the sensations, and then repeat the posture by balancing on the other leg.

If you have difficulty with this, use a wall for support. Rest your back and buttocks against the wall. The important thing is to keep your body aligned. As you begin to find balance in this posture, you will also find that you don't need to rely on the wall for support.

Tuning In

A good way to begin to tune in to the natural world, specifically tree energy, is through observation. Select one tree with which to begin this process. There may be a tree in your yard or nearby park to which you feel drawn. If you are attracted to a particular tree, check what type it is and what qualities are associated with it. This attraction may hold a message or solution to something in your life, or it may indicate a path you may want to explore. It may be appropriate to begin your work with that tree. Alternatively, you may want to begin with the current Celtic tree month—refer to chapter 3 for information.

If a type of tree has certain characteristics you want to foster, you may want to find one in your area and begin working with it. If you have not felt called to explore a particular tree, you may want to consider starting with your "birth" tree, especially if you can locate one growing in your area. Refer to appendix A for dates related to certain trees. A birth tree can inform you about some of your potentials. Alternatively, spell your name with the Ogham alphabet (refer to table 4.1 in chapter 4) and note the tree for the first letter of your first name. If that tree does not grow in your neighborhood, go to the next letter/tree until you find one.

If you feel that you will be guided to select a tree because you have something to learn from it, randomly select one by writing tree names on slips of paper and then picking one. Be sure to use the names of trees available in your area.

Take a notebook with you when you go out to visit your tree. Begin by observing it from a distance. What is its overall shape? What initial feelings or impressions come to mind? What descriptive words would you use? Vitality, peace, wisdom, nobility, humility? Write them down. Walk towards the tree and note if your impressions change.

Look at the pattern of branches and how they intertwine or how they are spaced apart. What type of leaves or needles does it have, or are the branches bare at the moment? Get to know the individual characteristics of the tree as you would another person. After visual observation, walk to within arm's length of the tree and then close your eyes. Imagine your energy expanding from your heart toward the tree. Send a greeting and tell the tree your name. Reach out and place the palm of your hand against the trunk. Send a welcoming flow of energy to the tree.

You may or may not sense the tree's energy the first couple of times that you do this. Trees are not used to humans slowing down enough to commune with them. They will be aware of you but detecting their notice of you may take time. Don't expect to hear a choir of angelic voices to herald your contact. It will most likely be subtle, but on occasion it can be a surprise. A particular phrase or image may suddenly pop into your mind. Once as I was visiting a place where I had not been for over twenty years, I was walking around putting my hands on the trees, as is my habit. I didn't "hear" anything, but the phrase, "We remember your spirit," suddenly came into my mind. I was surprised, because it was not the sort of thing I would have thought.

When something like this occurs, it is normal to question one's own sanity. However, it is important to trust what your "heart of hearts" tells you in each situation. If you truly believe that the source of the communication was not your own mind, then it probably was not.

An acquaintance told me of the time she was walking in the woods on a summer's day and noticed a severe gash in a tree. It was mostly healed, but she stopped and touched the tree. Suddenly she had an image of a snowmobile in her mind. First, she was surprised to suddenly think about snowmobiles in the middle of summer. Then she had an image of it hitting the tree. She thought it was odd, because the gash was so far above the ground. A moment later, when she thought about the previous winter she remembered that there had been quite a bit of snow on the ground for a long while. The path in the snow would have been at the level of the gash in the tree. When she realized that the tree had responded to her wondering about its wound, she spent more time sending it loving, healing energy.

Receiving clear messages from trees is not an everyday occurrence. However, it is important to remain open and aware, as most communication is subtle. We humans tend to be so used to the obvious—we like information to be handed to us in wide-screen, Technicolor, surround sound, action-packed entertainment. The natural world doesn't work this way, and so we need to slow down, empty our minds of the useless junk, and listen.

We must learn to listen with more than our ears and see with more than our eyes. In a conversation I had with R. J. Stewart[2] on this subject, he noted that we humans get so enthralled with visuals, but our eyes are not the most highly developed sense organ that we possess. Touch/skin is certainly our largest source for sensing the world around us, yet it takes a backseat to visual and aural sensation.

If you include the aura—the electromagnetic field that surrounds our bodies and is part of us—the sense of touch can be extended beyond the tips of our fingers. When you are working with trees (or anything in the natural world), be aware of your energy field and how it is part of your senses.

Since we are such visually oriented creatures, it may help to see tree energy first. Learning to see this energy is not difficult. The easiest part of the aura to see (be it a person's or a tree's) is the part closest to the tree (or person). It generally does not have color and will appear slightly white or gray and transparent, but it can frequently be yellowish or gold. When I first started doing energy work, I came across theories that this may be where artists of the Middle Ages got the idea for halos.

Observing tree energy is most easily done at a distance from the tree, especially if you can see the top part of it (or multiple trees) against the sky. The fading light of dusk is the best time of day when you are first learning to see auras. Spring and summer are the best times of year when there is more activity (above ground) to observe in trees.

If you have toyed with *Magic Eye* pictures, the concept is similar. It is like daydreaming when your eyes are open, but you are not really looking at anything. Start by softening your gaze so that you are not focusing on the tree's detail. Don't look at individual branches or leaves; just allow your eyes to see the outline of the tree against the sky. Slightly above this outline you will see the profile of the tree repeated as a whitish/yellow shadow that seems to radiate and move. That is the tree's energy field. During the summer, when the tree's vitality is at its height, the aura will seem to dance as though it has a life of its own. This is not unlike the movement of the aurora borealis.

When you look at multiple trees, their energy fields will be joined as one. If the trees are not close enough to each other that they touch, you may be able to see white or grayish wispy strands between them connecting their energy. This is also easy to observe with houseplants.

After you have been able to see how dynamic a tree's aura can be, go back to the tree you have already visited. Sit or stand near it and visualize its aura. Visualize your aura, and then visualize it connecting with the tree's energy field.

Hold the connection for as long as you can or however long it is comfortable. Make notes about any physical sensations or thoughts and feelings that you may experience. After you do this a number of times, and as you get to "know" different trees, you may want to review your notes. Do your experiences vary with different trees or different types of trees? Do your experiences vary with the same tree?

You may also want to log the time of day, the weather, and the season in your notes. This doesn't have to resemble a high school science project. Just noting things such as the date, that it's afternoon, sunny, and in the 60s will do. This way you can become familiar with the seasonal energy rhythm of the tree.

At times you may also want to note how you felt before visiting the tree and then how you felt afterwards. If you were feeling down, did your spirits lift after being with the tree? After a while you may find that your own energy resonates at a different level when you are interacting with trees and that you may experience a slight shift in consciousness.

Scientific research has found that meditation and prayer can change brain waves. At the frequency of 35 hertz, the mid-chakras "awaken" and come into balance. People in meditation and deep prayer reach 40 hertz where a cerebral resonance occurs, according to Dr. Andrew Newberg and others researching the physicality of consciousness.[3] It is not uncommon to experience a shift in consciousness during ritual, meditation, shamanic journeying, or in drumming circles.

There is a section of the forest where I like to walk that has become a sacred place for me. As I approach it and before I arrive at that spot, I begin to experience this shift. The effect can last a while after I leave the woods.

When this occurs as you are working with trees, it is important to "ground" the energy when you are finished so you can arrive back in your "everyday" consciousness. If you don't, you may experience an edgy or unsettled feeling. You may also have difficulty focusing or sleeping.

Just as you would at the end of a ritual, take time to find your center. Become aware of your feet on the ground and feel your connection with Mother Earth. Think of her energy as a ball of light below the surface of the ground, and feel a cord of energy running from the bottom of your feet into that ball. Imagine sending energy into the earth until you feel that you have arrived back to your usual state. Thank the earth for her help and the trees for making a connection with you.

If you are not experiencing this shift in consciousness, don't feel discouraged. This is not necessary for working with tree energy, but over time you may find that it will occur. The important thing is being able to sense the tree energy.

If you are not sure of what it feels like to detect the energy field of a tree (or person or animal), recall a time when someone felt good to be around. There may not have been anything spectacular going on but just the person's presence made you feel calm or vibrant. On the other hand, think about a person who gave you "bad vibes." Even though they did not do or say anything threatening to you, you felt certain negativity in their presence. You may also have met people who left you feeling "drained" without knowing why. You felt that way because they took energy from you and gave none in return. In both types of situations (positive and negative), it is the other person's energy that is affecting yours.

Tree Meditation

Utilizing trees in meditation is another way to access their energy. In meditation we close off the conscious area of our brains, which allows us to access the subconscious as well as shift into the 40-hertz space. Start by choosing a tree. Choose one at random or pick one that has attributes you want to foster. Refer to table 2.2 for a listing. Write the name of the tree on a slip of paper (perhaps cut in the shape of a leaf), or find a picture of that type of tree.

In order to do a tree meditation (or any type of meditation) be sure to allow yourself adequate time. If you have a gazillion things to take care of, don't try to squeeze a meditation in between other items on your agenda. It's important to allow time not only for the meditation itself, but also reflection afterwards. Taking a few minutes to jot down your thoughts and feelings afterwards is a good way to track the effects different trees may have on you. Schedule time in a place that is quiet and private. A loud television in the next room or the kids bounding around the house would be a distraction even for those experienced with meditation.

If you keep a meditation or ritual altar, light a candle and sit in front of it. Whether you have chosen a tree at random or selected one for a particular reason, sit with your hands cupped in front of you holding the piece of paper with the tree name. If you are using a picture, place it on your altar.

Begin by sitting comfortably and closing your eyes. Even if you plan to gaze at a picture, start with your eyes closed. This provides you with the opportunity to shift from the everyday outer world to your own interior space. Focus on your breathing and let each breath start from your belly. Slowly fill your lungs, then pause before you slowly exhale. The last air should leave from your belly. Pause again, and then start the next inhalation. When you feel that your energy is calm and grounded, allow your focus to move to the tree. If you are going to use gazing, slowly open your eyes. Keep your focus soft as you look at it and let your eyes rest on the nuances of color and form. Allow yourself to be receptive to energy, thoughts, messages, and feelings.

Don't approach the meditation with expectations of great, earth-shattering revelations about your life. Most information will come to you softly. And don't be disappointed if nothing seems to happen. Just allow yourself to relax and be receptive. If you are to learn something at that time, it will come. Taking time after meditation is important even if you do not keep track of your experience in a journal. Having time

TREE	ATTRIBUTES AND ASSOCIATIONS
Alder	Evolving spirit, foundation, protection, rebirth
Apple	Happiness, faithfulness, harmony, illumination, love, strength
Ash	Balance, communication, creativity, growth, healing, stability
Aspen	Courage, eloquence, endurance, protection, success
Bamboo	Flexibility, harmony, luck, protection
Beech	Manifest intentions, stability
Birch	Beginnings, blessings, change, growth, renewal
Blackthorn	Authority, protection, strength
Cedar	Calm and balance, longevity, prosperity, wisdom
Cherry	Achievement, joy, love
Chestnut	Healing, love, prosperity
Cypress	Healing, protection, strength
Elder	Abundance, good fortune, success, transition
Elm	Compassion, empathy, intuition, love
Fir	Cleverness, far sightedness, rebirth, transformation
Gooseberry	Challenges, gains, success
Gorse	Fertility, hope, prosperity, protection
Hackberry	Adaptability, creativity
Hawthorn	Fertility, hope, happiness, love, protection, reconciliation
Hazel	Inspiration, introspection, wisdom
Heather	Healing, luck, passion, spirituality, transitions
Hickory	Balance, discipline, flexibility, unification
Holly	Courage, divinity, luck, unity
Honeysuckle	Fidelity, love, psychic abilities
Hornbeam	Prosperity, protection, strength
Ivy	Growth, healing, love, transformation, vitality
Juniper	Healing, love, protection
Laurel	Expanded awareness, healing, poetic inspiration, wisdom
Linden	Attraction, love, peace, protection
Locust	Friendship, perseverance, strength
Magnolia	Clarity, love, self-awareness, truth
Maple	Abundance, balance, communication, creativity

Table 2.2: Basic associations and attributes of trees

Table 2.2 (continued)

TREE	ATTRIBUTES AND ASSOCIATIONS
Mesquite	Healing, protection
Mimosa	Happiness, love
Mistletoe	Birth/rebirth, fertility, healing, love, protection
Myrtle	Fertility, luck, money, peace
Oak	Fertility, health, loyalty, self-confidence, success, wisdom
Olive	Abundance, fidelity, hope, potency, reconciliation, victory
Palm	Fertility, protection
Pine	Good fortune, health, prosperity
Reed	Growth, harmony, healing, unity, will
Rowan	Dedication, expression, imagination, insight, healing
Spindle tree	Cleansing, honor, inspiration
Spruce	Intuition, versatility, well being
Sycamore	Communication, love, vitality
Vine	Fertility, happiness, intellect, wealth
Walnut	Change, inspiration, new perspectives
Willow	Flexibility, connections, knowledge, relationships
Witch hazel	Healing, inspiration, protection
Yew	Change, divinity, longevity, strength

for reflection allows information to settle. Things that may not be obvious during the meditation may come to the surface while you sit quietly. It may also take a day or two for you to recognize information that may have come to you during the meditation. Be patient and you will learn what you need to know.

Keeping in Touch

Use as many of your senses as possible when working with trees, especially touch. As mentioned, when visiting a tree put your hands on it or sit with your back against it. Get to know the feel of its bark. Pick up a fallen branch, leaf, nut, or fruit. How does it feel in your hands? Do you feel anything emotionally?

Use a piece of branch, thorn or nut as a talisman. Every part of the tree holds its spirit. Carry it with you to act as a reminder of your relationship with that tree. Keep it in your pocket or purse, in your car or at your place of work. Pick it up occasionally and let your senses remind you about the tree and how you felt in its presence. Also think about the characteristics embodied by the tree that you may be working to foster in your life.

Frequency is important. Whether you want to change an aspect of yourself or deepen your spiritual life, it is the subtle everyday contact or practice that brings about change. We are what we think.

---

1. Mira, Silva, and Shyam Mehta, *Yoga: The Iyengar Way* (New York: Alfred A. Knopf, 1995), 96. The Sanskrit name for the yoga handstand pose, *adho mukha vrikshasana*, means "downward-facing tree."

2. R. J. Stewart is a Scottish author and composer who has researched and written extensively on the Western Tradition. Some of his many books include *Earth Light*, *Power Within the Land*, and *The Underworld Initiation*.

3. Andrew Newberg, M.D., Eugene G. d'Aquili, Ph.D., and Vince Rause, *Why God Won't Go Away: Brain Science and the Biology of Belief* (New York: Ballantine Books, 2002) 1–8; Stuart Hameroff, M.D., "Breathrough Study on EEG of Meditation," *Science & Consciousness Review*, no. 1 (June 2005): 3.

THREE

The Tree Calendar

TREES WERE EXTREMELY IMPORTANT IN everyday life for people in earlier centuries. Tools, building materials, and medicines came from trees and were frequently believed to be potent because of the energy or spirit of the tree. In many cultures, before taking anything from a tree, an offering would be given to make an exchange. In addition to the mundane level of use, forests were sacred places for worship and learning, particularly to Celtic people.

According to historian Jean Markale, Druidic belief held that "divinity was accessible only in the midst of forests, in the nemeton."[1] The *nemeton* was a "sacred clearing" and sanctuary. The root of this word, *nem*, means "the projection of a part of the sky on earth." It is also related to the Latin word *nemus*, meaning "sacred wood."

Years ago, when I first heard the phrase "the memory of trees," it conjured images of a fantasy story set in some land where trees no longer existed and therefore were just a memory. When I began studying Celtic myth and culture, I learned otherwise. In Celtic legend, trees were not merely sacred static objects, but warehouses of memories—repositories of knowledge. We frail humans would come and go quickly upon the earth, but trees were here to maintain earthly wisdom with their longevity.

CALENDAR				OGHAM		
Letter	*Gaelic*	*English*		*Letter*	*Gaelic*	*English*
B	Beth	Birch		B	Beth	Birch
L	Luis	Rowan		L	Luis	Rowan
N	Nion	Ash		F	Fearn	Alder
F	Fearn	Alder		S	Saille	Willow
S	Saille	Willow		N	Nion	Ash

Table 3.1: Difference in letter order between alphabets

Throughout Celtic lore, the "great trees" are mentioned. Many stories refer to five great trees—an oak, a yew, and three ashes, each of which grew in one of the five provinces. These were separate from the *crann beatha* clan trees mentioned in chapter 1. Rather than allowing the great trees—and symbolically their culture and spirituality—to be desecrated by Christians, the Celts cut them down and thus short-circuited any triumph on the part of their opponents.

There are two systems associated with the Celts that utilize trees: the tree calendar and the Ogham alphabet. Each has its own system and set of associations with trees. The tree calendar has come to have the alphabet linked with it; however, debate surrounds the ordering of characters. The difference between the tree and Ogham alphabets is the order of the first five letters. The names of the letters are said to have been derived from the names of trees.

Not only has the order of the letters been hotly debated, but also whether or not the Celts actually used such a calendar system. Celtic scholar Peter Berresford Ellis and others claim that the tree calendar was unheard of before Robert Graves' book *The White Goddess* was published in 1948, and that Graves "lacked a linguistic knowledge" to study Celtic mythology on a deep level.[2] Ellis has also points out that Robert Graves did not appear to have called on the expertise of his grandfather, Charles Graves (1812–1899), who was a leading authority on the Ogham and ancient Irish law.

In my personal Celtic studies, I like to compare translations in order to understand as much as possible and not be swayed by popular belief. I refer to Mr. Ellis's work frequently and enjoy his beautiful translations, as well as his good, healthy skepticism. Given that much of Celtic society was rural and sylvan, I think it is quite possible that they looked to the trees for some type of time/seasonal reckoning, although it was most likely not as we envision it today. On the other hand, Robert Graves's work has been so widely adopted and integrated into modern Pagan practice that the tree calendar has become a system of symbols. Like all symbols, its purpose is to aid in accessing deeper levels of energy and consciousness. Whatever its true origin, I have attempted to relate as much fact with this symbolic system as possible, because I believe it provides a method for working with tree energy.

Tracking Time

The Celts reckoned time by darkness and their "day" began at sunset. We currently celebrate Beltane on May first, but Beltane is often referred to as May Eve because according to Celtic tradition, it actually begins the night before—April 30 by our current calendar. It is this difference in how the world is viewed that changed Samhain, October 31, into All Souls Day/Remembrance Day, November first.

Likewise, the Celtic New Year began at Samhain as the dark of the year began.[3] To our modern minds this may seem strange, but if you are in tune with the natural world, it makes perfect sense. Life begins in darkness. Seeds nestled in Mother Earth eventually reach toward the light, but first they need the darkness of her womb to germinate. We, too, begin in the darkness of our human mothers' wombs.

Reckoning time by the waxing and waning of the moon seems logical because it is regular and easy to observe. The Coligny calendar, which was discovered in 1897 near Lyons, France, is a sixty-two-month lunar calendar attributed to the Celts of Gaul. This calendar seems to indicate that a month began on the first quarter of the moon.

We should remember the significance of the moon to ancient people. In a world without bright artificial light, moonsheen pierced the darkness of night. There are thirteen lunations within the cycle of the year and each lunar month consists of twenty-eight days. This leaves an extra day that the Celts referred to as the "nameless day." From time to time, it coincided with the winter solstice. Because of the different calendars used at various times, dates have shifted, and so in the modern tree calendar we end up with winter solstice on December 23 instead of December 21, which is usually closer to the natural event. This extra day is said to have been the basis for the proverbial "year and a day."

MONTH TREES			SEASONAL TREES		
Date	*Letter*	*Tree*	*Date*	*Letter*	*Tree*
Dec. 24–Jan. 20	B	Birch	Post-Winter Solstice	A	Fir
Jan. 21–Feb. 17	L	Rowan	Winter		
Feb. 18–Mar. 17	N	Ash	Spring Equinox	O	Gorse
Mar. 18–Apr. 14	F	Alder	Spring		
Apr. 14–May 12	S	Willow	Spring		
May 13–Jun. 9	H	Hawthorn	Spring		
Jun. 10–Jul. 7	D	Oak	Summer Solstice	U	Heather
Jul. 8–Aug. 4	T	Holly	Summer		
Aug. 5–Sep. 1	C	Hazel	Summer		
Sep. 2–Sep. 29	M	Vine	Autumn Equinox	E	Aspen
Sep. 30–Oct. 27	G	Ivy	Autumn		
Oct. 28–Nov. 24	Ng	Reed	Autumn		
Nov. 25–Dec. 22	R	Elder	Winter Solstice Eve	I	Yew

Dec. 23   Mistletoe   Nameless Day

Table 3.2: Monthly and seasonal tree associations

The trees for each of the thirteen months are associated by the seasonal cycles as well as their vibrational energy that resonates more deeply at certain times of the year. For example, hazel is at its peak of energy in late summer, just as the hazelnut harvest begins.

The seasons were comprised of both solar and earth events, even though the trees that represent them are commonly called solar trees. Graves called them the "complimentary seasonal sequence."[4]

The information from table 3.2 is more easily perceived when displayed graphically as the Wheel of the Year. Viewing time as cyclical rather than linear appeals to the mind on a deeper level. The circle is a symbol of unity and completeness. Because it has no beginning or end we get a sense of timelessness and that we, too, can continue on forever.

Two of the season trees stand on either side of the winter solstice. One can understand the significance of the winter solstice, the point in the sun's cycle when it begins its

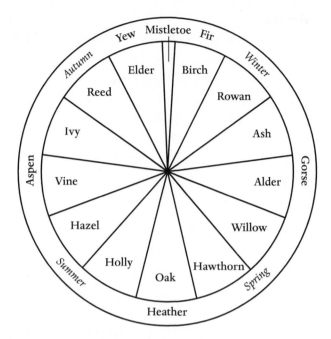

Figure 3.1: Time and the seasons viewed as cyclical rather than linear

journey back to the Northern Hemisphere. Once the longest night of the year passes, the days gradually lengthen. It is as if the breath of nature is suspended between these two trees, waiting for the sun to begin its return journey.

There are thirteen "month" trees and five "season" trees; together these are symbolic of the moon and the sun: the moon's thirteen lunations are contained within the five seasons of the year. This concept of the thirteen within the five comes from the Coligny calendar, which as mentioned, divided the year into thirteen months as well as five parts. It has been argued that this made perfect sense for our agrarian ancestors as seasons for sowing, growing, ripening, harvesting, resting.

The numbers five and thirteen appear to be significant in other traditions. The Gnostic Gospel of Thomas mentions five trees of paradise, which are symbols for Abraham, Elijah, Enoch, Isaac, and Jacob. Plants with five-pointed leaves are associated with various goddesses and gods and were believed to be especially magical.

The number five also held significance to the Babylonians whose moon tree, which also represented the year, was depicted with five fronds. While the Assyrian Tree of

PLANT	GODDESS / GOD
Ivy	Arianrhod, Bacchus, Cernunnos, Danu, Rhea
Vine / Bramble	Bacchus, Brigid, Freya, Llyr
Fig	Aphrodite, Demeter, Hathor, Juno
Plane tree / Sycamore	Cerridwen, Hecate, Morrigan

Table 3.3: Goddesses and gods associated with plants that have five-pointed leaves

Life is depicted with varying numbers of leaves and branches, it is also thought to have represented a calendar.

Throughout history and in many myths, thirteen is significant for the size of a group. King Arthur had twelve knights; Balder, twelve judges; Odysseus of Homer's *Odyssey* had twelve companions; Romulus, the founder of Rome, had twelve shepherds; and Jesus had twelve disciples.

Even though there have been many associations made with the importance of certain numbers, dates, and types of trees, the true origin of the tree calendar is unknown, and as previously mentioned, riddled with controversy.

The types of trees included in the calendar have also been debated. It has been noted that except for "vine," all of the trees are native to the British Isles, and there are no fruit / orchard trees included. One theory is that when the Celts occupied a large part of the European continent, trees native to that area became part of their culture. Archaeological evidence shows that the Rhine and Danube River area of Europe was the cradle of the Celtic civilization.[5] At the time when the Celts occupied that location, it would have been "thickly wooded . . . where the vine grew wild."[6] It would seem that this refers to brambles rather than grapevine, which has become a standard in many modern versions of the tree calendar.

Trees can serve as a grand-scale clock to anyone who can "read" their time signals. The Celts or any other earlier culture probably had little need for our type of calendar hung on the wall to count out days. They needed only to look at the world around them to know where they were in the cycle of the year. We struggle to imagine how rich it must be to exist in such finely tuned connection with the natural world. Getting aligned with the rhythms of trees is a place to start.

Candles to Focus Energy

At the beginning of each tree calendar month, take time to focus on the energy of that particular tree and ponder or meditate on its attributes. One way to focus on a tree and invite its energy into your life is to dedicate and light a candle to it.

With a thick needle, carve the name of the tree into the candle. In addition, you may want to use the Gaelic name for that tree or its related Ogham character. Refer to the next chapter for a listing of Ogham characters and their associated trees. Light the candle on the first night of the tree month. Take time to think about the tree's attributes and which one(s) may have meaning for you. Throughout the month, light the candle so it will be finished by the end of that tree's reign.

Tree Calendar Meditation

Once you have worked with several different types of trees and observed their various attributes and energies, you may want to do a seasonal meditation. For this you will need the name of the five "seasonal" trees (fir, gorse, heather, aspen, and yew) written on separate pieces of paper. Instead of just their names you can use pictures of them or create tree cards. Refer to appendix B for how to make these cards. Instead of sitting in front of your altar, you will be working in a circle. If you are doing this at night, you may want to use candles.

Place a chair or cushion on the floor in the center, where you will imagine a circle surrounding you. You may want to cast a circle as you would for ritual. Determine which way is north and, if you are using candles, place one there to mark that cardinal direction. Place the paper, picture, or card for yew to the left of the candle and fir to its right. If you are not using candles, simply place these cards side by side. Your card for heather goes in the south position at the opposite side of your circle. Place gorse in the east and aspen in the west. Take your seat in the center. From inside the circle, face the direction that corresponds to the current season. If it is midway through a season, face the midway point.

Begin as with other meditations, focusing on your breath and calming your energy. When you are ready, shift your focus to the tree of the current season. For example, if you are facing east, think of springtime and the attributes of gorse. Allow yourself to feel and experience the energy of this season and tree. Let the energy of the tree guide

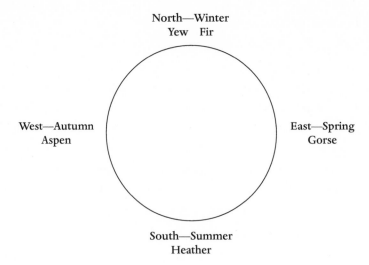

Figure 3.2: The seasonal trees as they relate to the cardinal directions

you. Moving clockwise, repeat this process for each of the other seasons. If it is winter, start with yew if it is before the solstice, or fir if it is after the solstice. The spring and autumn equinoxes are days of balance when light and dark are equal.[7] Take time to feel the equilibrium of these seasons. Spend as much time as you feel is appropriate on each one. With this meditation, you are connecting with the natural world and the cycle of the year. It provides a macroconsciousness of standing outside the circle of time. However, the circle is a spiral, and you are preparing to move within.

If you practice yoga, you might want to incorporate this into a session at home, or begin your seasonal meditation with a few yoga *asanas* (postures). Place the tree papers, pictures, or cards around your mat and do a specific posture that evokes each season for you. For example, you might do "downward-facing dog" for summer because the posture creates heat and warms the body. You might want to begin and end the yoga session with the tree pose.

Experiment with different forms of meditation, or sit with your tree cards or pictures to find what works best for you. Meditating, doing yoga, or just sitting with your tree cards or pictures will help you tune into the energy of each. You may also want to incorporate directions and seasons with the other trees of the calendar according to the time of year.

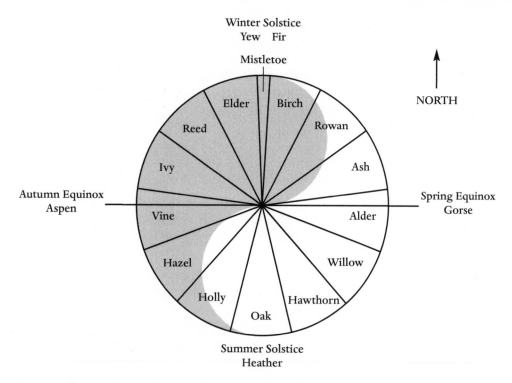

Figure 3.3: The trees of the calendar as they relate to the cardinal directions and seasons

Creating Your Own Calendar

Since coming into popular use, Robert Graves's calendar has raised awareness about trees and the cycle of the year. In order to tap into the strong annual cycle of tree energy, it is important to work with the ones you live among and become attuned with them by working with your own tree calendar.

Graves himself had suggested a different arrangement of some trees to more realistically fit with their cycles. For example, in one discussion on the order of letters in the Beth-Luis-Nion alphabet and relating associated trees with seasonal events, he stated that it would make more sense for apple and willow, hazel, and blackthorn to share months.[9]

The easiest way to begin making your personal tree calendar is to start with Graves's example. Make a list of all the trees and their associated time frames. Cross off the ones

SABBAT	TREE	ASSOCIATIONS
Yule Winter Solstice	Holly	Holly's bright, shiny leaves make the season festive. Their sharp points remind me of the protection we need through the cold winter ahead. The red berries symbolize the life-giving blood of the Goddess as she gives birth to the new sun/son.
Imbolg	Ivy	The evergreen ivy promises ongoing life. Its spiraling growth symbolizes life stirring beneath the surface and the need to begin spiraling back up out of winter's inward journey.
Ostara Spring Equinox	American Sycamore	Still bare of leaves at this time of year, sycamore's seed balls are noticeable. I am reminded that the Wheel is turning from one generation to the next.
Beltane	Crabapple	Spring is in full bloom, and life is bursting forth everywhere. It's a time of love, beauty, and enchantment. This tree is a symbol of the faery realm and the magic that is afoot.
Litha Summer Solstice	Linden	In this soft time of summer, the linden graces the landscape with its beautiful shape and delicate, fragrant flowers.
Lughnasadh	Oak	In full splendor, oaks are the tallest in the woods, offering a deep green backdrop for other trees. They provide cooling shade and food for animals at this early harvest time.
Mabon Autumn Equinox	Maple	Autumn colors begin to blaze as a night chill tinges the air. Maple sends out the last glory of summer's colors that will soon be lost to the grayness of winter.
Samhain	Weeping Willow	Willow holds its leaves long after others have fallen. Its downward flowing branches remind me that it is time to return to earth, spiral inward for winter, and remember those who have gone before.

Table 3.4: The author's personal tree calendar

SEASON	TREE	ASSOCIATIONS
Winter	Yew	Like this time of year, the yew symbolizes death and resurrection. Being an evergreen, it offers hope for the future while providing comfort before rebirth.
Spring	Birch	Its white trunk reminds me of the snow that has disappeared and the reward of having come through the dark of the year. The white also contrasts with the burgeoning green in the woods around it.
Summer	European Weeping Beech	This graceful tree offers shelter from gentle summer showers and large low branches upon which to rest.[8] Standing among these branches, one can feel a welcoming hug.
Autumn	Vine/Bramble	Its foliage fades from gold to brown, reminding me that winter is coming, while it also offers sweet fruits for sustenance.

Table 3.5: Supplemental season trees to the author's personal tree calendar

that do not grow in your area. Decide whether or not to keep the date ranges for the remaining trees. Consider: would shifting to a standard calendar month time frame feel right for you? Would an annual cycle with fewer trees make more sense? My personal tree calendar is based on the Pagan Wheel of the Year, with the time period for each tree beginning and ending on a sabbat.

I make it a point to visit each type of tree, and in some cases particular trees, as close to, if not on the sabbat and throughout its "reigning" period. This type of calendar can also be supplemented with four "season" trees.

1. Jean Markale, *Merlin: Priest of Nature*, trans. Belle N. Burke (Rochester, VT: Inner Traditions, 1995), 52.

2. Peter Berresford Ellis, "The Fabrication of 'Celtic' Astrology," previously published in *The Astrological Journal* 39, no. 4 (1997). It is available online at http://cura.free.fr/xv/13ellis2.html.

3. According to Miranda Green, the association of Samhain as the Celtic New Year has been questioned in recent years; however, no definitive conclusion has been reached. Miranda J. Green, *The World of the Druids* (New York: Thames and Hudson, Inc., 1997), 36.

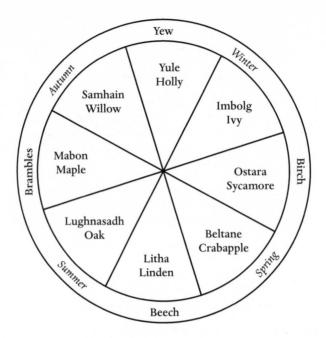

Figure 3.4: The author's personal Tree Wheel of the Year

4. Robert Graves, *The White Goddess: A Historical Grammar of Poetic Myth* (New York: The Noonday Press, 1975), 189.

5. Marija Gimbutas, *The Civilization of the Goddess* (New York: HarperCollins, 1991), 348 and 362.

6. Graves, *The White Goddess*, 201.

7. The balance of light and dark is vividly illustrated with the yin-yang symbol—see figure 3.4. Using an eight-foot pole and recording the length of its shadow through the course of a year, the ancient Chinese plotted it into a sun chart that became the yin-yang symbol. Allen Tsai, "Where Does the Yin Yang Symbol Come From?" http://www.chinesefortunecalendar.com/ yinyang.htm.

8. The town where I lived in Massachusetts had a wonderfully huge European weeping beech on the town common. During the summer its long sweeping branches had such thick foliage that it created a "living tent" under which a friend and I clandestinely conducted our rituals when we couldn't get out to the woods.

9. Graves, *The White Goddess*, 248.

FOUR

The Ogham

ALMOST EVERYTHING CONNECTED WITH THE Ogham—its name, characters, and origin—is in dispute. The idea of a mystical Ogham has captured the imaginations of many who have expanded and incorporated it into their practices. The age and original meaning of the Ogham is less important than the symbols it represents today. Like the tree calendar, it is the value we ascribe to them that has meaning for us. However, it is important to keep an open mind to new research and ideas and to be able to adjust our use and meaning of these symbols. Spirituality and reality evolve over time, and a living, breathing, advancing faith ultimately provides deeper meaning.

A History of the Ogham

The origin of the Celtic tree Ogham (also spelled Ogam) is unknown, but there is plenty of speculation about it. Even the simple fact of how to pronounce the word varies, from "Oh-m" to "Oh-wam" to "Oh-yam"—take your pick. One theory was that the Ogham was a way to write the Norse runes; another was that it evolved from the Latin and Greek systems of writing. The general consensus today is that its origin was completely separate. There is also an elaborate explanation on how the Ogham evolved from the Roman alphabet—this theory includes a convoluted description of adding and subtracting letters and sometimes working backwards to reach the correct order of letters.

There are several schools of thought concerning the name itself. One is that it comes from myth. According to legend, the Ogham was created by Ogma, the son of Breas. He was known as "Ogma the Eloquent" and is called the "God of Literature." Ogma's "golden speech" has been represented in artwork with a gold chain extending from his mouth to the ear of his listeners.

Some scholars claim that it has a Greek origin because of the Greek word *ogmos*, which means "furrow." When Ogham characters are carved into rock or wood, the strokes look like small furrows. Since the Celts of Gaul conducted a thriving trade with the merchants of Greece, they were not only familiar with the Greek language, but also used it in recording common transactions.

Because the first twenty characters of the Ogham are straight lines, rather than being written, carved, or painted on something, there is speculation that the characters were simply laid out on a flat surface using twigs or groupings of leaves. Carving the letters into wood is thought to have been a later development followed even later by carving them into stone, just as archaeological evidence has revealed that Stonehenge was preceded by a woodhenge.[1]

What we do know is that approximately 370 inscriptions exist in stone. These are standing stones that range from three to nine feet tall. Most of these are located in the southwest province of Munster, Ireland, with about one-third of the total in County Kerry. There is a scattering of these stones in Scotland, Wales, the Isle of Man, and Devonshire, England. Scholars disagree on the dates of these Ogham stones, but many place their timeframe from 300 to 600 CE. In Pembrokeshire, Wales, there are a few sixth century gravestones with both Latin and Ogham inscriptions.

Similar Ogham-like markings on standing stones found in Spain and Portugal have been dated to 500 BCE. It has been suggested that this may have been a precursor to the Ogham developed by the Celtic tribes on the Iberian Peninsula who migrated to Ireland. Harvard Professor Barry Fell, long-term president of the Epigraphic Society, took the risk of suggesting that markings on stones found throughout the United States are also a form of Ogham used by wide-ranging tribes of Celts.[2] Few people have taken this theory seriously and it unfortunately seems to have discredited some of this other work.

Many details about the Ogham come from *The Book of Ballymote*, which was compiled in 1391 for Tonnaltagh McDonagh of Ballymote Castle, County Sligo. This "book" is actually a collection of older manuscripts and documents on history, legend, and religion. Some of the manuscripts are thought to have been copied from ninth century sources. Other books that mention the Ogham include *The Book of Lecan* (1416), *The Book of Lismore* (late fourteenth/early fifteenth century), and *The Book of Leinster* (twelfth century). These books are similar to *The Book of Ballymote* in that they are manuscript collections of prose and poetry containing history, lore, legal, medical, and religious writings. Other twelfth-century sources for information on the Ogham include *Auraicept na nÉces* (*The Scholar's Primer*), *Lebor Ogam* (*The Book of Ogham*), and *De Duibh Feda na Forfid* (*Values of the Forfeda*).

While *The Book of Leinster* makes reference to the Ogham being in use centuries earlier, some scholars believe that these references and others, such as those contained in the *Táin Bó Cuailnge* (*The Cattle Raid of Cooley*), were twelfth-century additions to the manuscripts. According to Charles Graves, while the Brehon Laws[3] (circa 438 CE) mention the Ogham, the older volumes contained within, such as *The Book of Aicil* and the *Senchus Mor*, do not. However, according to Peter Berresford Ellis, there are at least four hundred Irish manuscripts that have not been translated[4]—more information on the Ogham could be awaiting discovery.

There are relatively few references to the Ogham being used for divination. Miranda Green suggests that the idea of divination is a mistaken translation of the word *for-cain*, which can mean "prophecy/predict" or "sang-over," referring to an oral teaching process of repeating lessons in chorus.[5]

A medical manuscript from 1509 (in the Library of the Royal Irish Academy, Dublin) mentions cures that included hitting an afflicted person with a rod marked with the Ogham. It was believed that this action would release the illness from the person's body. The type of wood depended on the cure needed, for example, elm for impotence. The Ogham inscription on the rod consisted of the person's name or, according to other sources, a spell.

A story in *The Book of Leinster* tells about a prince who went off to battle carrying a shield marked with Ogham characters. He was saved by a Druid who clued him in to the contents of the message, which were instructions to have the prince killed. In many stories of the Ulster Cycle, Cu Chulainn frequently leaves notices of challenge for his enemies on objects marked with Ogham.

A few sources mention the Ogham as a means to inscribe a person's name on a standing stone used to mark his or her grave. Concerning these, Caitlin and John Matthews noted that *The Book of Lismore* indicates "Ogham names were written" rather than saying that a person's name was written in Ogham.[6] Charles Graves also raised this point and suggested that a person's "Ogham name" was different from the name by which he or she was ordinarily known.[7] This brings up questions for which we have no answers: Does this indicate that people used clan or ceremonial names? Many of us today use magic names, so this may not be so extravagantly unusual. Magical uses of the Ogham are mentioned in several accounts.

Many of the standing stones marked with the Ogham do not seem to be burial markers. Charles Graves suggested that these pillar stones (called *Gallan*) were tribal boundary markers. He also points out that Celtic society was stratified and the common people would not have been able to decipher the Ogham messages. Graves suggested that the information on the pillar stones was understood by those who needed to know and that the information would not have been easily forged. The Ogham seems to have been understood by the "literary hierarchy" of bards, Druids and the upper ranks of warriors. The prince in the story from *The Book of Leinster* mentioned earlier was obviously not part of this elite. Graves also noted that an Ogham "inscription itself is called fair writing."[8] He considered the use of Ogham to have been different from the writing of books and documents.

One theory on the original use of the Ogham suggests that it was created for musical notation for the harp, perhaps because *The Book of Ballymote* refers to the various types as "Ogham scales." Some of these actually resemble written music more than an alphabet. Another is that it began as a sign language and that the written characters were merely an imitation of the hand and finger positions. R. A. Stewart Macalister based the latter theory on the fact that the Ogham's original twenty characters are grouped by fives because people have five fingers on each hand. There is also the theory that it served as a form of speech that was only understood by the initiated.

The nineteenth century Celtic Revival in literature and art not only fueled an interest in the Ogham but also romanticized the antiquity of it. Charles Graves declared that it was not an ancient alphabet and that it originated in the early Christian period. As previously mentioned, scholars today are leaning more to a 300–600 CE date range and some theorize that it could have been invented as a reaction to Christianity. While the Celts were quick to pick up some parts of Christianity, the overall change from a Pagan to Christian spirituality in Ireland took place over a long period of time—approximately from the third to eighth century. During this time there was a rich melange of ideas and faiths. Even as the Irish gravitated to the new religion, they took it on their own terms. For example, the Celtic cross is an integration of Pagan and Christian symbols, and outside of Ireland you certainly won't find the Sheila-na-gig in churches.

The Ogham and Poets

Ogham is sometimes referred to as the poetic alphabet because bards and people of learning used it. While we tend to think of a bard/poet as an entertainer (i.e. *the* bard Shakespeare), in Celtic culture a bard was more of a sacred storyteller, "musical dream weaver," and keeper of rituals. The next level in the Druidic order were the ovates, the shamanic journeyers who sought wisdom from the ancestors and the natural world. The third level, Druids, were the teachers, advisors and custodians of knowledge. It is important to note that native Celtic sources do not always make this distinction. Peter Berresford Ellis suggests that "Druids" were a class, the intellectuals of the Celtic social order.[9]

Many agree that the Ogham may have been used to pass information beyond a name or word written with its characters. In addition to being associated with a particular tree, each letter is believed to have also corresponded to certain people, locations, animals, and particular objects. References to the Ogham in *The Book of Ballymote* indicate that it was used for communications that could "pass unnoticed by the uninitiated." Rather than being an alphabet that was written and read like Latin and Greek, the cryptic characters of the Ogham were abstract symbols—"keys" to a wealth of information. If you have tried using the Ogham, you will have found that the letters are not practical for writing more than simple inscriptions.

Throughout history there have been secret alphabets devised for numerous reasons, but the Ogham was more wide-spread and seemingly in use for a longer time period than others. While not an alphabet, another example is Cockney rhyming slang[10] which has been around (and evolving) since the sixteenth century. Few people outside of England are familiar with it and can much less use it.

Robert Graves suggested that the Ogham was employed in its latest period of use as a method for secretly passing information by bards who did not agree with the poetic/spiritual themes proscribed by those in power. The Ogham could have been used to pass along, without detection, ideas that may have been deemed "inappropriate." This coincides with the British conquests of 1541–1691 when Ireland came under English rule and the Brehon Laws were replaced with the English rule of law. The use of the native language and circulating books in anything but English was difficult and punishable by law.[11] According to Peter Berresford Ellis, "Books in Irish were to be destroyed and all native centers of learning were closed."[12] This was a sad state of affairs for Ireland as it had been the beacon of education and learning for most of Europe during the Dark Ages.[13] The bards of Wales were fighting similar battles.

In its use as a sign language, each letter was assigned a point on the fingertips and joints of each hand whereby touching them could discreetly pass information. Robert Graves referred to this method as the "finger keyboard,"[14] Other similar methods are said to have been employed by touching the side of one's nose or shin with a part of a finger to indicate information embodied by the letter associated with that point on the finger. Curiously, only nineteen of the twenty core characters were assigned to the hand Ogham. It is not known why the twentieth letter or the other set of five characters were not used in this type of system.

Another theory put forth by Robert Graves for the possible use of this hand system is that it could have also served as a memory aid. History, myth and wisdom were passed on orally, and it is not inconceivable that many such *aide-mémoire* were developed and employed. Look at the length of the poems and ask yourself if you could learn, retain and recite these without some type of help. I don't think I could. One such long poem that Graves associated with the Ogham was *The Battle of the Trees*. Its title in the original Welsh is *Câd Goddeu*. This epic saga tells the story of Gwydion invading the underworld with a battalion of trees. Each type of tree exhibits a particular strength, and these strengths have come down through the centuries as aspects and powers associated with the trees.

The Battle of the Trees has also been interpreted as an intellectual battle rather than a physical one. Graves has suggested that it could have been a "mythographic shorthand" that relayed "an important religious event in pre-Christian Britain."[15]

Druidic training wasn't simply a matter of being familiar with all of the long poems—it was committing them to memory. According to Julius Caesar (102–44 BCE), the Celts of Gaul had an aversion to copying material into manuscripts. In his account, *The Gallic Wars*, he mentions that, "They are said there to get by heart a great number of verses; some continue twenty years in their education; neither is it held lawful to commit these things [the Druidic doctrines] to writing, though in almost all public transactions and private accounts they use Greek characters."[16] This supports the theory that the Ogham may have served as an aide-mémoire. It has also been cited as proof that the Ogham existed before the common era; however, Caesar does not mention the Ogham itself or other memory aids that the Druids may have used.

Caesar paints a broad picture that leads one to believe that the Celts recorded very little. Matters of spiritual significance were not committed to writing but other concerns were. In Italy Celts used letters based on Etruscan writing. In Gaul and the Balkan area, the Greek alphabet was used, and in Spain the characters from Phoenician script were used.[17]

Historical and spiritual matters may have been deemed too important to reduce to a document. The great Celtic legends were not written down until the Christian era. Words had a "mystic significance"[18] that would be dulled or less "alive" if they were static on a page. Knowledge tucked away in a book is not immediately available; however, if wisdom is held in the mind, one has total access to it. And, of course, another difference is that the spoken word is alive—full of depth, tone, and inflection.

I believe that part of the aversion to committing information to paper could have been an issue of trust. When you are speaking with someone you can make a judgment whether or not to trust him or her. When something is written you do not necessarily know the true source of the information and whether or not what is written is authentic. The Celts held the principal of truth in the highest esteem, and the power of truth was associated with divinity.

Depictions of Druids and bards usually include mention of the staves—*Taball-Lrog*—the poet's staff. This was not a simple walking stick, but rather a number of flat rods that were connected at one end and could be spread open like a fan. Descriptions mention that the rods were covered with Ogham characters, making the instrument a sort of multi-purpose shillelagh.

Since trees were believed to hold wisdom and teaching was done in groves, it would seem logical that tree names were used for the names of letters. Beith/birch is the first letter and it has been suggested that the Ogham was first written on birch. As usual, there is disagreement on this and the significance of the names. Ellis asserts that the characters were not assigned the tree names until the fourteenth century and then only for the purpose of teaching children—not unlike our modern alphabet songs.

The Ogham Characters

One point that most people agree on concerning the Ogham is that there were originally twenty Ogham characters and that an additional five (diphthongs) were added later to accommodate Greek and Latin characters. There is a marked difference between the first twenty characters and the other five. The first twenty are simple straight lines suitable for carving into wood or stone, while the others are more complex and would not lend themselves to be easily carved. The original twenty are called *feda* (*feadha*, plural) and the additional five, *forfeda*.

The characters are divided into groups of five—perhaps this division is symbolic of the five provinces of Ireland. The word for province in Modern Irish is *cuige,* which also means "a fifth." Of the original twenty characters, the first fifteen are consonants, the other five vowels. The original four groups are called *aicme* (tribes). Each aicme is named after the first character in the group, for example, *aicme beith, aicme huath,* and so forth.

Ogham can be written horizontally or vertically along a mid-line or stem line. This mid-line is also called *druim,* which means ridge or spine because the edge of a stone or flat rod was used instead of a carved mid-line. When written horizontally, the Ogham is read left to right. When vertical, it is read bottom to top. The starting point of the mid-line was often distinguished with a V shape (feathered arrow) or curlicues when written on paper as in *The Book of Ballymote.*

One difficulty in deciphering Ogham script on stones is discerning its course. In following the ridge or edge of a cut stone, the writing travels up one edge and down another. When all four edges of the stone contain Ogham, it's not simple to see where one begins reading and then continues after going up one side and down another. In some instances a dot on the stem line was used to indicate a break (space) between words. The effects of time and weathering complicate the task of reading the inscriptions.

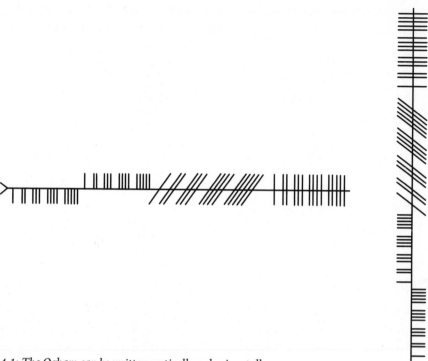

Figure 4.1: The Ogham can be written vertically or horizontally

The language represented by the Ogham on these stones is Primitive Irish, a forerunner of what is called Old Irish. The earliest known Irish literature was written between 600 and 900 CE in Old Irish. This does not mean that all Ogham stones were carved before 600 CE. Primitive Irish was still in use after the sixth century as there was a gradual evolution to Old Irish.

Like everything else with the Ogham, numerologists have had a field day with it. The number of consonants, fifteen, coincides with the full moon occurring on the fifteenth day of the lunar cycle. Fifteen is a multiple of three, and three and five are important numbers. Three is a magical number as the number of realms (heaven, earth, and underworld) and the aspects of the Goddess. Five represents the five provinces (ancient divisions) of Ireland, the mythical "well of wisdom" had five streams flowing into it, humans have five fingers on each hand, and we have five physical senses by which to perceive the material world.

The number four is also important. In the story *The Wooing of Etain*, four wands of yew with three Oghams each are mentioned. The use of four "fews" (generally squared pieces of wood no longer than your index finger that have an Ogham character carved or inscribed on them) and similar rods with characters on all four sides are mentioned in other sources. Four represents the four aicme of the original Ogham. These aicme have been linked with the four earth festivals of Imbolg, Beltane, Lughnasadh, and Samhain, as well as the four solar festivals of the solstices and equinoxes. There are also the four treasures of the Tuatha De Danann[19] and the four seasons.

Using Staves, Fews, and Cards

As previously noted, divination is not the most frequently mentioned use of the Ogham in ancient texts. However, these few instances have been latched onto, and divination by Ogham is about as popular as the use of Norse runes.

Instead of the usual "predict the future" or "who will I marry" sort of divination, I like to use the Ogham to search for messages or clues about what I may need to know about a particular situation. For example, if there is a problem or issue on my mind and I randomly select the Ur (U) Ogham character from a set of staves, I examine the attributes and associations of the related tree, in this case heather. Its basic associations are passion and generosity. This would indicate to me that I need to apply one or both of these attributes to help resolve the issue for which I am seeking guidance.

When working with the Ogham in this manner, there are several objects you can use: staves, fews, or cards. Staves or sticks are more or less the "classic" Ogham objects.

These can be bought or made and can be as elaborate or simple as you choose. Making your own tools imbues them with your energy, which personalizes and makes them more powerful. The stave is a small stick or twig approximately six inches long. A set will have one for each Ogham character. You can work with the original twenty *feadha* or all twenty-five. Refer to appendix B for instructions on making Ogham staves, fews, and cards.

You can use these tools for divination, but more importantly they can help you access the energy of the tree each Ogham character represents. Sit in front of your altar or wherever you are comfortable and light a candle. Take time to turn off the chattering "monkey brain" and let go of "left brain" activity. Let your mind be open to receive. When you feel relaxed, pick up one of the staves, fews, or cards. You can randomly

OGHAM CHARACTER	PRIMARY LETTER	SECONDARY LETTER(S)	NAME & VARIATIONS	ASSOCIATED TREE(S)	BASIC ASSOCIATIONS
The Feadha					
Aicme Beith					
⊤	B		**Beith**, Beth, Beithe	Birch	Beginnings, release, renewal, change
⊤⊤	L		Luis	Rowan	Quickening, insight, dedication, expression, blessings
⊤⊤⊤	F	V, GW	**Fearn**, Fern	Alder	Foundation, guardian, evolving spirit
⊤⊤⊤⊤	S		**Saille**, Saile, Suil	Willow	Intuition, flexibility, knowledge, relationships
⊤⊤⊤⊤⊤	N		Nion, Nuin, Nin	Ash	Transitions, connections, creativity
Aicme Huath					
⊥	H		**Huath**, Uath, Huathe	Hawthorn	Protection/defense, hope, healing, spiritual energies
⊥⊥	D		**Duir**, Dair, Daur	Oak	Strength, self-confidence, justice
⊥⊥⊥	T		**Tinne**, Teine	Holly	Hearth and home, unity, protection, courage, guidance
⊥⊥⊥⊥	C	K	Coll, Call	Hazel	Wisdom, knowledge of secrets, creativity
⊥⊥⊥⊥⊥	Q	CC	**Quert**, Ceirt, Queirt, Cert	Apple	Eternity, love, faithfulness, rebirth

Table 4.1: The Ogham

(continued on next page)

Table 4.1 (continued)

OGHAM CHARACTER	PRIMARY LETTER	SECONDARY LETTER(S)	NAME & VARIATIONS	ASSOCIATED TREE(S)	BASIC ASSOCIATIONS
Aicme Muin					
	M		**Muin**	Vine/Bramble	Inward journey, lifting confusion, opening, learning lessons
	G		**Gort**	Ivy	Growth, wildness, development confronting the mystical
	Ng		**Ngetal**, nGétal, Ngeadal	Reed	Health and healing, adaptation, gathering
	St	Z, SS	**Straif**, Straiph, Straith	Blackthorn	Authority, control, strength in adversity
	R		**Ruis**	Elder	Maturity, abundance, awareness, transition
Aicme Ailm					
	A		**Ailm**, Ailim	Fir, Elm, Pine	Perspective, reaching, rising above
	O		**Onn**, Ohn	Gorse (Furze)	Hope, persistence
	U	W	**Ur**, Ura	Heather	Passion, generosity
	E		**Eadhadh**, Eadha, Edad	Aspen	Endurance, communication, courage, success
	I	J, Y	**Iodho**, Idad, Iodhadh, Ido	Yew	Death, transition, endings

The Forfeda

Symbol	Letter	Name	Tree	Meaning
	EA	**Éabhadh,** Ebad	Honeysuckle, Aspen	Attracting sweetness of life
	OI	**Oir,** Or	Spindle tree, Ivy	Creativity, inspiration
	UI	**Uilleann,** Uilen, Uileand	Honeysuckle, Beech	Manifesting intentions
	IO	**Ifin,** Iphin	Gooseberry, Beech	Clarity of vision, second sight
	AE	**Amhancholl,** Eamhancholl	Witch hazel, Pine	Cleansing, purifying, releasing

select one, or if there is a particular tree that you want to work with, choose that one. Think of how that tree looks. Ponder its attributes and how they fit into your life. Feel the energy of the tree in your hand. When you feel that you have a sense of that tree's energy, you can end the meditation. Place the card, stave, or few you were holding where you will see it frequently for a day or two as a reminder. If you keep a journal, you may want to note any sensation or imagery that arose during your meditation.

Cultivating Traits

Another way to invite tree energy into your life to engender certain traits is to wear or carry something from a tree. The Ogham fews and cards can be small enough to carry in a purse or pocket. For example, if your life is in transition you could carry your card or few for the *beith* (birch) Ogham. If maturity is an issue, use *ruis* (elder). If you feel bogged down and you need to rise above whatever is causing a problem in your life, you could carry the *ailm* (fir) Ogham. Alternatively, since *ailm* is represented by fir or pine you could carry a few needles from a tree. If strength is what you are looking to emphasize, carry an acorn to represent oak. If you're worried about traveling, tuck a holly leaf into your suitcase. If you don't have access to real holly use a picture or cut out a holly-shaped leaf from a green piece of paper and then write its Ogham character on it. Alternatively, jewelry is available in many leaf, flower, and acorn motifs; however, this could potentially get pricey if you want something for each tree with which you intend to work.

At home if you keep an altar or have a special place where you meditate that has a flat surface, use twigs to lay out the Ogham character of the tree whose traits you are cultivating. Let it be a reminder of the tree's energy and what you are working toward.

---

1. Alastair Service and Jean Bradbery, *The Standing Stones of Europe* (London: Weidenfeld & Nicolson, 1996), 248–249.
2. Barry Fell, "Old Irish Rock Inscriptions from West Virginia: Ogam Translated" *The Epigraphic Society Occasional Papers* 11, no. 252 (1983): 1–37. The Epigraphic Society was founded in 1974 by Dr. H. Barry Fell of Harvard University and Norman Totten of Bentley College for the purpose of supporting the discovery and decipherment of ancient inscriptions.

3. The Brehon Laws are a testament to the advanced thinking and belief of the Celts. In these laws, men and women were co-equals. They gave women more protection and rights than any other system of law until recent times. James MacKillop, *Oxford Dictionary of Celtic Mythology* (Oxford: Oxford University Press, 1998), 53.

4. Ellis, *The Chronicles of the Celts*, 9–10.

5. Miranda J. Green, *The Celtic World* (New York: Penguin, 1995), 431.

6. Caitlin and John Matthews, *The Encyclopedia of Celtic Wisdom* (Rockport, MA: Element Books, Inc., 1994), 29.

7. Charles Graves, "On the Ogam Beithluisnia." Excerpted in Matthews, *The Encyclopedia of Celtic Wisdom*, 30.

8. Ibid.

9. Ellis, *The Druids*, 70.

10. Cockney rhyming slang originated in London's East End and is a method of code speaking where a word is replaced by another word or phrase that rhymes with it. For example, bank is "tin tank," boots are "daisy roots," and cigarettes (smokes) are "ash and oaks."

11. Roderic O'Flaherty (1629–1718) wrote a "mytho-historical" account of Ireland, *Ogygia, seu Rerum Hibernicarum Chronologia*, in Latin during the Cromwellian oppression, in which the cryptic name "Ogygia" meant Ireland, the name Plutarch used for it. During the nineteenth century Celtic Revival, many mistook this word to mean Ogham. Ellis, *The Druids*, 225, and Seumas MacManus, *The Story of the Irish Race* (Old Greenwich, CT: The Devin-Adain Co., 1990), 19.

12. Ellis, "The Fabrication of 'Celtic' Astrology."

13. For more information, see Thomas Cahill's *How the Irish Saved Civilization: The Untold Story of Ireland's Heroic Role from the Fall of Rome to the Rise of Medieval Europe* (New York: Nan A. Talese/Doubleday, 1995), 181–186.

14. Graves, *The White Goddess*, 115.

15. Ibid., 38.

16. T. W. Rolleston, *Celtic Myths and Legend* (New York: Dover Publications, 1990), 37.

17. John Davies, *The Celts: Prehistory to Present Day* (London: Cassell & Company, 2001), 60.

18. Ellis, *The Chronicles of the Celts*, 5.

19. The four gifts are La Fal (Stone of Destiny), the Sword of Nuada, the Spear of Lugh, and the Cauldron of Dagda. MacKillop, *Dictionary of Celtic Mythology*, 415; Rolleston, *Celtic Myths and Legend*, 105–106.

FIVE

Exploring the Range of Oghams

WHILE SCHOLARS AND OTHERS CONTINUE the debate about its origins, there is a modern purpose that the Ogham has come to serve. Similarly, archaeologist Marija Gimbutas's life work of deciphering ancient "decorative patterns" into a complex range of meaningful symbols was never fully accepted by her colleagues. However, her interpretations of material from ancient Goddess-worshipping cultures hold a great depth of meaning for many people today.

Interpretations and use of the Ogham hold a similar position. We use products of the past not to return to earlier days but to tap into a rich body of knowledge that continues to grow. I believe it is important to continually reevaluate our beliefs because, as we grow spiritually and in years, our perspective shifts. We evolve, as does the knowledge base we draw upon thanks to ongoing research and translation. As trees teach us, flexibility is key.

Whatever its age and original purpose, the Ogham, like the tree calendar, has acquired a meaning and use for people today. As Marija Gimbutas pointed out, knowledge and emotion are deep within the psyche and respond to symbols. I personally believe that symbols and practices can be used as tools to enrich my life as I continue to explore myth and historical fact for the kernels of truth that feed my intellect. This gives me balance.

Symbols help to access meanings that linger on the edge of consciousness. They help us to hear the whispers from the woods and elsewhere, but we must be ready to listen and ready to do some work.

In our modern world we have grown so accustomed to information being handed to us as analyzed, pre-packaged sound bites. We learn a little about a lot, but rarely "get under the hood" to understand. For deep-felt meaning in spirituality, we need to delve below the surface. We need to search and work and learn as we go along.

We talk about our spirituality as a path. Like any path that is interesting, the scenery will change as we move along. There are decisions to make when we arrive at any sort of crossroad. Most importantly, we are each on our separate paths, so in a sense we are all trailblazers. I may follow the same tradition as you, but our paths will be different because we look out at the world with different eyes and with different souls.

As trailblazers, we must each adapt the tools we find along our paths. One size does not fit all because everyone's energy, everyone's path is unique. Something that is meaningful to you does not have to be meaningful to anyone else and vice versa.

The Ballymote Scales

The set of Ogham characters that is most well known is the simple, straight-grooved alphabet carved into standing stones. This Ogham is also easy to use when scratching the characters onto a candle or carving them into a wand or other tool. One of the manuscripts in *The Book of Ballymote* has become known as the "Ogam Tract" because it contains ninety-two versions of Ogham characters. I was delighted to find the rich diversity and creativity of the Oghams.

While most of them follow the pattern of one stroke for the letter *B*, two for *L*, three for *F*, and so forth, a few of the Ogham scales are constructed differently (each set of Ogham characters is referred to as a "scale"). For example, scale 33 reverses the strokes in each aicme and gives the letter *N* one stroke, *S* two strokes, and so on, ending with *B* having five strokes. In order for the Ogham to have deep meaning for us, we need to make it personal.

If the Ogham contains the letters representing all the trees with which you are working (or intend to work) and you like the simplicity of the single strokes, then continue to work with it. Alternatively, you may find a set of Ogham characters that is more aesthetically pleasing and choose to use those symbols to aid you in accessing the corresponding tree's energy.

The following Ogham samples are just a few select examples of the many that exist in a wide range of styles.[1] Most of the Oghams are written along a single stem line with the starting point marked by a curlicue bracket. When necessary, the stem lines in the samples are broken and continued underneath to fit the page.

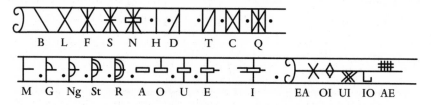

Figure 5.1: Scale 1, **Aradach Finn,** *"Ladder of Fionn"*

A number of Oghams relate to Fionn Mac Cumhaill who was the leader of a great standing army called the Fianna (also Fian) in third-century Ireland. The Fianna served Cormac Mac Art, one of the greatest kings of Ireland. Under his rule the island enjoyed a period of peace and prosperity. During the era of the Fianna, Ireland had no foreign invaders.

Figure 5.2: Scale 3, **Luthogam,** *"Hinge Ogham"*

Scale 3 (figure 5.2) is illustrated in two parts to fit on the page. Normally when it is written out with all characters it would be done so as scale 1 (figure 5.1). Like scale 1, scale 3 uses a double stem line in between which the characters are written. The *forfeda* has its own separate stem line inside the other two. Other sets of Ogham, such as scale 5, have multiple (sometimes up to four) stem lines and resemble musical notation.

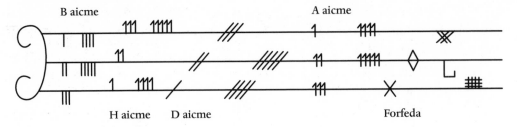

Figure 5.3: Scale 5, Trelurgach Find, *"Three-stemmed Ogham of Fionn"*

Dr. Fell translated scale 5 as an Ogham of Fionn; however, Lugh was also known as Find, "Fair One." Some scales were said to have been secret Oghams used by warriors and created for one-time use, perhaps as codes for certain battles.

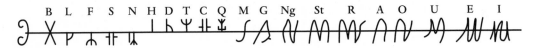

Figure 5.4: Scale 14, Runugam na Fian, *"Running Ogham of the Fianna"*

Scale 13 (figure 5.5) is attributed to Ilann, son of Fergus Mac Roich, a king of Ulster. It is not clear if Ilann (or Illann) who is sometimes referred to as Ilann the Fair created this for one-time use. He and his brother were killed at the Red Branch hostel defending the lovers Deirdre and Naisi (or Noíse) in their flight from King Concho-bar.[2] The story is part of the Ulster Cycle. The story is part of the Ulster Cycle.

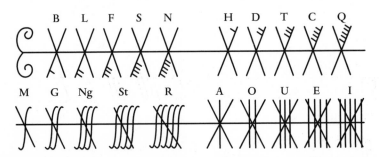

Figure 5.5: Scale 13, Ebadach Ilaind, *"Created by Ilann"*

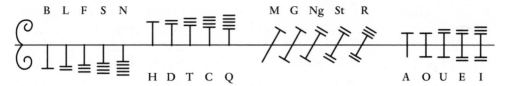

Figure 5.6: Scale 17, **Ogam adlenfid,** *"Letter rack Ogham"*

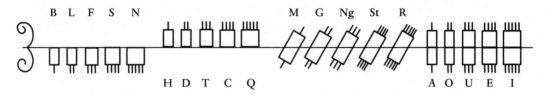

Figure 5.7: Scale 19, **Crad cride ecis,** *"Anguish of a poet's heart"*

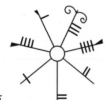

Figure 5.8: Portion of scale 25

Although scale 25 is rather complicated, part of it is reproduced here (figure 5.8) to illustrate how an Ogham can be unique and dynamic. Previously mentioned, scale 33 (figure 5.9) reverses the number of strokes for the characters in each aicme. In scale 49 (figure 5.10), dots take the place of multiple lines for each character.

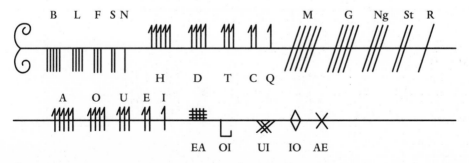

Figure 5.9: Scale 33, **Ceand ar nuaill,** *"Head on Proscription"*

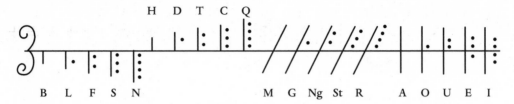

Figure 5.10: Scale 49, **Brecor beo,** *"Lively dotting"*

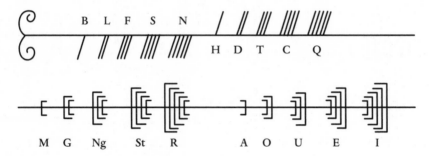

Figure 5.11: Scale 50, **Ceand imreasan,** *"Strife head"*

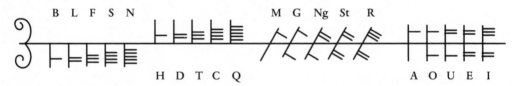

Figure 5.12: Scale 51, **Ogam Dedad,** *"Ogham of Dedu"*

The Clan Dedad were followers of Cu Roi Mac Dairi, a giant hero who was a master sorcerer and warrior. Cu Roi Mac Dairi and the Dedad are associated with County Kerry. Their stories are part of the Ulster Cycle.

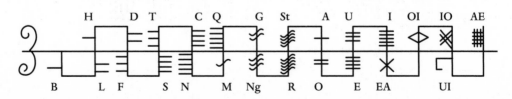

Figure 5.13: Scale 52, **Ceand debtha,** *"Head of dispute"*

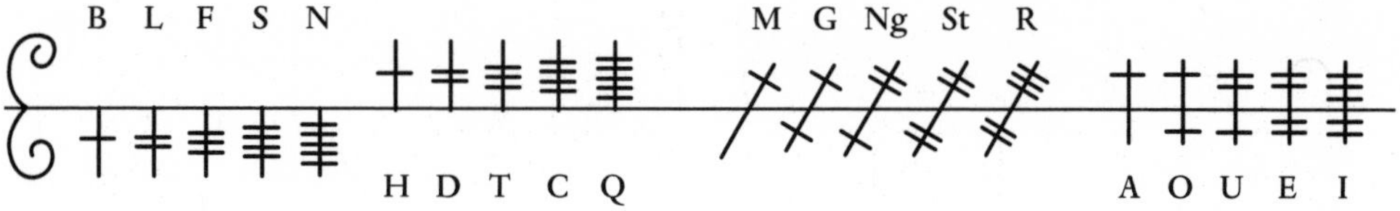

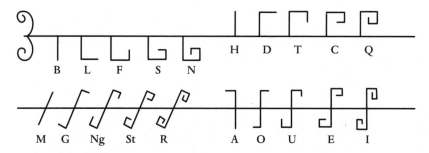

Figure 5.14: Scale 53, Unnamed

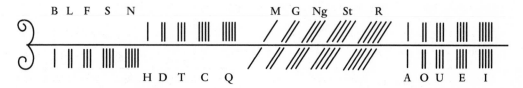

Figure 5.15: Scale 54, Unnamed

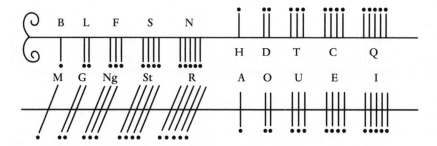

Figure 5.16: Scale 55, **Didruim,** *"Ridgeless"*

Figure 5.17: Scale 56, **Ogam focosach,** *"Well-footed Ogham"*

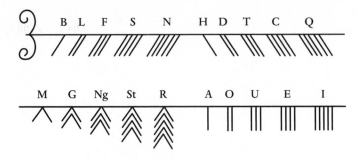

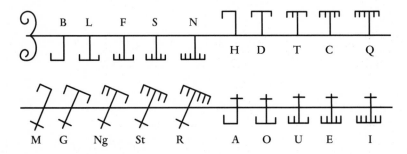

Figure 5.18: Scale 61, Taebogam Tlachtga aentaeb uile na fega-sa sis, *"Side Ogham of Tlachtga, on one side all these letters below"*

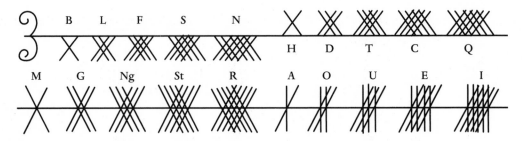

Figure 5.19: Scale 62, Unnamed

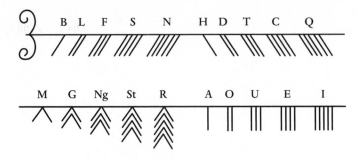

Figure 5.20: Scale 64, Snaithi snimach, *"Interwoven thread"*

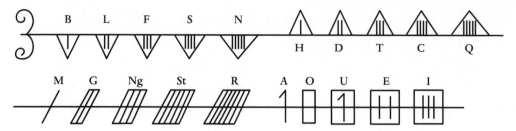

Figure 5.21: Scale 68, Unnamed

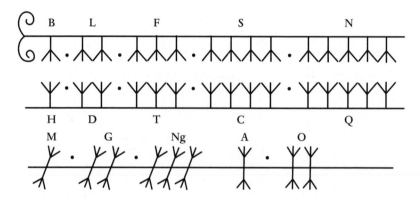

Figure 5.22: Scale 70, Unnamed

In scales 70 and 73 (figures 5.22 and 5.23) not all of the characters were illustrated but one can see how the last two aicme would progress.

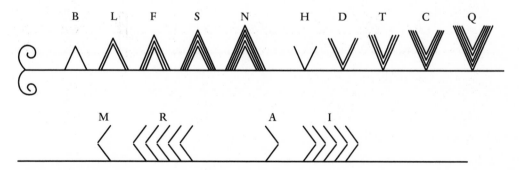

*Figure 5.23: Scale 73, **Ogam airenach**, "Shield Ogham"*

According to R. A. Stewart Macalister, several of the Oghams, including scales 75 and 76, were magical and used for divination.[3] Scale 75 has been called Fionn's wheel as well as Fionn's window.

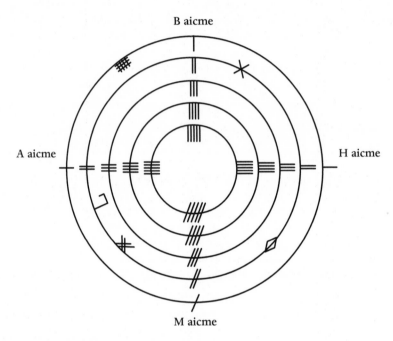

Figure 5.24: Scale 75, **Fege Find,** *"Fionn's Wheel"*

Searles O'Dubhain suggests that the aicme as laid out on Fionn's wheel represents four spiritual paths and that the letters within each carry information to guide the seeker.[4] As mentioned earlier in this chapter, the Fianna were an elite group of warriors. In addition to passing (surviving) a number of difficult physical trials in order to join their ranks, potential recruits needed the literary savvy to master the twelve books of poetry. Not only were the Fianna soldiers, they were also bards.

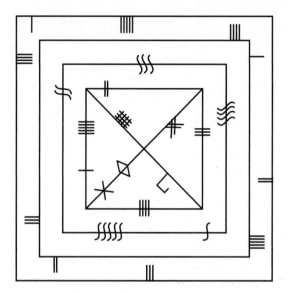

Figure 5.25: Scale 76, Traig sruth Ferchertne coig feda in gach snaithi, *"Stream strand of Ferchertne—five letters in each thread"*

Ferchertne (also spelled Fercherdne and Feirceirtné) was the son of Medb (Maeve) and Ailill, the queen and king of Connacht, and a contemporary of Ilann and Cu Roi Mac Dairi mentioned earlier. Ferchertne was one of great poets in the story "The Colloquoy of the Two Sages," which appears in both *The Book of Leinster* and *The Book of Lecan.* He is reported to have said, "I swear by the letters of my Ogham." One's personal Ogham may have been something of serious importance.

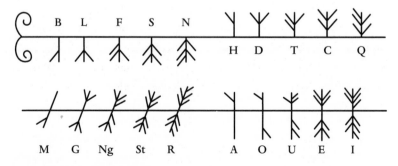

Figure 5.26: Scale 89, Unnamed

Scales 70 and 89 are both unnamed in *The Book of Ballymote* but they have become known as the "sacred branch Oghams" partly because their characters resemble tree branches. Scale 70 follows the pattern of the standard Ogham with its set of branching characters occurring in multiples to distinguish each letter. Scale 89 uses the number of branches on each "trunk" to indicate the letter. The *M* and *A* aicme use multiples above and below the stem line rather than the total branches on the trunk.

Creating Your Own Ogham

As with the tree calendar, you may find that many of the trees represented by the Ogham are not commonly found in your area and that some trees with which you want to work are not represented. As with the tree calendar, the solution is to develop your own.

Before charging ahead and designing a set of characters, decide how you are going to use your Ogham. As a tool it has to have function. The standard Ogham is convenient because it has enough letters with which to form words. Determine whether or not this is important for you to access tree energy. If it is, create an Ogham that can provide enough letters for your use.

You may find that after developing your own Ogham, and after it becomes your "permanent" set of letters, that you need other characters as you work with more trees. New trees can replace ones that you no longer work with and assume those letters, although you may need to assign new letters to accommodate the names of the new trees. If you don't want to delete any trees/characters, you can add new ones like the *forfeda* diphthong characters which were added to the original Ogham. You could also develop temporary Oghams for use while "getting to know" certain trees.

I have a permanent set of Ogham characters based on my tree calendar, which will be used as an example. I found the branch Oghams (scales 70 and 89) appealing and have used them as my "sabbat" tree characters. My "season" trees are represented by spirals. The spiral is a fundamental form found in nature. To ancient people it was a sacred symbol of the Goddess and her transformative powers.

The characters in the *H* aicme are above the stem line because from Yule to the time of Beltane (just before the summer solstice) is a time of growth. I look at these characters as trees with branches stretching to the heavenly realm. The characters of the *L* aicme fall below the stem line and represent roots reaching to the underworld.

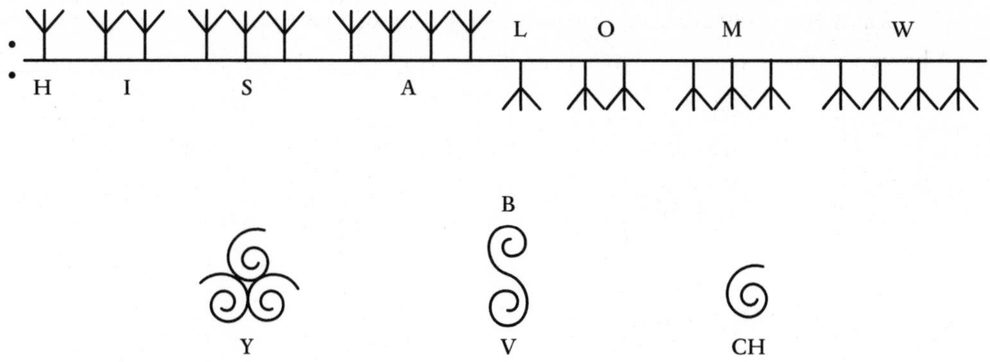

Figure 5.27: The author's Ogham

CHARACTER	LETTER	TREE	ASSOCIATION
H aicme			
	H	Holly	Yule
	I	Ivy	Imbolg
	S	Sycamore	Ostara
	A	Apple	Beltane
L aicme			
	L	Linden	Litha
	O	Oak	Lughnasadh
	M	Maple	Mabon
	W	Willow	Samhain
Season Trees			
	Y	Yew	Winter
	B	Birch	Spring
	V	Vine/Bramble	Autumn
	CH	Beech	Summer

Refer to chapter 3 for details on each tree's relation to its associated sabbat and season.

Table 5.1: Associations of the author's Ogham

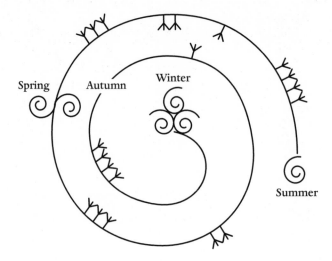

Figure 5.28: The author's Ogham as a spiral

My view of life's flow is more of a spiral than a circle. Energy spirals into the center for winter. We turn inward for reflection and renewal. That same spiral that leads us downward, inside ourselves in the dark of the year, eventually leads us up again toward the light and growth in spring.

The three spirals of winter remind me of the ancient site at Newgrange in Ireland. A set of triple spirals on the back wall, sixty-five feet from the entrance, is illuminated by the light of the rising sun on the three days of the winter solstice. It marks one of the turning points of the year. Spring and autumn are mirrored thresholds of life and death. The single spiral of summer marks the other turning point of the year.

I use my Ogham by carving them into my sabbat candles. Because the candles do not burn down completely during my sabbat rituals, I continue to use them to keep in touch with each particular tree during its time according to my tree calendar. I like to also keep season candles, and I usually inscribe two with the season Ogham character since one candle does not get me through a season. In addition, I have plans to put the spiral of Ogham characters on an altar cloth. Be creative and you will find many ways for your personal Ogham to bring you into rhythm with tree wisdom as you travel your spiritual path.

1. The names of the scales were translated by Dr. Barry Fell in his paper "The Ogam Scales of the Book of Ballymote," found in *The Epigraphic Society Occasional Papers* 22, part II (1993): 87–132.

2. This is part of the story called "Deirdre and the Sons of Usna" (which is also known as "The Exile of the Sons of Uisnech"). One version is recorded in *The Yellow Book of Lecan* (circa 1390) and is considered part of a prologue to the *Táin Bó Cuailnge* (The Cattle Raid of Cooley).

3. R. A. Stewart Macalister, *The Secret Languages of Ireland* (Cambridge: University Press, 1937), 40.

4. For more on this, please refer to http://www.summerlands.com.

Trees in Ritual
and Spellwork

TWO OF THE MOST IMPORTANT ingredients of spellwork and ritual are energy and spirit. The first few chapters of this book dealt with tree energy, and if you have followed at least some of the meditations and exercises you have found how to tap into this rich source of energy. Trees also embody spirit, and like us, they thrive best when the four elements are in balance.

Associating the three permanent elements of water, air, and earth with trees is easy to understand, but fire seems quite a different matter because of its destructiveness. However, fire is only temporarily damaging. It keeps a forest healthy by getting rid of underbrush that can create a tinderbox that burns too hot and too long. The most important reason is that fire adds nutrients to the soil and trees respond with lush new growth. Certain types of pine seeds are only released after a fire. From a Pagan perspective, fire plays the part of death in the cycle of life, and drives the cycle of rebirth.

Ritual

When in ritual, we seek a balance with the elements and we use various objects to evoke their presence. You may not want to replace these elemental objects with things from trees, but you may find that leaves, twigs, nuts, and fruit will compliment, boost, and balance the energy of your circle. On the other hand, you may want to see how the elements feel when evoked with tree energy (some trees are strongly associated with an element), or you may want to follow your intuition about which tree to use where in your circle.

You probably already incorporate some tree energy in your rituals with flowers in the spring, fruit in summer, nuts and fallen leaves in autumn. Refer to appendix B for information on how to preserve leaves and flowers to keep them looking fresh.

If you are using Robert Graves's tree calendar, you may be in the practice of honoring each tree in your moon circles. If you are developing your own tree calendar, bring those trees into your rituals and you will discover a new pathway into the natural world.

If you use a wand for casting a circle, you may want to consider working with one that is special for each sabbat, tree "month," or whatever time frame you employ for your tree energy work. These can be in addition to a wand to which you are already attuned. Building a collection of wands is not a weekend project, but the time you invest in finding and working with the right wood will reward you with a rich depth of energy. Refer to appendix B for information on wand making.

Magic

When we work magic, we move energy from one plane of existence to another. A spell creates a gateway for energy to move as it brings your intention into the physical realm. To do this requires focusing your mind and personal energy toward what you want to manifest. You must be very clear in your intention in order for it to take shape in this world. As the activity of a spell is performed and you sing or say an incantation, you need to have the result clearly in your mind.

A few basic types of spells include love, health, protection, success/luck, abundance/wealth, healing, fertility, sex, banishing, release, binding, and divination. There are, of course, many subcategories.

Objects used during spellwork aid in directing the energy for your intended purpose. As in ritual, objects used or created in spells are symbols of the energy we want to move or affect. Visualizing what we want to change as well as meditating on symbols imbues energy into the object(s) with which we work.

Spells can be simple or elaborate. However, the saying "less is more" can be good advice. The actions and words in a spell are meant to focus the mind and energy for visualizing the outcome. Picturing your desire in your mind is the most important part. Sometimes if a spell is too complicated, energy can be wasted on getting it right and it can end up as a performance. However, if elaboration helps you focus your mind and energy, then it is right for you. Try different approaches until you find the balance you need for your spellcraft.

Repetition is important, not only in the number of times you sing or say a chant/incantation, but also in the number of times you do the spell itself. I usually prefer doing them at least three times (the magic number three) or a multiple of three—usually nine since it is a significant number in Celtic lore and works well for me. Other people use different numbers for the times to repeat a spell. This is a personal choice—use whatever number is significant and works for you.

Repetition opens the subconscious part of the mind, which is essential for any type of creative energy to flow. Repetition also helps bring out the necessary emotions that aid in manifesting intentions.

Some spells may work quickly while others may take time or need multiple repeats. If things are not moving for you, it could be that your intention is not meant to happen at this particular time. Also check that you are being clear about what you are doing and then follow your inner voice. If it seems that you should drop it, do so. Alternatively, if you feel strongly about what you want to manifest, you may need to reexamine how you are asking for it and try a different approach. As already mentioned, the most important ingredient in a spell is belief in what you want to manifest as well as belief in yourself. Be truthful with yourself.

A great deal has been written on the ethics of spells. For example, a love spell to make someone fall for you could be construed as making a person do something that is not of his or her own free will. Spellcraft involves personal ethical decisions. My advice is to be truthful and responsible and to remember the old adage: be careful what you wish for as you may get it.

Spells and magic are a personal matter, so if you haven't already, it is a good idea to develop your own way of doing them. Samples and ideas from others can serve as a basis for your own spells. The spells offered here are suggestions on how to incorporate trees into your craft. Expand upon them and make them your own. Let them spark your imagination. Experiment and be creative. It is your unique energy that will manifest your desire.

Timing and Preparation

Coordinating spellwork with the phases of the moon adds energy to your intent. In addition to the moon, some people also take planetary positioning into consideration. While this can give your spells a boost, need dictates the proper time for spellcraft as well as your schedule. Squeezing your spellwork into a busy day or evening just to do it within a certain phase of the moon would be less effective than doing it another time when you are not rushed and can put your full focus and energy into it. As always, follow your inner voice.

If you have flexibility of scheduling, table 6.1 offers a brief overview of what spells to do at which moon phase. Again, if other timing works better for you, use it.

If you are working during a full moon you may want to work where you can see the moon. Moonlight provides a special ambiance, although this is not necessary for the success of your spell. The energy of the moon is all around you and so working in moonlight is a personal preference. Even on a cloudy night the full moon is just as powerful.

If moonlight is important to you but you do not have a place to work a spell that is in its direct light, go outside or into another room where you can see it and meditate on your purpose. Visualize what you will be doing and then go inside (or into another room) and do your spell. After your workings, you may want to take any symbols or objects created during the spell outside to "bathe" in the moonlight for a few minutes.

With spells that are worked over the course of several days, especially nine-day spells, you may find that timing it to end on the full moon will give a boost that seals your intention.

As you would for ritual or meditation, find a place that is quiet and private. This can be indoors or outside. Assemble everything you will need before casting a circle. You may also want to have your Book of Shadows or a journal handy to record infor-

MOON PHASE	TYPE OF SPELL
Waxing	Growth, invitation, gain, money, love, fertility, health, success
Full	Maximum power for sending out and drawing to, love, sex, health, protection, and any type of spell that needs a culminating boost
Waning	Removal, endings, release, binding, banishing
Dark	Finding inner wisdom, germination

Table 6.1: Moon phases for timing spells

mation. If you are working outside, your setup can be as simple as a circle drawn on the ground with a stick of the type of wood with which you are doing a spell.

When burning anything, be sure you have an iron cauldron or some other fireproof vessel, and that it is placed on a safe surface. Make sure it is big enough to accommodate anything you burn. You do not need great amounts of things for spells because you are working with symbols and intent. Always be safe.

As in ritual, placing an image or figure of a deity on the altar helps focus attention and draw energy. Similarly, a picture of the type of tree with which you are working can be placed on the altar. When employing tree energy in a spell, you can use a twig, leaf, nut, flower, fruit, piece of bark, or anything else from the tree that embodies the energy of that tree. In some instances you may not have access to the part of a tree that you want to use, or you may not have the type of tree in your area. In this situation, you can simply raid your local arts and crafts store. While the real thing may be preferable, it is intention that counts.

Spellwork

Candle magic spells are simple and you can easily enlist the aid of a tree by scratching its name into the candle. This can be in a standard alphabet or Ogham. When you give voice to your intention, call on the tree spirit, otherwise known as a *dryad*, to add its energy to yours. For example you can begin with: "Dryads of the _____ tree, I call on you to aid me." Then continue with the rest of your incantation.

Generally a short, two or four-line incantation works well because it is easy to memorize and the repetition of something so brief works to access your subconscious energy and emotions. For rhythm, you may want to try doing a two or six line incantation that consists of a line with eight syllables followed by one with four. The incantation does not have to rhyme, but like repetition, it seems to cut to the chase, and access that part of the mind that opens to inner energy.

If you feel comfortable "ad-libbing" a spell, do it that way. I have frequently found that when energy flows in sacred space, words will come naturally and smoothly. I have also found that in these circumstances I can rhyme my speech very easily, but after the circle is dissolved I cannot recall the rhyme. If this method works well for you, don't worry about trying to record your incantation in your journal. If it is meant to be remembered, it will be. If spirit flows through you serendipitously in spellwork, then that is the way for you to work. You may find that you will use different methods and approaches for different types of spells.

Simple and spontaneous poetry has been considered oracular when it occurs under certain circumstances, such as that 40-hertz brain wave mentioned previously. Messages from the Pythia (priestesses) of Delphi were delivered in verse. The Celtic poet Cinaed was said to have spoken in quatrains when he stepped upon Lia Fáil in ritual.[1]

Since a big part of spellwork is done in the mind, it is important to prepare yourself for it. Do not do spells when you are upset, distracted, or depressed because it is next to impossible to properly focus under these circumstances.

You may find that setting up your things and preparing your space gives you enough time to begin the transition to your pre-spell meditation. If not, take time for a cup of herb tea or a warm bath to calm and balance your energy.

When you are ready to start, cast a circle. This is not so much for protection (although this can make you feel safe), but rather to create a neutral space that will act as a cauldron for the energy you raise. Holding and building the energy prior to sending it out can give your spell more of boost. Calling the quarters and/or calling on the Divine is a personal choice.

Bring your body and mind to stillness and then visualize your intention coming to fruition. As you go through your visualization, feel your energy, your power rise within you. Once you have the image clearly in your mind, begin your incantation or chant and any symbolic activity. When you finish, continue to hold an image of your desired intention in your mind. Thank the tree and tree spirits for their help just as you would deity in ritual. Take time to ground excess energy and then open your circle.

Spellwork takes energy and you may feel slightly drained afterwards. If you find this happening you may want to have a light snack prepared before you begin. Sipping a cup of tea as you record your spell is a nice way to make the transition back to your everyday world.

It is assumed that the following spellcraft activities will be done while saying or singing your incantation. Where it is suggested to write something in Ogham, use whatever alphabet is appropriate for you.

General

The following objects and activities can be used for a variety of spells.

Birch

Gather strips of fallen birch bark and let them dry out. Using dragon's blood ink[2] (or whatever ink may be more appropriate for your spell), write the keywords of your intention. As you do this, keep an image of it in your mind. As you say your incantation, pass the birch through a candle flame and drop it into your cauldron.

Balance and Harmony

Ivy and Holly

At Yule, ivy and holly symbolize the struggle for balance. If you are seeking to balance your energy or that of your household (at any time of year), make a small holly wreath or use a small branch and lightly wind a length of ivy around it.

Reed or Bamboo

Both of these plants are used to make flutes and a small piece from either can be used to symbolically invite sweet harmony into your life. Sing your incantation to it and then place it where you will see it often.

Banishing and Releasing

Gorse or Heather

These classic "broom" plants work well but any type of supple twigs can be used. If you are working on a carpeted floor, you may want put a protective cover over your circle area. Bundle a handful of gorse or heather twigs to create a small ritual hand broom. Write the name of what you want to release or banish from your life on a piece of paper and burn it. When the ashes are cool scatter them on the floor around your altar. Take the broom and sweep the ashes from the center out to the edge of your circle. Gather the ashes and then scatter them to the wind.

Alternatively, if you don't want to scatter ashes around the floor, burn the paper as above and simply sweep the floor with the broom. Take a few pieces of the broom and burn it in your cauldron. When all the ashes are cool, scatter them to the wind for final release.

Witch Hazel

Write the name or keyword of what you want to remove from your life on a small slip of paper. Place the paper in a cup and pour in enough witch hazel to submerge it. Position the cup where it can stand in the light of the waning moon overnight.

Binding

Ivy

Take a strand of ivy that is long enough to form a small circle. Write the name of what, or whom, you seek to bind with on one piece of paper and your name on another. Place them both in the center of the ivy ring. Do this on three consecutive days and then burn all the slips of paper.

Blessings

Fir or Pine

Gather needles and cones. Tie a small bundle of needles together with thread and burn them in your cauldron. Pass the cone(s) through the smoke and then place them in a location where you will see them frequently and be reminded of your blessings.

Divination, Communication, Psychic Work and Travel to Other Realms

Aspen

To improve communication with someone or aid in interaction with other realms, gather two aspen leaves. On one, paint your initials in Ogham and on the other, the name of the person or realms with which you seek communication. Wrap them in a cloth and place them under your pillow for three consecutive nights.

Bay Laurel

Bay leaves were said to have been burned in the temple at Delphi. Place several leaves on your altar and burn one as you employ your favorite method of divination.

Sycamore

Create this charm prior to divination or traveling to other realms. Collect three (or whatever number is appropriate for you) seed balls. Place them in a pouch and tie it shut. Hang this from your belt or around your neck during divination or shamanic travel.

Female Fertility and Sexuality

Holly

Red holly berries symbolize the life-giving blood of the Mother Goddess. Gather three berries (or a multiple of three) and carry them in your hand to a body of water. As you say your incantation, drop the berries into the water. In this situation where casting a circle may be difficult, visualize a circle of light surrounding you as you go through your spell.

Male Fertility and Sexuality

Mistletoe

Empower a sprig of mistletoe with an incantation and then hang it near your bed or over the doorway into the bedroom.

Oak

Hold an acorn in the palm of your hand (the one with which you write) and direct your energy into it as you say your incantation. Afterwards, carry it with you for nine days and then bury it in the ground.

Health and Healing

Cedar

Use a piece of cedar wood or scent a symbolic object with cedar oil as you visualize recovery from an ailment. Afterwards place it in the bedroom (place of rest) or kitchen (place of nourishment). When the scent has faded bury it in the ground. If you used an object you want to keep, cleanse it in salt or earth and then let it stand in the light of a full moon.

Rowan

Use a handful of dried rowan berries or rowan berry tea. Place them in the center of a small square of white or purple cloth. Gather the cloth over the berries and tie it into a bundle with white or purple ribbon. Hang this in your kitchen during flu season or keep it for the entire winter.

Love

Apple

Use a crabapple, or a cultivated apple if you don't have crabapples available. If possible, use one that you have hand picked. In Ogham, carve the initials of the one you desire and your own in a ring around the apple. Bury it in the ground or commit it to a body of water.

Birch or Hazel

Do this just before or on Valentine's Day if the catkins of the birch or hazel are available. Light a red or pink candle and then gather the catkins together into a piece of pink or red tissue paper. Hold this in your hand over your heart as you recite your incantation. Continue to visualize your desire as you burn the bundle.

Willow

Take three long supple branches of willow, braid them together and then fasten it into a circle with pink, red, or white ribbon. Place a picture or the name of the person you love in the center and then put it next to your bed.

Protection

Blackthorn, Hawthorn, or Locust

Carefully gather a few thorns from the tree. Write the name of the person or situation from which you seek protection on a piece of paper and then wrap it around the thorns. Bury this in the ground—if possible near the tree from which the thorns were collected.

Holly

Place an image of a holly tree or a sprig on your altar. Cut out a piece of paper in the shape of a holly leaf and write what you want protection from on it. Burn it and when the ashes are cool sprinkle them in front of your house.

Ivy

This is similar to the ivy binding spell. Take a strand of ivy that is long enough to form a circle. Write the name of the person or situation that you seek protection from on a slip of paper. Write your name on another slip. Place your name in the center of the ivy ring and the other outside the ring. Do this for three consecutive days and then burn all the slips of paper.

Remembrance

Any type of tree

This can be done at Samhain to remember ancestors and loved ones who have passed on or recently after someone has died. You can utilize something from a tree that you associate with a particular person or a tree that holds significance at Samhain. Refer to the individual tree listings in part 2. As you hold something of the tree in your hand, visualize that person in your mind as you speak his or her name. Ask that the tree aid in sending loving energy to that person so they may find their way as their journey continues in a place different from yours.

Success

Hazel

Use this for success in tests or any situation that requires knowledge. Prepare a candle with the Ogham for hazel and a keyword for your situation. In Celtic legend, the salmon of wisdom fed on the nuts from nine hazel trees that stood beside the pond where it lived. Using a sturdy needle (i.e., one for leatherwork), string nine hazelnuts together to form a ring. Place it around the base of the candle. If this spell is being used for success in an exam, do it nine times before the exam. Ideally, keep the spell brief and perform it just before studying.

In Conclusion

These sample spells are intended to spark ideas and illustrate how simple it is to incorporate tree energy into your spellcraft and rituals. The associations and attributes of trees in part 2 of this book can be used as a guide for the type of spells in which they can be employed. The listing is by no means a limitation. Be creative and explore, and you will be rewarded.

---

1. Tomá Ó Broin, "Lia Fáil: Fact and Fiction in the Tradition," *Celtica 21* (Dublin: Dublin Institute for Advanced Studies, 1990), 395. Lia Fáil, or La Fal, is also called the Stone of Destiny; it was the ancient coronation stone of Ireland, which according to legend, sang or cried out when the man destined to be king sat or stood upon it. Mackillop, *Dictionary of Celtic Mythology*, 298.

2. Dragon's blood ink contains the resin of the palm tree called "dragon's blood" (*Daemonorops draco*) to give it color as well as power. According to Scott Cunningham, dragon's blood is powerful when used as incense and with other incense to increase their potency. Scott Cunningham, *Encyclopedia of Magical Herbs* (St. Paul, MN: Llewellyn, 1998), 95.

SEVEN

Wood as an Element of Change

IN THE ANCIENT CHINESE SYSTEM of feng shui, wood is classified as one of the five elements: water, earth, fire, metal and wood. This may seem strange to Westerners who are accustomed to working with three or four elements, but in feng shui the elements are symbols of archetypal energies. These energy types are used as a way to understand the actions and changes that can shape and transform one's life. When I developed the method of gemstone feng shui,[1] I discovered that an alternative feng shui practice could bring remarkable results. This chapter is not intended to provide instruction for a complete traditional feng shui practice; instead, it is offered as a guide for adapting a few feng shui techniques and tools for inviting tree energy into your environment to foster change.

Adapting Feng Shui Tools

There are two feng shui tools that can be adapted easily for working with tree energy in your environment: The compass and the magic square. The first step in working

Subtract the century from your date of birth.

$$1947$$
$$- 1900$$
$$47$$

FOR MEN		FOR WOMEN	
Add the digits until you get a single digit number.	$4 + 7 = 11$ $1 + 1 = 2$	Add 5 to the date.	$47 + 5 = 52$
Subtract from 10.	$10 - 2 = 8$	Add the digits until you get a single digit number.	$5 + 2 = 7$
If your result is 5, use the number 2.		If your result is 5, use the number 8.	

Table 7.1: Determining your compass number

with these tools is to determine your compass number. Table 7.1 shows you how to calculate it. The nine directions on the compass are used to chart the direction that holds the most power for you, as well as other significant directions. These directions are determined by your energy group, which is either east or west. Follow the steps in table 7.1 to calculate your compass number, and then locate that number on the wheel in figure 7.1. The outer circle of the wheel indicates your power direction.

The compass layout of nine directions was derived from the *lo shu* grid, which was based on the pattern found on the back of a tortoise that the first emperor of China found in the River Lo. The grid itself resembles our modern pound sign (#) as well as the *kangi* character for the Well hexagram[2] of the *I Ching*.

After extensive analysis, ancient Chinese scholars believed that the markings on the tortoise provided a perfect three-by-three magic square. The numbers, if added in any direction, equal fifteen. This is also the total number of days in a complete waxing or waning cycle of the moon, which includes the dark and full phases of Luna.

Working with the Directions

The magic square, combined with the compass, produces a matrix of attributes and associations for each of the directions. This matrix is used to map out areas in your environment that correspond with certain life aspects.

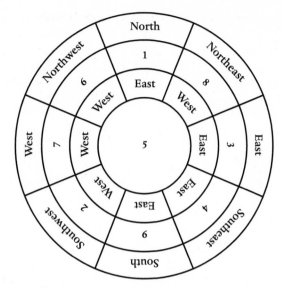

Figure 7.1: The tree energy compass

6	1	8
7	5	3
2	9	4

Figure 7.2: The lo shu grid

6—Northwest	1—North	8—Northeast
Achievement	Career	Wisdom
Benefactors	Personal Journey	Knowledge
Assisting People	Foundation	Self-cultivation
Father		
7—West	**5—Center**	**3—East**
Creativity	Balance	Family
Projects	Harmony	Ancestors
Children		Community
2—Southwest	**9—South**	**4—Southeast**
Relationships	Illumination	Prosperity
Love, Romance	Fame / Success	Blessings
Marriage	Reputation	Self-/Net worth
Mother	Respect	Resources

Figure 7.3: The magic square

The aspects embodied by these sectors include:

East—Those you love—from your immediate family to the family of humankind, your ancestors and friends. This area is also about growth and vitality.

Southeast—Wealth and abundance on all levels from self-worth to monetary worth and blessings received. Personal resources and anything that enriches your life. Go here to recover your self-worth.

South—To be known in your community or field of employment; garner respect and recognition. This is concerned with your outward self as well as self-actualization. If you want to shine, work on this area.

Southwest—Encompasses love, romance, marriage and all types of relationships: personal and business. Many times we learn about relationships through our mothers. This direction is also associated with being receptive.

West—If you want to have children, help your children or stimulate your creative impulses, activate this area. This is where you nurture all manner of things to which you "give birth."

Northwest—Achievement also includes those who help you achieve: benefactors, mentors, and your father. It is about responsibility—giving, as well as receiving.

North—Careers and personal journeys symbolize progress in our lives. Progress is not always about moving forward; at times we must stand still and assess ourselves before we can move onward. Think of this as your area of foundation.

Northeast—Wisdom, knowledge, and self-cultivation also encompass turning points. Gaining self wisdom can bring about revolutions in our lives.

Center—Place of balance, harmony, and spirituality, this is also considered the prosperity point. To attain balance and harmony requires joy.

Trees have attributes and associations that can be applied to your environment through the magic square. To begin mapping the square to your environment, you will need a magnetic compass. Determine which direction is north and then orient the magic square to it. Imagine superimposing the magic square over a room in your house. It may be easier to draw a floor plan of the room where you are working. Draw the magic square on a piece of tracing paper and then lay it over the room sketch. This divides the room into nine sectors—each corresponding to a direction and specific life aspects.

If there is an area of your life that holds issues for you, check which sector of the magic square it would fall into. For example, if a love relationship is causing difficulty, the southwest sector is the area in which you would want to concentrate your efforts. A few trees associated with love include apple, juniper, and pine. If it is a communication issue, elm and sycamore could bring help.

To enlist the aid of a tree, first make sure that energy is calm and free flowing in that area of the room where you are doing your energy work. If necessary, remove

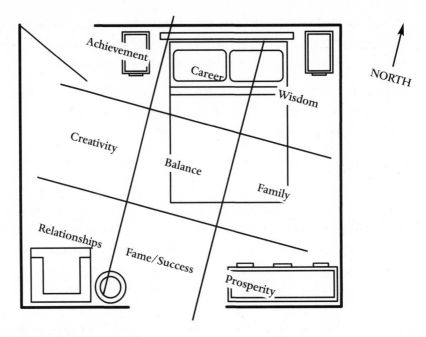

Figure 7.4: The magic square superimposed over a room

clutter. The area does not need to be stark and bare, but it should be free of any "rats' nests." Decide which tree you are going to work with and then place something of that tree in that sector.

If you have an object made from that tree's wood, place it there. Following the example in figure 7.4, if the small round table is made from an appropriate wood, move it so that it is completely in the southwest sector. If it is not of the type of wood with which you want to work, use it as a place to locate objects such as a small branch, leaves, nuts, or fruit from the appropriate tree. Refer to appendix B for information on preserving and using leaves. If natural items are not available or would not be appropriate, a picture of a tree can be used. If it is one for which you have a tree card, Ogham stave, or few, use that instead. If you want (or need) to be a little more subtle with the object, use a candle (brown or green) with the name or Ogham character of the tree inscribed on it. To strengthen your intention, you could also inscribe a word or name relating to the issue on the candle. If you maintain an altar, you may want to temporarily move it to the area where you are doing your feng shui energy work.

When you place an object, take a few moments to visualize the issue or person, and then bring an image of the tree into your mind. Think of that tree's energy glowing and expanding to encompass you and the person with whom you are having issues. After you do this, you may want to say something such as:

"I call on _____ (name of tree)
to bring to me
help with _____ (issue or person).
So mote it be."

Continue your visualization for as long as it feels appropriate. In the following days or from time to time as the issue requires, repeat your visualization.

Table 7.2 provides a listing of trees by direction for use with the magic square. Just as the magic square was applied to a room, it can be expanded to encompass your entire home and property. Alternatively, you can go smaller and work with the magic square in miniature on a desk or tabletop. As in ritual and spellwork, intention plays a major role.

EAST

Alder—rebirth
Ash—ancestors, communication
Aspen—ancestors, rebirth
Beech—ancestors
Gooseberry—ancestors

Hawthorn—ancestors, family, growth
Hickory—unification
Ivy—fertility, growth
Locust—friendship
Oak—ancestors

Reed—growth, unity
Spindle tree—community spirit
Willow—connections
Yew—ancestors

SOUTHEAST

Apple—prosperity
Aspen—money
Birch—blessings
Cedar—prosperity
Chestnut—prosperity
Elder—abundance, blessings, prosperity
Fir—prosperity

Gorse—prosperity
Hawthorn—prosperity
Heather—self-worth
Hickory—abundance
Hornbeam—prosperity
Maple—abundance, money
Myrtle—money, luck
Oak—prosperity

Olive—abundance, fruitfulness, prosperity
Palm—abundance
Pine—abundance, prosperity
Sycamore—abundance
Vine / bramble—wealth
Walnut—wealth

Table 7.2: Trees for the nine directions   *(continued on next page)*

Table 7.2 (continued)

SOUTH

Apple—illumination	Birch—growth, renewal	Olive—success, potency,
Ash—illumination	Elder—success	victory
Aspen—success	Gooseberry—success	Spruce—enlightenment
Bay laurel—expanded awareness	Oak—success	

SOUTHWEST

Apple—love	Hornbeam—spiritual love	Myrtle—love
Ash—communication	Ivy—fidelity	Oak—loyalty
Cherry—love	Juniper—love	Olive—marriage
Chestnut—love	Linden—love, attraction	Pine—love
Elm—love, compassion, empathy	Locust—love	Reed—loyalty
Hawthorn—love, marriage	Magnolia—love	Sycamore—communication, love
Hazel—marriage	Maple—love, communication	Willow—relationships
Heather—passion	Mimosa—love	Witch hazel—love divination
Honeysuckle—love	Mistletoe—love	

WEST

Ash—creativity, fertility	Hackberry—creativity	Olive—fertility, rebirth
Bay laurel—poetic inspiration	Hawthorn—fertility	Palm—fertility, rebirth
Beech—creativity	Hazel—fertility, inspiration, creativity	Pine—fertility
Birch—arts, crafts, fertility	Honeysuckle—creativity	Rowan—imagination, poetry, music, fertility
Elder—creativity	Maple—creativity	Vine/bramble—fertility
Elm—birth/rebirth	Mistletoe—fertility, birth	Walnut—inspiration
Fir—birth/rebirth	Myrtle—fertility, youth	Willow—birth, fertility
Gorse—birth, fertility	Oak—fertility	Witch hazel—inspiration

NORTHWEST

Birch—travel	Hickory—giving/charity	Rowan—strength
Cherry—achievement	Oak—father, strength	Willow—connections

NORTH

Ash—personal growth	Heather—spirituality	Pine—emotions, regeneration
Cherry—awakening	Hickory—discipline, strength	Rowan—grounding
Elm—grounding stability	Holly—rebirth	Spindle tree—seeking self
Fir—rebirth	Maple—grounding	Spruce—grounding
Gorse—hope	Mistletoe—rebirth	Walnut—inspiration
Hazel—introspection, inspiration	Olive—rebirth, security	Yew—rebirth, change

Table 7.2 (continued)

NORTHEAST

Apple—knowledge	Hawthorn—wisdom	Maple—transformation,
Ash—knowledge	Heather—transition/	wisdom
Bay laurel—wisdom	changes	Oak—wisdom
Cedar—wisdom	Hazel—knowledge, wisdom	Spindle tree—self-cultivation
Elder—transitions	Hickory—transformation	Walnut—change
Elm—wisdom	Ivy—transformation	Willow—knowledge
Fir—transformation	Magnolia—self-awareness	Yew—change

CENTER

Alder—balance	Cedar—balance, calm	Myrtle—peace
Apple—harmony	Elm—grounding	Olive—balance, harmony,
Ash—balance	Hickory—balance	peace
Aspen—harmony, peace	Linden—peace	Reed—harmony
Bamboo—harmony	Locust—balance	Rowan—centering
Beech—balance, stability	Maple—balance, grounding	Spruce—grounding

If you are working on a tabletop and using small objects, a tic-tac-toe gaming board can easily serve to define your magic square. These are usually six-by-six inch squares and come in a wide range of styles, some of which are attractive. I have one that is a mirror beveled into nine sectors. Look around and you will probably find one that suits your taste, or consider making your magic square.

Energy Groups

As previously mentioned, your number on the compass indicates multiple directions that hold importance for you. The "east" or "west" on the compass refers to the energy groups. Your power direction can also be referred to as your "life" direction. The other directions in your energy group constitute health, abundance, and longevity. These four are your positive directions.

The directions in the opposite energy group can hold potential challenges. More accurately, these are directions that you can use to bring healing and protection into your life as needed.

EAST ENERGY GROUP	WEST ENERGY GROUP
East	West
Southeast	Northwest
South	Northeast
North	Southwest

Table 7.3: Energy Groups

Life—This sector is concerned with abundance/prosperity in family and career; things that constitute "the good life."

Health—This area is connected with vitality and good health; a zest for life. If you are ill or low on energy, this is a good area with which to work.

Abundance—This area is concerned with well being, prosperity, and blessings.

Longevity—As its name implies, this area has to do with long life and good health.

Loss—This area is connected with the loss of prosperity and property through events such as theft or financial problems.

Misfortune—This area is associated with accidents or illness and a general lack of energy and vitality.

Setback—This area is connected with unexpected events, disruptions, and disputes.

Difficulty—This area is concerned with disappointments and annoyances.

Like the life aspects associated on the magic square, these directions can be used to deal with problems. For example, the area called "misfortune" is associated with illness and accidents. If you are experiencing these you could call on tree energy in the related sector to help. Ash, birch, and chestnut are a few of the trees associated with healing. Hazel is associated with healing as well as protection. As described previously, go through a visualization as you place something of your chosen tree in that sector. Using table 7.4, find the column with your compass number to determine your directions.

If you are dealing with setbacks or losses, you may want to invoke tree energy that could provide protection, such as hawthorn or spruce, or use trees to invite luck, such

COMPASS NUMBER	I	2	3	4	6	7	8	9
Life	North	SW	East	SE	NW	West	NE	South
Health	East	West	North	South	NE	SW	NW	SE
Abundance	SE	NE	South	North	West	NW	SW	East
Longevity	South	NW	SE	East	SW	NE	West	North
Loss	NE	SE	NW	SW	East	South	North	West
Misfortune	SW	North	West	NE	South	East	SE	NW
Setback	West	East	SW	NW	SE	North	South	NE
Difficulty	NW	South	NE	West	North	SE	East	SW

Table 7.4: Determining your positive and challenging directions

as bamboo or myrtle. Sometimes just getting positive energy moving can help stimulate an area—use maple or elder for this.

To apply energy to these areas, create a wheel with your specific directions according to table 7.4. Like the magic square, superimpose this wheel over your floor plan (one room or your entire home) to determine where these areas fall in your environment.

Don't limit yourself by only using these directions to cope with challenges because they can also be used to enhance the good things in your life. For example, we might all want a little more abundance, and by inviting more into our lives we also help bring abundance to others. Use your four positive directions to keep the good energy flowing. When you place objects in these directions, meditate on your blessings and send some of your positive energy back to the tree with which you are working. This will help strengthen your relationship with that particular tree or type of tree and further your abilities as you work with other trees.

As you work with various trees using these techniques, keep in mind that your energy is unique, as is the energy of each tree. Experiment using different trees in the various magic square and direction wheel sectors. If you find that something is not working for you, discontinue it and try another tree's energy. The tables in this chapter are intended to provide a starting point. As you read through part 2 of this book, you may find other trees that are more suitable for your specific purpose and situation. Above all, don't be afraid to try something different. You are the only one who can

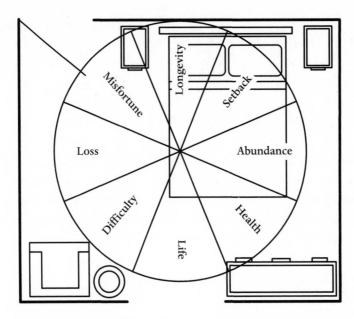

Figure 7.5: Like the magic square, the direction wheel is superimposed over a room

judge how well a method or technique is working, or not. Perhaps the best advice comes from Obi-Wan Kenobi of *Star Wars*: "Trust in the Force." Or, more appropriately: Trust in the Forest.

Alder—protection

Apple—healing, protection

Ash—healing, protection, dispersion of negativity

Aspen—protection

Bamboo—luck, good fortune, protection

Bay laurel—healing, protection

Beech—aiding energy flow

Birch—healing, protection, purification

Blackthorn—protection

Cedar—healing, protection, purification, repelling negativity

Cherry—overcoming obstacles

Cypress—healing, protection

Elder—good fortune, healing, positive change

Elm—healing

Fir—protection

Gorse—protection

Hawthorn—cleansing, lifting depression, luck, protection

Hazel—healing, luck, protection

Heather—luck, protection

Hickory—flexibility, protection

Holly—healing, luck, protection

Hornbeam—protection, removing the unwanted

Ivy—healing, luck, protection

Juniper—cleansing, healing, protection

Linden—luck, protection

Locust—protection

Magnolia—protection

Maple—positive energy

Mesquite—healing, protection, purification

Mimosa—protection, purification

Mistletoe—protection

Myrtle—luck

Oak—healing, luck, protection

Palm—protection

Pine—good fortune, healing, protection, purification

Reed—healing, willpower

Rowan—counteracting negativity, luck, protection

Spruce—healing, hope, safety, protection, well-being

Sycamore—perseverance, protection, shelter

Walnut—change, healing, protection

Willow—flexibility, healing, protection

Witch hazel—banishing, protection

Table 7.5: Trees for protection and dealing with negativity

LIFE	ABUNDANCE	LONGEVITY	HEALTH
Apple	Apple	Apple	Apple
Cedar	Fir	Bamboo	Chestnut
Fir	Gorse	Cedar	Cypress
Ivy	Hickory	Cypress	Elder
Sycamore	Maple	Elm	Elm
	Palm	Fir	Hazel
	Pine	Linden	Heather
	Sycamore	Maple	Juniper
		Oak	Mistletoe
		Olive	Oak
		Pine	Pine
		Yew	Witch hazel

Table 7.6: Trees to enhance positive aspects

1. Gemstone feng shui can be used as an alternative or supplement to a traditional practice. It is based on the theory that the energy of the five elements can be evoked and worked with through the use of crystals and gemstones. Sandra Kynes, *Gemstone Feng Shui* (St. Paul, MN: Llewellyn, 2002).

2. The Well hexagram represents a method for drawing upon the deep strength within the mystery of life. The Well hexagram is connected with feng shui in that it is a symbol of reaching deep inside oneself to connect with one's own energy, which is necessary in order to touch the energy (and essence) of life.

The Shamanic Journey

As we find our place in the web of life, we can also feel the various subtle movements of this web. When we realize that consciousness and reality are fluid, we find the undercurrent of spirit, music, and the energy that runs through the web and our souls.

Shamanism has been practiced in many cultures all over the world and is still used by indigenous people, including the Campa Indians of Peru, Australian Aborigines, the Batak of Malaysia, and the !Kung of the Kalahari in Africa.[1] The word "shaman" comes from the Tungus people of Siberia and means "seer in the dark." Shamanic practices in Western Europe are believed to date back at least twenty thousand years. Shamanism is going through a revival and has been incorporated into various modern practices.

Even though shamanism is a spiritual practice, it is not rooted in any particular religion. It is not a spiritual belief, but rather a tool that can be used to deepen spiritual experience. Shamanism acknowledges that everything is spiritually alive. The shamanic journey is a methodology that involves a shift in consciousness to otherworld energies— the network that underlies the world of our "everyday" consciousness. This type of journey provides access to a different reality as well as a way to function in that reality.

The shamanic journey is a method for connecting with the spirit realm. The purpose for shamanic journeys has generally been for divination, healing, deepening of spiritual life, acquiring guidance or knowledge, and bringing that information back to the conscious plane. It does not require an intermediary because anyone can tap into other realms, including the realm of self. By balancing the deep inner realm of self, one can then bring the rest of one's life into balance more easily.

The shamanic journey does not require special equipment or drugs. It is a naturally occurring spiritual state, if we allow it to happen. While it may take a little practice, the technique lies in letting go of your ordinary state of consciousness. As mentioned in chapter 2 in the discussion on seeing auras, it is a matter of allowing the monotony of outside stimulus to lull our chattering monkey brains into the 40 hertz range. This can be accomplished with mesmerizing sounds such as drumming, rattling, or chanting.

I accidentally discovered the power of chant to shift the level of consciousness. I had a tape of chants that I wanted to learn and popped it into the cassette player in my car while I was driving. When I realized that I was beginning to slip out of mainstream reality, I quickly switched to the radio and loud, jarring music to pull me back.

Reaching Other Realms

Shamans generally work with the three realms of upperworld, middleworld, and underworld. These are sometimes associated with the mental, physical, and emotional states. The spirit realms encompass all three.

In a journey we ascend or descend within ourselves to find the inner realms. It is through this inner place that we can connect with other realms. The common entry points into these realms frequently incorporate a tree, pole, ray of light, mountaintop (upperworld), or cave (underworld).[2]

As mentioned in previous chapters, the concept of the World Tree or cosmic tree was prevalent in many cultures. A tree was and still is used to balance or bring into balance the shaman's energy with the earth and spirit world because the tree is rooted in the dense matter of earth yet extends to the ether above. This is appropriate for journey work with tree energy. Using different trees at different times will aid in bringing your energy into balance. As we free our minds with these shamanic techniques, we tune into the energy around us and open our inner channels to receive.

Odin experienced a shamanic journey when he suspended himself from the World Tree and perceived the knowledge of the runes. Similarly, the hanged man in the classic tarot deck is suspended, like Odin, upside down from a tree. Like the shaman, he sees the world completely differently from the "normal" perspective.

Jean Markale said ". . . the shamanic experience is equivalent to a restoration of that primordial mythic time." He associates this to the idea of the Celtic nemeton being "a piece of Heaven on earth . . . or rather a magical orchard of the sort encountered in legend."[3] It is this view of a World Tree from which Merlin, as shaman, makes his prophesies. Because the sacred clearing, the nemeton, and most sacred trees are associated with a holy spring or well, the three permanent elements of earth, air, and water are an integral part of the shamanic experience.

The example provided in this chapter of the World Tree as entry point is based on a real forest where I frequently hike. I have used this visual approach as a pattern to begin some of my journeys; however, it is offered here merely as an example. It is important for you to develop your own entry points because they will have greater significance for you and it will be easier for you to attune all of your senses with them. My sample also utilizes an oak tree, which most people are familiar with, as it is helpful to visualize it clearly.

At times you may feel the need to work with a particular type of tree to access its particular attributes. Follow your intuition and visualize it as your World Tree. If you do not have that type of tree in your area or if you are not familiar enough with the details of the tree, start with a picture. Study it until you feel that you know that individual tree and feel that you are standing beside it. Alternatively, as you use this practice, you may visualize an approach to a tree but not know or "see" it until you get close to it. Allow your inner forces to choose the type of tree you need to work with.

The sample journey provided here portrays a descent, but whether you climb the tree or descend through its roots is a personal choice. Going to the upper branches or into the higher realms does not equate with better or more enlightened journeys. The idea that God and goodness resides above and evil, the devil, and hell below is a Christian construct that has no place here.

In preparing for a journey, give yourself plenty of time without interruption in a place that is private and quiet. If you choose to journey during the day you may want to darken the room. At night you may want to light a candle or use very soft light. For a start, you may want to tape the sample journey and use it as a guided mediation. A place is indicated in the text where you may want to insert fifteen to twenty minutes of music or drumming to aid in your journey.

Shamanic drumming and rattling tapes and CDs are widely available. Some people find the drumming more distracting than helpful in shifting levels of consciousness. The rattling is a softer sound. I have found that drums and rattles provide slightly different qualities for journeys—neither one is better, just different. It is important to experiment to find what suits you best. My only suggestion is to get a recording with a "call back." (In a guided visualization, the guide tells you when it is time to return to the everyday realm.) The call back on a drumming or rattling tape/CD provides a noticeable change that gently breaks the mesmerizing effect of the rhythm. This helps you to adjust and begin to shift your level of consciousness gradually, which is preferable to being startled by an abrupt ending or a tape clicking off.

Avoid jumping straight into a journey. Take time to prepare yourself and your space as you would if you were taking a physical journey. I like to have a cup of herb tea beforehand, especially in the winter. It gives me a nice cozy feeling that helps me start the process of focusing inward as I set up my space. I keep a permanent altar and I like to do my journeys beside it because of the energy that has accumulated there.

Wear comfortable clothing so you will not feel restricted. If the weather is cold, you may want to cover yourself with a light blanket. Decide if you are going to sit up or lie down. If you plan to sit, use a comfortable chair or place pillows on the floor where you will have support for your back. If you lie on the floor, use a pillow and a blanket or something soft underneath you. Consider these things as you prepare because physical discomfort during a journey can be distracting. Have a journal or pad of paper and pen, or a tape recorder close by to document your journey afterwards. This process of recording your journey will also aid in the transition back to your everyday world.

Once you and your area are prepared, cast a circle as you would for ritual. This is not so much for protection as it is to create a cauldron/container for the energy. Just as for ritual, take time to ground and quiet your energy. Take a few deep breaths and bring your awareness to the present moment.

In journeying, as in meditation, it is important to set your everyday concerns aside. This is not always easy, even for the experienced practitioner, so have patience. One method for doing this is to envision tying your worries into a bundle and then dropping it into a well or pool of water at the start of your journey. In chapter 2, where sacred water and trees were discussed, we learned that it is a custom to tie a piece of cloth to a tree after visiting a well or spring. I like to use this method in my journey, and tie my bundle of concerns on my way to the World Tree. Again, I have used one way in the sample visualization, but you may want to experiment to find what works best for you. As in meditation, if a thought from the everyday realm comes to mind, gently acknowledge it and set it aside.

As you prepare your space, have a question in mind or a reason for your journey, but do not go with any particular expectation about what you will see or learn. Be flexible and accept what you find. Shamans generally meet up with spirit helpers or guides that can take the form of humans or totem animals. In your journeys with trees you may meet certain tree spirits, dryads, or other beings. Be open. Do not be shy about asking questions of them, but do not demand answers. Be respectful and always thank any spirits you meet, but don't go overboard and feel you have to prostrate yourself before them in praise.

Remember to always do what is comfortable for you. If for any reason you feel uneasy, end the journey by climbing down the tree or back up the roots, or just imagine that you are standing beside the tree. You have free will and can do this at any time. No one or other energy can control you or take over you when you journey. Always remember that you are in control. If you encounter other beings/inner contacts who may seem belligerent, be polite but stand your ground. This does not often occur so do not go into a journey with fear—just know that you have control of yourself.

Journey

[Begin recording here.]

Close your eyes and get comfortable. Become aware of your feet or body on the floor. Feel your energy move through you, down through the floor, down through the building to the earth. Feel Mother Earth's energy join with your energy. Your body may feel heavy as it becomes grounded.

Now, draw the energy up through your body. Feel the vital life-force move through you. As you feel this movement, become aware that you are walking through a forest. Leaves blanket the ground and the air is crisp. The smell of rich soil fills your nostrils as a light breeze stirs the fallen leaves. Squirrels and chipmunks noisily rush through the underbrush.

You walk along a path that follows a small ridge overlooking a slow-moving river. There are several trees with low-hanging branches that are festooned with colored strips of cloth that have been tied onto many twigs. Some of the branches dip into the water. As you leave the path you pull a piece of cloth from your jacket pocket. You pause and hold it between your palms in front of your chest. Let all the burdens of your heart flow into this cloth, and then fasten it to one of the tree branches. Walk away and don't look back.

The path splits to skirt around two tall oak trees that grow in the middle of it. These trees are about four feet apart. These are the gateway trees. Stop in between them, raise your hands to shoulder height and place a palm on each tree.

Say to yourself, "And so, I enter." Feel the energy of the trees move through your hands. When you are ready, continue on your way.

The path curves to the left, but you continue forward. You see that the ground slopes into a small valley where a stream trickles down a little stepped waterfall. The splashing water is musical, and at times it sounds like laughter. You move forward down the steep slope where bare rock provides rugged steps. You begin to feel the energy of the land. As you climb down you notice a large gnarled oak tree growing from the rock. This is the World Tree that guards this enchanted valley.

The only sound is the trickling water farther down the slope. When you reach level ground beside the tree, you find a parting in its great exposed roots where they cradle a nest of ferns. The opening at first seems small but when you pull some of the fern fronds aside you find that you can fit inside.

You enter what appears to be a tunnel. It does not go very far horizontally. You notice a soft glow coming from below and realize that you can descend a narrow shaft by climbing down the tree's roots. You continue down until you reach a level corridor with ceiling and walls created by the roots interspersed with rock. There is a soft light from the rock, just enough to allow you to see your way, and even though it is autumn, this underground route is not cold. It is as if the earth itself is providing warmth.

At the end of the corridor you find yourself in the vestibule of a large chamber with decorative Celtic-style artwork covering the walls and ceiling. On closer inspection you see that these designs are formed by the tree roots and that they slowly move in ever-changing twining patterns. As these designs evolve, you may see animals, faces or symbols that hold meaning for you.

As the root patterns change they also pulse with energy. You may see sparkles or light moving along the roots or a flow of color. You may also hear music or a soft buzzing.

The floor is bare earth and in the middle is a pool of shimmering water that reflects the flowing patterns of the walls and ceiling. There is a bench formed by large roots at the other side of the chamber. You walk around the pool and sit on the bench. Watch and listen. Remain alert because the strongest energy may come through other senses. What you hear, see and feel may hold messages for you; things that may guide you or answer your questions.

A being or animal may come and sit beside you, or you may simply feel the sentient presence of the great tree that is above and surrounding you. You may ask questions, but do not demand answers. Even if you are not spoken to directly, anything that is said may hold information for you. Listen and feel the warmth of the energy that surrounds you. If you are compelled to walk around the chamber, do so.

[Insert fifteen to twenty minutes of drumming or rattling audio here, and then slowly lower the volume when you are ready to record the remaining text.]

It is time to begin your return journey. Thank anyone who has spoken to you for their gift of wisdom. In return, offer them a gift. It may be a piece of jewelry that you wear, something in your pocket, or a piece of your clothing. Give something that has value to you and give it freely. Retrace your path around the pool. When you reach the vestibule you may want to pause a moment and look at the chamber before you begin your ascent. Does the place seem different from when you entered?

Retrace your path up the roots and along the passage, then through the entry where you find yourself standing next to the great oak tree. Climb up the slope, using the roots of the tree to steady you. When you reach the top of the slope, look back at the little valley and the oak tree. Do you feel closer to the web of existence than when you entered?

Continue on your way. Find the path and follow it. At the gateway trees in the middle of the path, pause again. Place a palm on each tree and say to yourself: "And so I leave, to return again."

The forest around you slowly fades. Become aware of your room. Feel the floor underneath you. Become aware of your energy and the earth energy that has been holding you. Let excess energy flow to Mother Earth as you return to your everyday consciousness. When you are ready, open your eyes.

[End recording.]

After the Journey

It is important to take your time and not rush to re-cross the threshold into your everyday world. It is not unusual to feel a little disoriented when you return, especially from your first journey. Even if you have previously journeyed, when you begin to move deeper you may feel slow or displaced when you come back. The Celtic bards of Wales called this *awen*, which means a state of inspiration.[4] This may seem like a fine line to tread, but this in-between state can be a muse. That's why journaling your experience aids in this transition and allows you to access the events, sights, and conversations that took place in your journey. Try to record as much detail as you can. Even if you do not recall everything in chronological order, it is important to get information down on paper (or recorded on an audiotape) because it will quickly slip from your everyday consciousness.

During your post-journey, take time for a light snack and something to drink such as herb tea. If you have difficulty grounding, eat a small piece of chocolate. Chocolate is so sensual that it almost never fails to bring you completely into your physical body.

Various types of birds are associated with certain trees, and in general are considered to be messengers. In your journey work, take note of any bird that appears as it may be a key to certain trees and their energy, which may be relevant to you.

In Celtic legend, a silver branch with sweetly tinkling bells acted as a passport into other realms—most notably the faery world. Greek legend tells of a similar golden bough. Likewise, a sacred branch at the entrance to the underworld is used in Virgil's *Aeneid*. These are all symbols of the cosmic/World Tree. You may find it helpful to hold a branch as you embark on your journey. This can be from the same type of tree that you envision as your World Tree or it can be from a type of tree that has qualities you find helpful. As in ritual, employing a symbol aids in unlocking information.

If you have a wand, carry it with you when you journey. Alternatively, you could make a special wand that you use only for your journeys. Refer to appendix B for information on wand making.

TREE	TYPE OF BIRD
Alder	Hawk, seagulls (especially herring gull), raven
Apple	Grosbeak
Ash	Common snipe
Aspen	Mourning dove, swan
Beech	Bluebird
Birch	Eagle, pheasant, egret
Blackthorn	Thrush
Cedar	Goldfinch
Cherry	Red-tailed hawk
Chestnut	Blue jay, grouse, swan
Cypress	Owl
Elder	Pheasant, raven, rook
Elm	Lapwing, ruffled grouse
Fir	Sparrow
Gorse	Cormorant, harrier hawk
Hackberry	Cedar waxwing, quail
Hawthorn	Blackbird, owl, purple martin
Hazel	Crane
Heather	Red grouse
Hickory	Peacock, phoenix
Holly	Cardinal, starling
Honeysuckle	Hummingbird, lapwing
Ivy	Lark, mute swan, swallow
Juniper	Cedar waxwing, goose
Linden	Turtle dove
Locust	Finch
Maple	Horned owl
Mimosa	Hummingbird
Oak	Oriole, wren
Olive	Dove
Pine	Crow, jackdaw, raven
Reed	Geese, kingfisher
Rowan	Duck, quail
Spruce	Grouse, mallard duck
Sycamore	Goldfinch
Vine/bramble	Eagle, titmouse, white swan
Walnut	Eagle
Willow	Hawk, snowy owl
Yew	Eagle, hummingbird

Table 8.1: Birds as messengers associated with trees

In the beginning, you may find it easier to visualize the path you walk in your journey in idyllic conditions. If autumn leaves underfoot or the bright colors of summer help you attain a sense of place, use these visual and audio clues. As you become more comfortable with journeying, let your imagery adapt to the current season and weather conditions. This will help you more fully tap into the experience and energies around you. Learn to appreciate the feeling of rain or the harsh barren beauty of winter and delve into the special energy that unfolds. It helps to take walks for the purpose of observing how trees, or a special tree, are affected by different weather. Notice how its energy affects yours.

Study the natural world so you can adapt it to your journeys and engage all of your senses. If you are in the woods, hear the leaves swish as you walk through them and fallen branches crunch if you step on them. If you are near water listen for softly lapping waves of a pond or the trickle of a small stream down a rock face. Take note of what odors are in the air. Do you smell sweet spring blossoms or earthy late autumn decay? Is it summer and muggy? Can you feel the anticipation of a thunderstorm brewing? Let your senses come alive.

As mentioned, the sample journey is intended to help you on your way. It is important for you to develop your own entryway. Use or model it on a real place you've visited or a place from childhood memory. It can be a place that you completely create in your mind. As long as it seems real, it becomes your reality.

An Alternative Journey Method

In the mid-1990s, Belinda Gore wrote a book entitled *The Ecstatic Body Postures*, which was based on Professor Felicitas Goodman's research into shamanic journeying and ritual body postures. Starting with postures found in prehistoric cave paintings, their work expanded to include the postures of ancient statues. They experimented and found that these ritual body postures functioned as a "doorway" into specific areas of reality.

This type of journey and its preparation are done in the same way described earlier in this chapter but when you are ready to begin, you assume the posture of the statue instead of sitting or lying down in a comfortable position. Actually, as part of your preparation you may need to try out the posture. Several of my friends and I experimented with a number of postures and found that at least two of us and sometimes all three of us had strikingly similar journeys. Following these journeys we read the description of the reality Goodman and Gore had experienced in the particular posture we had just used, and we found that most of the time our encounters were comparable.

Recalling these experiences, I decided to try something similar with my tree journeys. To do this you will need to have an individual tree in mind. Get to know its shape and "posture." I started with the willow that stands in front of my house. It's small for a willow of its age, but its shape / posture has always fascinated me because the trunk grows almost horizontal to the earth. I knew to imitate this position standing up while journeying would be nearly impossible, having worked with some ecstatic ritual postures that were exceedingly uncomfortable. However, since above and below are debatable directions when journeying, lying on the floor allowed me to assume the shape of the tree. As I did this I also focused on an image of the tree in my mind. I very quickly began to feel the fluid motion of willow branches.

If you decide to try this method, begin by deciding what you need to work on, bring into your life or heal. Determine the attributes you want, and then match them up with a type of tree. Individual trees can teach individual lessons. For example, two willows can give you different information. For this reason I think it is best to find a tree in your area that you can go to and get to know. Become familiar with its "posture." Do a little sketch, but don't worry about being artistic and capturing elegant details because all you want is to know the basic shape. If you need to work with a tree that is not in your area, find a picture of one and get to know it as well as you can. This will be easier after working with several trees.

When you are ready to journey with this tree, prepare your space and start your drumming or rattling tape or CD. Instead of approaching it as you would your World Tree, simply go into the posture of the tree as you hold a question or thought in your mind. Take as much time as you need. You may get to meet the specific dryads of that tree. When you are ready to return to your human form, simply think of your own shape and move into a posture more normal for you. After doing this, thank the tree and any dryads who may have spoken with you.

As you continue to work with trees in this manner, you will build a group of tree helpers to whom you can turn for aid in solving issues or seeking knowledge.

---

1. Tom Cowan, *Fire in the Head* (San Francisco: HarperSanFrancisco, 1993), 11; Paul Devereux, *Shamanism and the Mystery Lines* (St. Paul, MN: Llewellyn/Quantum, 1993), 102.

2. The Maypole can be considered a shamanic tool used when the veil between the worlds is thin.

3. Markale, *Merlin*, 120.

4. *Awen* was known as a mantic (sometimes borderline mad) state of poetic/creative inspiration that marked the threshold of wisdom and access to the spirit realm. In Wales, people who embarked on these shamanic journeys were called *awenyddion*, which meant "people inspired." MacKillop, *Dictionary of Celtic Mythology*, 29; Matthews, *Encyclopedia of Celtic Wisdom*, 1, 219.

In Summary

IF YOU ARE NEW TO working with tree energy, begin with the exercises in chapter 2. Find a place where you can be near trees and open your energy to their presence. Touch a tree trunk, or reach up and hold onto a branch as you feel your energy field merge with that of the tree. Take notes so that as you work with various trees you will be able to see how they may have completely different energy and other characteristics.

Get to know the types of trees in your neighborhood. Take time to observe them. Observe how they react in wind, rain, and snow. Know when they come into flower, bud, and leaf. If you have pine trees nearby, note how the cones behave in various weather conditions.

You don't need to trek out to a state forest or remote wilderness to work with tree energy. If you have a backyard with a tree or two, you may find what you need there. If you live in a city, find a park where you have comfortable access to trees. In our fast-paced lives it is so easy to lose that delicate thread of contact with the natural world, so don't make it a major expedition to find the idyllic spot, because frequency of contact is important for keeping in tune. On the other hand, as you continue to work with tree energy and need to expand your range, make a longer trip a special occasion.

If you have been using the Celtic tree calendar, try substituting other trees, especially for the calendar trees that do not grow in your location. Experiment with your own cycle of tree energy based on the sabbats, or create one that coincides with the full moons, dark moons, or the zodiac. Use whatever sequence of time reckoning works most comfortably in your life and coordinate a set of trees that embody that energy for you. Use ritual, meditation, and/or shamanic journeying to make this a part of your consciousness.

Utilizing the Ogham alphabet can be combined with other methods to honor and access the energy of particular trees. By inventing your own Ogham—whether you substitute other trees with the standard Ogham characters or develop your own version of the letters—you can create a link with tree energy that is uniquely yours. As with the tree calendar, your Ogham can be changed to accommodate your growth and evolving needs. Alternatively, using the same one over time creates a meaningful tradition that is very personal. If you develop an Ogham that works well for you, you can always create a temporary one for short-term use.

Incorporating tree energy into spellwork can bring more depth, added energy, and a vast range of possibilities to your magic. Working with any type of spirit ally will boost your intentions, and trees can be particularly powerful. Reverently handling their leaves, nuts, fruits, and branches, and bringing them into your home imbues you and your environment with their spirit. Bring tree energy into your sabbat rituals as you celebrate the cycles of renewal. It is in the forest that we find the clearest example of life, death, and rebirth working in harmony.

Whether or not you have experimented with feng shui, using a few of the tools to apply tree energy to your environment can bring many positive results. As with all energy work, intention plays a major role. Most importantly, keep in mind that your energy and your home are unique and your intuition is the key. Combining symbolic tree objects that you create for ritual and spellwork with feng shui can bring a new (or renewed) magical aspect to your home.

If you already use shamanic journeying, you may want to jump right into the alternative tree posture technique. Either way, journeying can bring rewarding results that may help you move deeper into your spiritual path with the assistance of some very special allies.

Whether you incorporate all of these methods or just a few of them into your life, don't be shy about modifying them to fit your needs. As they become a regular part of your practice, it is not unusual to find that your relationship with the forces of the natural world (not just trees) will deepen.

There was an article in my local newspaper about a man who had worked for almost twenty years as a tree cutter. When his company was contracted to take down a 300 to 450-year-old oak that was "in the way" of a housing development, he quit his job and started a campaign to save the tree. The man explained that he was not out to save every tree, but he could not stand by and let this majestic beauty be taken down just to widen a road.[1]

Like any relationship, one with a tree is also a two-way street and we must give as well as receive. It is important to examine how we live and take responsibility for the resources we use, and come to terms with the fact that our spiritual lives are intimately bound to the integrity of the natural world.

The more we open ourselves to the energy around us, the more mystical our relation with the land and elements becomes. It is as though the more we learn, the more we find that there is to learn. As we learn (and speed is not important), we are able to see and appreciate the mysteries of the natural world. It is not important to reveal everything so much as it is important to acknowledge and appreciate the beautiful mystery and wisdom of the soul.

Trees—these beautiful giants—bear silent witness to the quick passing of us humans. They remain as living memorials to those who planted them as well as those who protect them so they can continue to live in "quiet wisdom in the forest."[2]

---

1. The tree became known as the Snowstorm Oak, because when the tree cutting was first scheduled, snow prevented the crew from taking it down. Other locals got involved and the tree has been spared—at least for now. Patrick Jenkins, "Ex-Tree-Cutter Works to Save the Giant," *The Star Ledger* (Newark, NJ), April 1, 2003, Middlesex County Edition.

2. Jeremy Harte, *The Green Man* (Andover, Hampshire, England: Pitkin Unichrome Ltd., 2001), 18.

PART
TWO

This section contains information on fifty trees. It is not offered as a comprehensive field guide, but simply provides details for basic identification as well as information to help you get acquainted with their associations and energy.

As in the chapters on the tree calendar and the Ogham, the word "tree" applies to plants that are not trees but have woody stems. They are included here to accommodate the standard calendar and Ogham. Additional trees were chosen because they are common and easy to find in many locations and will help in expanding your work with tree energy. You may consider using this format for adding others not included here.

To dwellers in a wood,
almost every species has its voice
as well as its feature.

THOMAS HARDY
Under the Greenwood Tree

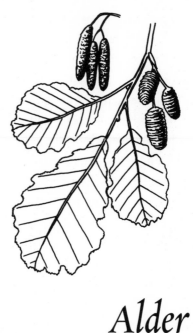

Alder

Derived from the tree's gaelic Irish name of *fearn*, the place name of Burrisnafarney in Ireland means "the borough of the alder plain," Mullafernaghan means "hill of the alder," and Cloughfern means "stone of the alder." In the second branch of the Welsh Celtic myth, *The Mabinogion*, Gwern's (the son of Branwen and Matholwch) name means "alder."

Medicinally, alder has been used as a substitute for quinine, as well as to reduce fever and inflammation. Alder has also been used to treat parasites such as lice. Its inner bark is a natural pesticide. Since ancient times in Europe and North America, its bark, twigs, and flowers have been used for dyes (brown, green, and red) and its wood for smoking meats.

The wood from young alder trees is easily worked. Mature alder wood is attractively tinted and veined. In Scotland, where alder is frequently used for making chairs, it is called Scottish mahogany. Alder has been used for barrel staves, spinning wheels, bowls, spoons, cigar boxes, clogs (in Holland and Lancashire, England) and fish weirs. One reason that alder has been considered magical is due to the way its cut wood changes from white to red. Alder logs retrieved from bogs have the color but not the hardness of ebony.

Alder has an interesting relationship with the three elements of air, water, and fire. Young, green branches can be easily turned into whistles by cutting both ends and pushing out the pith with a smaller stick. These hollow branches can be cut to various lengths and tied together to create "Pan" pipes. Whistles made from this wood are said to be magical and can summon the four winds.

Alders thrive near streams, but alder logs are water-resistant and have been used for pilings (most notably in Amsterdam and Venice). Alder branches have been used for divining rods, which are sometimes called "wishing" rods.

Concerning fire, alder does not burn well as fuel, but an excellent grade of charcoal can be created from it. According to Elizabeth Pepper and John Wilcock, people doing ceremonial magic were at one time advised to burn incense on alder charcoal.[1]

Alder is a healer for its companion trees in the aftermath of trauma such as a flood, logging, or mining operations as noted by the seventeenth-century poet, William Brown, who wrote: "The alder, whose fat shadow nourisheth / Each plant set neere him long flourisheth."[2] This is scientifically explained by alder's ability to enrich soil with nitrogen, which trees and other plants need for healthy growth.

Latin Name: *Alnus glutinosa* (European, black, or common alder), *A. serrulata* (smooth alder), *A. maritima* (seaside alder), *A. crispa* (mountain alder), *A. incana* (gray alder)

Seasonal Details: flowers with slender drooping male catkins[3] and small female pinecone-like catkins on slender stalks February–May; mountain alder flowers, June–August; seaside alder flowers, August–September; rounded toothed leaves

Powers/Attributes: banishing, divination, foundation, guardian, healing, intuition, protection, rebirth, resurrection, transformation

Elements: air, water, fire

Celtic Calendar Dates: March 18–April 14

Ogham Character: ᚛ᚃ᚜ **Name:** Fearn **Letters:** F, V, GW

Rune Character: ᛁ **Name:** Is **Letter:** I

Rune Character: ᛗ **Name:** Man/Mannaz **Letter:** M

Feng Shui Sectors: center, east

Goddesses: Cailleach Beara, Branwen, Freya

Gods: Bran, Manannan Mac Lir, Proteus

Other Beings/Characters: archangel Raphael, elves, faeries, Gwern, Gwydion, Taliesin

Zodiac: Pisces

Celestial Bodies: Mars, Venus

Plant: broom

Gemstones: beryl (sea green), ruby, serpentine

Wildlife: fox, herring gull, hawk, raven, seagulls

Other Trees: birch, hazel, hornbeam, willow

Colors: light green, deep red

Energy: feminine

Other Associations: evolving spirit; leadership; the pentagram; Saturday; north; Celtic peasant/common tree[4]

Spellwork and Ritual: banishing rituals and spells; protection spells; healing spells and meditations; water, wind, and general weather magic; divination, especially scrying; moderation of the four elements

1. Elizabeth Pepper and John Wilcock, *The Witches' Almanac* (Newport, RI: The Witches' Almanac, Ltd., Spring 1998–1999), 44.

2. William Cullina, *Native Trees, Shrubs and Vines* (New York: Houghton Mifflin, 2002), 41.

3. Catkins are clusters of tiny flowers.

4. MacManus, *Story of the Irish Race*, 129–144. The ancient Brehon Law of Ireland levied fines against anyone who damaged or cut down trees. The amount of the fine depended on the type of tree. Trees were divided into four categories: chieftain/noble, peasant/common, shrub, and bramble. There are various interpretations for some trees as to which category they belong in. Where there are discrepancies, I have made note and included both.

Apple/Crabapple

APPLES ARE ONE OF THE oldest cultivated fruits and have a long association with magic, the faery realm, and the Isle of Avalon. Its connection with illumination/understanding is included in the Bible in the story of the Garden of Eden: eating an apple gives Adam and Eve knowledge of good and evil. This tree's association with the Goddess is also present in the story with the serpent curling around its trunk. The snake was a symbol of the Great Mother Goddess.

In many folktales, eating an apple opens the gateway into other realms—most often into faeryland. Again, the apple provides illumination and the gaining of knowledge. A wand made of apple wood also aids in opening the faery realm for the person who wields it.

In the Celtic epic *Táin Bó Cuailnge*, a silver branch with three golden apples hung on the wall above King Conchobor's head and was used for "keeping order over the throng." Whenever the branch shook on its own accord, everyone fell into a respectful silence.

Jean Markale asserts that Merlin passed into another realm as a shaman, not in a crystal cave, but in the magical apple tree where he waits and watches.[1]

In Elizabethan England, apples were served at the end of a big meal along with a dish of caraway seeds to help digestion. Forked branches from apple trees are frequently used as divining rods. The wood is hard and strong and is used for tool handles and carvings. It takes a deep polish, but is not weather resistant.

Apple is one of the nine sacred woods for a sabbat fire, in which it represents love. At Yule, it was customary to "wassail" apple trees, which would encourage a good harvest of apples in the following autumn.[2] A bowl of frothy wassail was taken into the orchard on Yule, and the tips of the tree branches were dipped into the liquid. Some of it was also sprinkled on the soil around the base of the tree to bless the ground. Wassail is traditionally a hard cider that is warmed over a fire with spices and a few whole apples, which burst and produce a white foam over the liquid.

Apples are common in Pagan ritual and for general spellwork. Slicing an apple in half across its middle displays its seeds laid out in a pentagram design. A symbol of regeneration, apples are used in Samhain rituals as offerings to the dead to aid the process of rebirth.

At Samhain, winning the game of bobbing for apples (or capturing an apple suspended by a string) meant that you would be blessed by the Goddess for a year. It was also said to bestow the power of foresight. Since apples were symbols of Avalon, capturing one from the water was representative of crossing to the holy isle. Emain Ablach, the "Island of Apple," is the equivalent to the Isle of Avalon.

Derived from the tree's Gaelic Irish name *abhall*, the place name of Magherally means "plain of apple trees," and Derrylisnahavil means "oakwood of the fort of apple trees."

Dreaming of apples symbolizes prosperity and the good life.

(continued on next page)

Latin Name: *Pyrus coronaria* (American crabapple), *P. malus* (domestic cultivated apples), *P. ioensis* (prairie crabapple); *P. baccata* (Siberian crabapple)

Seasonal Details: white or pink flowers, March–May; fruits, September–November; crabapples usually less than two inches across, cultivated apples more than two inches across; leaves, rounded base and sharp tip

Powers/Attributes: attraction, beauty, choice, faithfulness, fertility, generosity, happiness, harmony, healing, illumination/knowledge, immortality, love, perpetual youth, prosperity, protection, regeneration, strength, wealth

Elements: air, water

Ogham Character: ⦀⦀
Name: Quert
Letters: Q, CC

Rune Character: ◊
Name: Ing/Ingwaz
Letters: Ng

Rune Character: ⟨
Name: Peorth/Pertho
Letter: P

Feng Shui Sectors: center, northeast, southeast, south, southwest

Goddesses: Aphrodite, Athena, Diana, Freya, Hera, Iduna, Rhiannon, Venus

Gods: Abellio, Apollo, Dionysus, Lugh, Vertumnus, Zeus

Other Beings/Characters: archangels Gabriel and Radrael, elves, King Arthur, Olwen, unicorns

Other Names for Tree: silver bough, silver branch

Zodiac: Aquarius, Taurus

Celestial Body: Venus

Gemstone: rose quartz

Wildlife: butterflies, cedar waxwing, grosbeak

Other Trees: hazel

Colors: pink, yellow-green

Energy: feminine

Other Associations: eternal life; adventure; dates: December 23–January 1, and June 25–July 4; the faery realm; Friday; sabbats: Beltane, Lughnasadh, Samhain, Yule; Celtic chieftain/noble tree; east

Bach Flower Remedy: cleansing (all apples); self-hatred (crabapple)

Spellwork and Ritual: attracting abundance; attracting a lover; crossing into the faery realm; love spells; seeking strength and protection

1. Markale, *Merlin*, 153.

2. Apple trees were wassailed on Christmas Eve, New Year, and Twelfth Night (January 6th) from medieval times through the Victorian period in England. Diana Ferguson, *The Magickal Year: A Pagan Perspective on the Natural World* (London: Labyrinth Publishing, 1996), 66.

Ash

The ancient Egyptians imported ash and used the wood for bows and arrow shafts. In medieval Europe, ash wood was used for wheel spokes and other products that required strength and flexibility. Today, ash's strong, shock-resistant wood is used for tool handles, bats, snowshoes, and other sports equipment.

Ares, the Greek god of war and son of Zeus, was said to favor the ash because it produced excellent spear shafts. In an ancient Greek creation story, humans were formed from ash and oak trees.

Since it was known as the "Venus of the Woods" in England, an ash leaf placed in the left shoe was believed to result in a person meeting his or her future spouse. Finding an ash leaf with an equal number of sections on both sides of the center vein was considered lucky and was often used in love charms. A double leaf was also considered lucky. In medieval folklore, the person on whose property an ash tree stood would be unlucky in love if seeds did not appear each year. An ash leaf placed under the pillow at night is said to aid in dreamwork.

In Norse mythology, Yggdrasil is a fantastic ash tree that connects heaven and earth. Its leaves provided shade and shelter for the entire earth and was known as the World Tree. This immortal tree carried the destiny of the world; if the tree was destroyed, the world would perish. In many legends, an evil serpent dangerously threatened to destroy the roots of Yggdrasil.

The underworld goddess, Hel, is said to have had her palace beneath one of the roots in the realm of Helheim. As Odin hung upside down from Yggdrasil, he drank from the Spring of Destiny that bubbled up at the base of the tree. This water is said to have given him great knowledge and revealed the mystery of the runes to him. Because of this, ash wood is popular for rune tiles. In alternate versions of this story, Odin is said to have hung himself from his spear of ash.

In the ancient *Eddas*,[1] the oral literature of Iceland, the wise eagle observed everything in the world from atop the sacred ash tree. Two streams flowed from the roots; one contained the knowledge of the past and the other the knowledge of the future. According to the stories, humans were created from the wood of the tree.

Three of the five great trees of Ireland were ash: the Tree of Uisnech, the Tree of Tortu, and the Tree of Dathi. The five trees were located in each of the five provinces and symbolized guardians who protected the sovereignty of the land. They were destroyed in 665 CE by the Celts themselves, rather than surrendered to the encroaching Christians.

Irish emigrants to America took pieces of an ash tree called the Tree of Creevna in Killura with them as protection against drowning.

Along with oak and hawthorn, ash was considered part of the triad of powerful faery trees. In the traditional besom broom, ash is used for the handle.

Derived from the Gaelic *fuinnse* and *fuinnseóg* for ash tree, the name of the town Funshin in Ireland means a "place of ash trees." The city of Fresno, California, gets its name from the Spanish word for ash tree because of the number of white ashes that grew there when the area was first settled.

Latin Name: *Fraxinus americana* (white ash), *F. excelsior* (common ash), *F. quadrangulata* (blue ash), *F. nigra* (black ash), *F. pennsylvanica* (green ash/red ash); *F. caroliniana* (water ash)

Seasonal Details: clusters of small flowers, April–May; one-inch long winged seeds that stay on the tree until autumn; multiple oval leaflets on stalks that turn orange to purple in autumn

Powers/Attributes: ambition, balance, communication, creativity, fertility, growth, healing, illumination/knowledge, love divination, peace of mind, poetry and storytelling, prophecy, protection (especially from drowning), rebirth, stability, transitions

Elements: air, earth, fire, water

Celtic Calendar Dates: February 18–March 17

Ogham Character: ᚍ
  Name: Nion
  Letter: N

Rune Character: ᚨ
  Name: As/Asa
  Letter: A

Rune Character: ᛗ
  Name: Ehwaz/Eh
  Letter: E

Rune Character: ᛉ
  Name: Gyfu/Gebo
  Letter: G

Rune Character: ᛗ
  Name: Man/Mannaz
  Letter: M

Rune Character: ᚹ
  Name: Wunjo/Wyn
  Letter: W

Feng Shui Sectors: north, northeast, east, south, southwest, west

Goddesses: Eostre, Frigg, Hel/Holle, Minerva, Nemesis

Gods: Ares, Dagda, Frey, Llyr, Neptune, Odin, Poseidon, Thor, Woden

Other Being/Character: Gwydion

Other Names for Tree: hoop ash (black ash); tree of water (Teutonic)

Zodiac: Capricorn, Libra, Taurus, Virgo

Celestial Bodies: Mercury, Neptune, Sun, Venus

Plants: wood anemone

Gemstones: clear quartz, coral, zircon

Wildlife: butterflies, common snipe

Color: pale blue

Energy: masculine energy

Other Associations: connection with astral realm; doorway to other realms; dates: May 25–June 6 and November 22–December 1; sabbats: Ostara/vernal equinox, Beltane; Celtic chieftain/noble tree; Celtic Abred (Ireland) or Annwn (Wales), the innermost circle from which all life sprang; Norse Asgard, the home of the gods which included Valhalla

Spellwork and Ritual: attraction spells; dispersion of negativity; divination (especially the seeds); protection spells; boosting the energy of spells; sea magic; solar magic; use in meditations, spells and rituals for seeking creative inspiration

---

1. Like many ancient cultural myths, the *Eddas* were not written down until the Christian era. The Prose Edda was recorded by poet, historian Snorri Sturluson circa 1222–1223. The Poetic Edda was recorded during the second half of the thirteenth century by unknown authors from material that dates to 800–1100 CE. *The New Encyclopedia Britannica*, 15th ed., s.v. "Eddas."

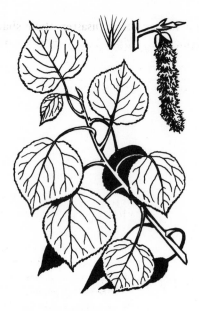

Aspen

THE ASPEN IS FREQUENTLY KNOWN as the "trembling aspen" because of the way the leaves seem to constantly quiver. One of the many beliefs about this tree is that it was the wood used for Christ's cross. Another story relating to Jesus that attempts to explain the quivering action of the leaves is that the aspen was the only tree in the forest that did not bow down to the holy family. Jesus is said to have put a curse on it, which caused the tree to tremble in fear.

According to *Cormac's Glossary*,[1] a rod of aspen, called a fé, was used to measure a fresh grave to ensure its occupant would fit. This is said to have given rise to aspen's association with death. In the *Táin Bó Cuailnge*, aspen was cut for the charioteers of the sons of Gárach for spears to slay the Ulster hero Cu Chulainn.

Medicinally, aspen has been used to alleviate fevers. The black poplar is used for skin abrasions and to relieve pain and inflammation. The buds, bark, and leaves contain salicin, which is similar to aspirin. It has also been used for earaches, asthma, and coughs.

During time of famine, Native Americans used the inner bark of the aspen as food. This was preferable over some other available foods because of its sweetness. It was also used to feed animals.

Aspens have soft white wood that is prone to breaking in storms. They are one of the early trees to repopulate a forest after a fire or other disaster, their shade providing a gentle "nursery" for other trees. Aspens stabilize a damaged ecosystem, and like alders, they are healers.

Latin Name: *Populus tremuloides* (quaking aspen), *P. alba* (white poplar), *P. nigra* (black poplar), *P. canescens* (gray poplar)

Seasonal Details: long clustered catkins that often release "cottony" seeds March–May; small oval/heart-shaped leaves that turn vibrant yellow in autumn

Powers/Attributes: ancestry, astral projection, communication, courage, eloquence, endurance, harmony, healing, money, peace, protection, rebirth, rejuvenation, success

Elements: air, water

Ogham Character: ᚉ
  Name: Eadhadh
  Letter: E

Ogham Character: ᚕ
  Name: Éabhadh
  Letters: EA, CH, K

Rune Character: ᛈ
  Name: Peorth/Pertho
  Letter: P

Feng Shui Sectors: center, east, southeast, south

Goddesses: Calypso, Frigg, Hecate, Morrigan, Persephone

Gods: Apollo, Hercules, Tyr, Zeus

Other Names for Tree: trembling aspen, shivering tree, poplar

Zodiac: Capricorn, Libra

Celestial Bodies: Mercury, Saturn, Venus

Gemstone: gray topaz

Wildlife: butterflies, mourning dove, swan

Other Tree: willow

Colors: gray, silvery white

Energy: masculine (white poplar), feminine (black poplar)

Bach Flower Remedy: fear of unknown things

Other Associations: death; dates: February 4–8, May 1–14, and August 5–13; west; sabbats: Mabon/autumn equinox; sources disagree whether this is a Celtic peasant/common tree or shrub tree

Spellwork and Ritual: protection spells (especially against theft); traveling to or communicating with other realms; spells to help get you through difficult times, as well as when you just need a boost in specific aspects of life

---

1. This was an Irish/Latin dictionary compiled by Cormac Mac Cuilennain of Cashel circa 900 CE. Ellis, *The Druids*, 150.

Bamboo

ABLE TO GROW IN BOTH tropical and temperate climates, bamboo is indigenous to Africa, Asia, Australia, and both North and South America. Over a thousand species of bamboo have been identified, and more are being discovered. "Gregarious flowering," or synchrony, is an unusual behavior of bamboo in which many of the plants of a particular species will come into bloom at the same time even if they have not bloomed for decades. Some species flower only once in a hundred years.

Bamboo was formerly thought to be a primitive grass, but after studies of its DNA, it is now considered to be a highly evolved plant. Bamboo species range in size from one foot to over one hundred feet tall. Bamboo was among the first plants to reappear after the atomic bombs were dropped on Hiroshima and Nagasaki.

The hardy varieties of bamboo can tolerate almost any type of soil, as long as it is not waterlogged. A water barrier such as a small stream helps to contain the spread of a grove. A solid barrier in the ground will also halt its proliferation.

Bamboo wood has been put to a wide range of uses, from baskets to furniture, and from decorative fencing to industrial barriers for concrete pouring, and, of course, bamboo flutes and fishing rods. Its flexibility and durability has made it useful in sports such as Kendo (Japanese fencing) and Kyudo (Japanese archery). Bamboo baskets and combs dating to the Jomon Period (circa 10,000–300 BCE) were found at geological sites on both the Honshu and Kyushu Islands of Japan, and many believe that bamboo was used in ritual as well as everyday life.[1] In the Yayoi (300 BCE–250 CE) and the Kofun (circa 300–710 CE) cultures, bamboo was used for fish traps, sieves, and baskets. In the eighth century, large bamboo canes were used as drainpipes. Through the ages, bamboo has also served as both subject and material for Japanese artists.

In many Asian cultures, bamboo is considered sacred. The *Guicang*, or "Book of Concealment," a manuscript from the Shang Dynasty of China, explains implements of divination that include a set of bamboo sticks called "counters." Bamboo was also used in a method called "bamboo root divination." The ancient Chinese believed that to study bamboo and master its lessons was time well spent. Bamboo is still a symbol of nobility, virtue, and respectability. However, dreaming of a bamboo stalk means you may be involved in a lawsuit.

I first got to know bamboo when I bought a small cutting at a fundraising event for a local school. The plant seemed very hardy and didn't mind where I placed it—shade or sun. Its energy was very comfortable, and at the next opportunity I bought another one. Several months later, while hiking with a friend, I was pleasantly surprised to discover a bamboo grove with culms over twenty-five feet tall. The energy was so uplifting that I was soon running among the towering bamboo like a little kid.

The sound of wind through its leaves is a beautiful, soothing symphony.

(continued on next page)

Latin Name: *Bambusa vulgaris* (common bamboo), *B. oldhamii* (giant timber bamboo), *B. multiplex* (golden goddess), *Gigantochloa atroviolacea* (tropical black bamboo), *Thyrsostachys siamensis* (monastery bamboo); *Otatea acuminata* (Mexican weeping bamboo)

Seasonal Details: an evergreen that flowers periodically; rapid bursts of growth in the spring, summer and autumn; colors range from yellow, green, reddish, black, and sometimes with variegated patterns

Powers/Attributes: good fortune, flexibility, harmony, longevity, luck, protection,

Element: air

Feng Shui Sectors: center, longevity, negative areas

Goddesses: Hina, Izanami

God: Thoth

Celestial Body: Sun

Energy: masculine

Other Association: divination, wisdom, strength

Spellwork and Ritual: breaking negative energy and spells; use making a wish in ritual; divination; drawing energy into your rituals and meditations if bamboo plants are positioned beside or near your altar

1. Ronald E. Dolan and Robert L. Worden, eds., *Japan: A Country Study* (Washington, DC: Federal Research Division of the Library of Congress, 1992), 5–6.

Beech

Beech bark, leaves, roots, and sap have been used for medicines for burns, ulcers, bladder and liver problems, and tuberculosis. Its bark and leaves have astringent properties and are used in skin care products. Beechnuts have served as food for humans and animals, and in the Middle Ages, they were a main source of food for domestic swine.

While beech wood is strong, it tends to split easily. It has been used for indoor applications, but not outdoor ones since it does not weather well. A great deal of paper is produced from beeches. The bark is excellent for carving, and unfortunately many people like to leave their initials and other messages on these trees. This practice dates back to Roman times.

The beech does not do well in cities as it does not tolerate pollution as well as other trees. However, young beeches are tolerant of shade and wait patiently in the forest for older trees to fall, allowing sunlight to finally reach them.

When oak groves were not available, beech was a suitable substitute for Druidic ritual because of its majestic bearing. Along with oak, beech trees were included in the sacred grove of Dodona at the temple of Zeus in Greece. Crispus, a Greek orator, was known to take solace under a beech, with which he also shared his wine by pouring it on its roots.

Along with apple, alder, and hazel, forked beech branches have been popular as divining rods. Beech is one of the trees considered protective against lighting because lighting tends to strike maples, oaks, and pines more often. The beech is actually a good conductor of electricity and harmlessly grounds lightning bolts.

Associations with rebirth, transformation, and ancestors may have come from the common occurrence of dried, brown leaves remaining on the tree from one year to the next. This provides a clear illustration of cycles and generational change.

Beech has been called the "mother of the woods" and queen to the king oak.[1] As mother, her lofty branches provide protection and shelter for smaller trees, and sustenance for humans and wildlife with her sweet beechnuts. Like hazelnuts, beechnuts were believed to impart wisdom and were used as amulets. The visible roots of the beech have been compared to serpents—a fitting connection, since the snake was a creature associated with the Great Mother Goddess.

Latin Name: *Fagus grandifolia* (American beech), *F. sylvatica* (European beech)

Seasonal Details: yellowish female flowers and male catkins April–May; triangular-shaped nuts called masts September–October; coarsely toothed oval/elliptical leaves that turn golden in autumn

Powers/Attributes: ancestry, companionship, creativity, mental balance, protection, second sight, stability, wisdom

Elements: fire, water

Ogham Character: ᚖ
Name: Uilleann
Letters: UI, PE

Ogham Character: ᚗ
Name: Ifin/Iphin
Letters: IO, PH

Rune Character: ᚾ
Name: Nyd
Letters: Ng

Rune Character: ᛈ
Name: Peorth/Pertho
Letter: P

Feng Shui Sectors: center, east, west, negative areas

Goddesses: Athena, Cerridwen, Diana, Freya, Frigg, Hel/Holle

Gods: Apollo, Loki, Odin, Tyr, Zeus

Other Beings/Characters: archangels Hayriel and Jophael

Other Names for Tree: copper beech (English), white beech (American)

Zodiac: Gemini, Virgo

Celestial Body: Saturn

Gemstones: azurite, blue topaz

Wildlife: bluebird, deer, fox, wild turkey

Other Tree: oak

Color: light blue

Energy: feminine

Bach Flower Remedy: intolerance

Other Associations: patience; rebirth; transformation; date: December 22; aiding energy flow; southwest; sabbats: Litha/Midsummer, Samhain

Spellwork and Ritual: bringing stability to your life; manifesting intentions into the physical world; cleansing ritual space; making offerings to the Goddess; enhancing contact with ancestors at Samhain using leaves

1. In the woods where I hike, which is mostly oak and beech, I found a pair of trees that I call "the lovers." It consists of an oak and upon one of its roots a beech has grown. The limbs of both trees have become intertwined into a beautiful embrace.

Birch

AMERICAN BIRCH PRODUCES A HARD, heavy wood that is used in construction and for carving. European birch wood is soft and fibrous and used mainly for firewood. The sap of the black birch contains wintergreen oil and has been used for food flavorings as well as to produce birch beer. The sap can be boiled down like maple syrup.

The birch is associated with renewal because of its ability to take hold and grow more quickly than other trees. It is a cold climate tree that can compete with evergreens. Often it is the first to spring up after a forest fire, seemingly as a herald of the great woods that will eventually return. Birch is a hardy tree that can do well in many types of conditions. It is most often found in groves rather than individually.

Birch was frequently used for Maypoles and is one of the nine sacred woods for a sabbat fire, in which it represents the Goddess. In the traditional witches' besom broom, a bundle of birch twigs can be used for the brush. Because of the belief in its protective qualities, baby cradles were commonly made of birch.

According to Jean Markale, birch was a tree dedicated to the dead.[1] Since death was believed to be a passage into another life, it was also associated with rebirth. In Celtic burials, bodies were transported to their graves with bushy birch branches for a covering, which was called a *strophais*.

In England and Ireland, December 26 included the custom called "the hunting of the wren," which marked the transition of old year to new. The wren represented the old year and was said to be hunted down by a robin (the spring bird) that carried a birch rod in his claws.

In thirteenth- and fourteenth-century Wales, lovers met in "the house of leaves," which meant under a birch tree. Birch wreaths were given as love tokens to remember these meetings. Going "a-maying" referred to these trysts and meant birch trees as often as hawthorns. (Another name for the hawthorn is "May tree.") During the Victorian era, birch was a symbol of grace and meekness.

Derived from the tree's Gaelic name, *beith*, the place name of Aghavea (Achadhbeith) in Ireland means "the field of the birch trees."

In ancient Rome, birch, along with oak and yew, represented the three pillars of wisdom. In Slavic folktales, the Genii of the Forest, or *Ljesch*, and other mythical beings favored the birch. The tree is a symbol of the country Estonia and its culture.

Archaeologists have found birch bark with inscriptions. The bark easily peels from the tree and has a smooth surface on its inner side. I have found birch an interesting surface for artwork, which also makes it useful in spellcraft and ritual.

(continued on next page)

Latin Name: *Betula papyrifera* (American white birch or paper birch), *B. alba* (European white birch), *B. pendula* (European weeping birch), *B. lenta* (black birch or sweet birch), *B. nigra* (river birch)

Seasonal Details: yellow-green catkins in March; oval/heart-shaped, finely serrated leaves; bark colors range from drab gray to salmon, or cinnamon-red (river birch) to white (paper birch); the river birch has shaggy bark

Powers/Attributes: beginnings, birth, blessings, creativity, crafts, fertility, growth, healing, inspiration, love, protection, purification, renewal

Element: water

Celtic Calendar Dates: December 24–January 20

Ogham Character: ⟙
    Name: Beith
    Letter: B

Rune Character: ᛒ
    Name: Beorc
    Letter: B

Rune Character: ᚢ
    Name: Ur/Uruz
    Letter: U

Feng Shui Sectors: southeast, west, northwest, negative areas

Goddesses: Audhumla, Cerridwen, Fand, Freya, Frigg

Gods: Angus Mac Og, Dagda, Lugh, Thor

Other Beings/Characters: Ljesch, Taliesin, wood nymphs

Other Names for Tree: Lady of the Woods, silver birch

Zodiac: Sagittarius

Celestial Bodies: Jupiter, Moon, Sun, Venus

Plants: daisy, fly agaric mushroom

Gemstones: fluorite, quartz

Wildlife: eagle, pheasant, white cow, white egret, white stag

Other Trees: fir, spruce

Colors: dark green, white

Energy: feminine

Other Associations: the arts, travel to the faery realm, date: June 24; sabbats: Ostara/vernal equinox, Beltane; springtime in general; north; Sunday; Celtic peasant/common tree

Spellwork and Ritual: celebrating a birth; moon rituals; blessing the beginning of a project, relationship, new home, or making any kind of fresh start

1. Markale, *Merlin*, 117.

Blackthorn

Archaeologists have found that our relationship with the blackthorn dates back to the Neolithic period (9000–7000 BCE).[1] This tree was used by the ancient Greeks, Romans, and Arabs for medicine as well as food. Blackthorn's astringent and diuretic properties have made it useful in treating stomach and bladder trouble, as well as skin problems and sore throat. Blackthorn's fruit, sloes, are rich in vitamins and have been used in jams, jellies, and for flavoring in liqueurs, most notably sloe gin. Its black bark and sturdy wood makes it an attractive walking stick. The bark has also been used to create a rich red dye for linen and wool.

Blackthorn has been used for divining rods. As a method of trial (according to Irish legend), when Mochta's axe was heated in a fire of blackthorn, it would burn the skin of a liar but others were unharmed.

Along with gorse and linden, blackthorn is associated with Walpurgis, also called Valborg. Walpurgis is said to have originated with the Vikings and was their celebration of spring, which took place in late April. As Christian and Pagan traditions became entangled, this celebration evolved into Valborgsmäss to honor a revered eighth century German abbess (whose name may have been Valborg or Walburga). The mass was celebrated on May Eve to commemorate her sainthood on May 1, 779. As Christian influence grew and the drive to convert people from Paganism intensified, Walpurgis became an event to drive out witches. It was believed that May Eve was the witches' last big blowout of the year (especially since it was directly opposite Samhain in a cyclical calendar). Walpurgis became known to the wider world after Goethe wrote of it in *Faustus*. Blackthorn came into use for exorcism rituals because of its connection with Walpurgis.

Derived from *draeighean*, Gaelic for blackthorn, the name of the town Aghadreen (Aghadreenagh) in Ireland means the "field of the sloe bushes," and Clonarney (Cluain-airne) means "meadow of sloes."

Blackthorn and hawthorn were used together for hedges to keep animals out of orchards and gardens. It is still part of many hedgerows. During my pilgrimage in Ireland, I noted that blackthorn and gorse seemed to grow near many of the sacred sites I visited.

Latin Name: *Prunus spinosa*

Seasonal Details: white flowers in late winter/early spring; small round, blue/black fruit (sloes) ripen in October after the first frost; spiny branches

Powers/Attributes: authority, control, protection, strength, truth

Elements: earth, fire

Ogham Character: ᚎ
Name: Straif
Letters: St, Z, SS

Rune Character: ᚦ
Name: Thorn
Letters: Th

Rune Character: ᚹ
Name: Wunjo/Wyn
Letter: W

Feng Shui Sectors: negative areas

Goddesses: Banba, Bertha, Brigid, Hel/Holle, Macha, Ran

Gods: Bel, Dagda, Loki

Other Being/Character: faeries

Other Names for Tree: sloe, sloe plum, wishing thorn, faery tree

Zodiac: Aries, Scorpio

Celestial Body: Saturn

Plant: houseleek

Gemstones: agate, bloodstone

Wildlife: bees, butterflies, thrush

Other Trees: gorse, hawthorn, linden

Colors: dark purple, gray, white

Energy: masculine

Other Associations: fate and other powers that must be followed; Walpurgis; winter; south; sabbats: Imbolg, Samhain; Celtic shrub tree

Spellwork and Ritual: giving strength to spells; protection

---

1. Brenda Fowler, *Iceman: Uncovering the Life and Times of a Prehistoric Man Found in an Alpine Glacier* (New York: Random House, 2000), 193.

Cedar

In the Middle Ages and the Renaissance, the durable cedar was used in Europe for furniture, chest lining, and musical instruments. The mythical unicorn was said to keep treasure in a cedar wood chest. Cedar wood is currently used for fencing and furniture. Used for brooms in Canada, cedar branches clear the air as they clean the floor.

Medicinally cedar incense was used to treat colds and scurvy. Cedar fragrance is still used to keep moths away from clothing and other fabrics. The northern white cedar (*Thuja occidentalis*) has been a favorite wood of shipbuilders on the East Coast of the United States because it is light and buoyant. Although not a true cedar, it is called such because its oil is very similar to that of the cedar. The Latinized Greek *Thuja* in its name means "to fumigate." The Greek word *thuo*, meaning "to sacrifice," is also thought to be a root word for the name because cedar was frequently burned in temples.

Although there are a number of trees called cedars, only those of the genus *Cedrus* are true cedars. In the Middle East, cedar wood from the famed Cedars of

Lebanon was used to build the Temple of Solomon. It was also known as *arbor vitae*, the Tree of Life. Cedars were associated with the Divine because they seemed to grow out of the rocks without need of soil or water, and they flourished under difficult conditions.

In ancient Egypt, cedar oil and incense were used as offerings to the gods. The sun god Ra was mentioned as "he who dwelt among the cedars."

Native Americans used split cedar roots to weave baskets, and burned cedar twigs to give food a spicy, smoked flavor. Boughs of cedar were placed on top of tepee poles to ward off lightning. Boughs also functioned as mattresses, over which hides would be thrown to create a comfortable bed. The legendary Thunderbird was believed to nest in cedar trees high in the mountains.

Cedar became associated with Imbolg because it represents coming into the light from darkness.

Latin Name: *Thuja occidentalis* (northern white cedar), *Chamaecyparis thyoides* (Atlantic white cedar); true cedars: *Cedrus libani* (cedar of Lebanon), *Cedrus atlantica* (blue atlas cedar)

Seasonal Details: barrel-shaped cones that stand upright on the branch; scalelike flattened leaves that hug twigs and branches; true cedars have clusters of needles

Powers/Attributes: calm and balance, dreaming, eternal life (evergreen), healing, longevity, preservation, prosperity, protection, purification, removal or repulsion of negativity, wisdom

Elements: air, earth, fire, water

Feng Shui Sectors: center, southeast, northeast, longevity, life, negative areas

Goddesses: Arianrhod, Arinna, Astarte, Brigid, Calypso, Persephone

Gods: Aegir, Osiris, Ra, Thunderbird

Other Beings/Characters: archangel Tazkiel, elves, faeries, unicorns

Other Name for Tree: *Arbor vitae*

Celestial Body: Sun

Gemstone: yellow chrysoprase

Wildlife: goldfinch

Other Trees: fir, larch, spruce

Color: light yellow

Energy: masculine

Other Associations: passing from darkness into light; the self; dates: February 2–18 and August 14–23; sabbat: Imbolg; throat chakra; Babylon

Spellwork and Ritual: attracting abundance (in the form of property); protection spells; purifying space before ritual; removing negativity and recovering balance

Cherry

The cherry's red wood, which darkens with age, is a favorite for carving, furniture, cabinetwork, and paneling. In the Middle Ages and the Renaissance it was used for musical instruments. Medicinally, the aromatic inner bark has been used in cough syrups and tinctures for sore throats, respiratory ailments, and poor circulation. Chokecherries were widely used by Native Americans for syrups and dye for clothing, baskets, and feathers. Biscuits made from chokecherries were dried and stored for winter food. Native Americans in Oregon mixed chokecherries with salmon and sugar to treat dysentery.

During the Victorian era, white cherry flowers were a symbol of deception. Cherry stones have been used as talismans to attract lovers.

The cherry tree appears in Danish and Lithuanian folktales in connection with a spirit or guardian of the forest. In Lithuania it was called *Kirnis*. In Serbian tales, beautiful faery-like beings known as the Vila lived in the forests and loved to play near cherry trees.

The Kodokan emblem used by those who practice Judo is a stylized cherry blossom. For the Japanese samurai, this blossom was the epitome of purity and sacrifice. The Samurai used it as a focal point for meditations on the meaning of life and death. Today, the cherry season in Japan is heralded with festivals, parties, and a special beer brewed for the occasion.

Dreaming of cherries on a tree indicates a potential loss in business. Dreaming of a cherry tree without cherries indicates that you will have good health.

Latin Name: *Prunus serotina* (black cherry), *P. virginiana* (chokecherry), *P. pennsylvanica* (pin cherry/fire cherry), *P. padus* (European bird cherry), *P. avium* (sweet cherry), *P. cerasus* (sour cherry)

Seasonal Details: white or pink flowers, May–June; fruit ripens in July–October; long and narrow, blunt-toothed leaves

Powers/Attributes: achievement, action, awakening, divination, joy, knowledge and learning, love, playfulness

Elements: fire, water

Feng Shui Sectors: north, northwest, southwest, negative areas

Goddesses: Artemis, Morrigan, Persephone, Yaya Zakurai

Gods: Herne, Mars, Pan, Thor, Vertumnus

Other Beings/Characters: phoenix, unicorn

Zodiac: Aquarius, Aries

Celestial Body: Venus

Gemstones: obsidian, sard

Wildlife: red fox, red-tailed hawk

Other Tree: plum

Color: burnt umber

Energy: feminine

Other Associations: communication with animals; love; overcoming obstacles; peace; the will; root chakra; transformation; the cycle of life and death; youth; Celtic shrub tree

Spellwork and Ritual: attraction and love spells; seeking wisdom and awakening to new levels; meditation to find inner peace with this tree

---

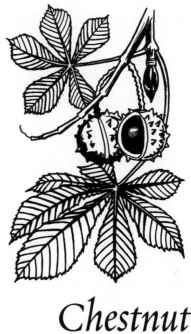

Chestnut

AT ONE TIME, CHESTNUT LUMBER was valuable and it was widely used for furniture, musical instruments, and fences. During the Middle Ages and the Renaissance, chestnut wood was used as a substitute for oak in the Mediterranean area. (The grain and color of the Durmast oak is very similar to chestnut.) Prior to a fungus epidemic in the early 1900s that almost completely eliminated it, the chestnut was a dominant woodland tree in North America.

Roasted chestnuts are a popular winter snack that contains vitamins B1, B2, and C. The nuts are sometimes ground into flour for baking. Chestnut meal has also been used to make starch to whiten linen cloth. In medieval Europe, horse chestnuts (*Aesculus hippocastanum*) were widely used for food by the poor as well as fodder for domestic swine. The word *Aesculus* in its name comes from the Greek *esca*, meaning "food."

Containing sulfur, chestnuts aid in removing toxins from the body. The leaves, bark, catkins, and nuts have been used medicinally to relieve coughs and diarrhea. The horse chestnut has been used to treat fever, rheumatism, and arthritis. Its many medicinal uses were first recorded by the ancient Greek physician Dioscorides.

The Celts who spoke Brythonic Gaelic (especially those of Wales) used and revered chestnuts in place of hazelnuts.

The horse chestnut is native to the Balkans and was slowly adopted as an ornamental tree throughout Europe. They were well known for lining the beautiful boulevards of Paris. Chestnut trees were introduced into the British Isles by the Romans. In Victorian England, the Sunday before Ascension Day was called Chestnut Sunday. This was a special day for middle-class Londoners to visit Kew Gardens and enjoy the horse chestnuts in bloom. The horse chestnut's upright catkins inspired the nickname "Candle Tree." In southern England, chestnut trees were planted for coppicing to create fencing and stakes to hold up other plants.

There are several theories to explain the word "horse" in its name. One is that "horse" simply meant "coarse"—it is not a delicate tree. Another theory is that young branches sometimes carry markings that look like tiny horse hooves. Others believe that "horse" was mistaken for the Welsh word *gwres*, which can mean "hot" or "pungent."

Latin Name: *Castanea sativa* (European chestnut), *C. dentata* (American chestnut), *Aesculus hippocastanum* (horse chestnut)

Seasonal Details: pale yellow (male) flowers and green (female) flowers in upright catkins, May–June; nuts flattened on at least one side in spiny husks

Powers/Attributes: healing, love, prosperity

Elements: air, fire, water

Feng Shui Sectors: southeast, southwest, health, negative areas

Goddesses: Artemis, Boann, Diana

Other Names for Tree: candle tree, sweet chestnut

Zodiac: Cancer, Gemini, Sagittarius, Virgo

Celestial Bodies: Jupiter, Sun

Gemstones: milky quartz, moonstone

Wildlife: blue jay, grouse, swan

Other Trees: beech, oak

Color: silver

Energy: masculine

Bach Flower Remedies: failure to learn from mistakes; overconcern for the welfare of loved ones (red chestnut); extreme mental anguish (sweet chestnut); unwanted thoughts and mental arguments (white chestnut)

Other Associations: dates: May 15–24 and November 12–21; sabbat: Yule/winter solstice

Spellwork and Ritual: purging and banishing rituals and spells; blessing a new home to attract abundance and prosperity; peace of mind

Cypress

THE CYPRESS IS BELIEVED TO have originated in Persia and Syria and then introduced into Italy by the Etruscans. It was a tree that the Roman upper classes liked to plant around their villas and have trimmed into exotic shapes. Its use for topiary reemerged in seventeenth century France and England. In Greece, a sacred grove of cypress once grew at the ancient Nemea sanctuary of Zeus, southwest of Corinth. The ashes of those killed in battle were kept in cypress chests to honor them as heroes. It was thought that cypress was one of the four woods, along with palm, cedar, and olive, used for the cross of Jesus. This could be the reason that cypress was frequently used for the coffins of popes.

Cypress trees are tolerant of harsh conditions and symbolize persistence under adversity. The wood is hard, close-grained, and has a reddish hue. During the Middle Ages and the Renaissance, it was used for musical instruments. Imported from Italy, cypress chests were popular in England in the fifteenth and sixteenth centuries. In the late nineteenth century, cypress wood for cabinetry and furniture was an important part of the economy of the American southeast.

Cypress is a tree of mixed messages. In ancient Egypt, cypress wood was used for coffins, which began its association as a tree of death. Because it can live up to a thousand years, cypress has also been associated with immortality. However, once a cypress is cut down, it does not come back, which to the ancient Romans symbolized the finality of death. In addition to using cypress wood for coffins in southern Europe, garlands of branches were draped on funeral biers and sometimes placed in the coffins. In Turkey, cypress trees were planted in and around graveyards to neutralize unpleasant odors.

In *Metamorphoses*, Ovid recounts the legend of Cyparissus, an attendant to Apollo who accidentally killed a pet deer. The youth was so grief-stricken that he laid down on the ground in despair and, weeping inconsolably, turned into a cypress tree.

Dreaming of cypress trees means that a friend is trying to secretly help you.

Latin Name: *Cupressus macrocarpa* (Monterey cypress), *C. arizonica* (Arizona cypress), *C. sempervirens* (Italian cypress—common in Europe and the Middle East), *Taxodium distichum* (bald cypress—not a true cypress)

Seasonal Details: tiny, scalelike leaves that grow around the branches in all directions; knobby round cones usually in pairs that stay on the tree for several years

Powers/Attributes: comfort in grief, healing, longevity, persistence, protection, solace

Elements: earth, water

Feng Shui Sectors: longevity, health, negative areas

Goddesses: Artemis, Ashtoreth, Diana, Hebe

Gods: Apollo, Cupid, Hercules, Jupiter, Mithra, Osiris, Zeus

Other Beings/Characters: Cyparissus, Zoroaster

Other Names for Tree: tree of death

Zodiac: Aquarius, Pices, Taurus

Celestial Body: Pluto, Saturn

Gemstone: turquoise

Wildlife: owl

Other Trees: pine, juniper

Energy: feminine

Other Associations: grief and death; life after death; peace; dates: January 25–February 3 and July 26–August 4

Spellwork and Ritual: past-life workings; rituals for healing sorrows and loss; quiet ritual and meditation when moving inward

Elder

ELDER BRANCHES HAVE BEEN USED for musical pipes which gives it the name "pipe tree." Music played on a flute of elder wood is said to have the same power as a wand. Its wood has also been used for butchers' skewers and shoemakers' pegs.

The berries are used for wine, jam, vinegar, and syrups. Medicinally, the flowers have been used as a sore-throat remedy, an expectorant, as well as a lotion for healing and soothing irritated skin. Elder has also been used to treat rheumatism, warts, and the flu. The bark, root, berries, and leaves have been used for dyes. The Romans used elderberry juice as a hair dye. The flowers and leaves are used for consecration and blessings.

Elder trees have been cultivated in some places solely for their berries to make wine. Not only were they used for elderberry wine, but also to provide more color in other wines. The practice of doctoring clarets, Bordeaux, and port became so widespread that in 1747, the Portuguese forbid any use of elderberry juice in their products.

In Ireland's oral tradition, it is said that if you stand under an elder tree on Midsummer's Eve you will be able to see the faeries. Cutting down or burning elder was not recommended, as this action would not please the faeries who take shelter there. A woven crown of elder twigs worn at Beltane is said to provide second sight. A branch used in the Beltane procession consecrates the circle.

Elder symbolizes the Goddess's roles as life-giver, death-wielder, and transformer. At one time, the odor of the elder flowers was thought to cause death. This made it an appealing wood for battle shields.

Elder is believed by some to be the type of tree used for Jesus' crucifixion cross. Aspen, oak, and fig are other trees said to have been used for this as well; however, sources vary and many types of trees are said to have this distinction.[1] In medieval Europe it was considered to be unlucky because of the belief that Judas Iscariot hung himself from an elder. For a time, elder was a symbol of sorrow and death,

and branches were carried in funeral processions. The driver of the carriage would frequently carry an elder whip. In Austria it was planted on graves—if it bloomed, it meant that the deceased was happy.

In Sicily, elder wood was used to ward off snakes and thieves. This belief has also been connected with St. Patrick as the type of wood used for his staff, which was instrumental in driving the snakes from Ireland.[2] In Denmark during the Middle Ages, elders were called guardian trees because sailors entrusted part of their soul to an elder tree for safekeeping and to ensure that they would return from sea.

Dreaming of elderberries indicates pleasant social events are ahead. If you are picking them in your dream, you will have financial gain. Eating them in a dream symbolizes abundance.

Latin Name: *Sambucus nigra* (European elder), *S. canadensis* (common elder), *S. pubens* (red elder)

Seasonal Details: small fragrant white flowers in dense flat-topped clusters, June–July; purple-black berries, August–October; the red elder tree blooms April–July, and bears fruit, usually red, in June–September

Powers/Attributes: abundance, blessings, consecration, creativity, good fortune, healing, knowledge of magic, positive change, prosperity, protection, sleep, success, transition

Elements: air, earth, fire, water

Celtic Calendar Dates: November 25–December 22

Ogham Character: ⁓
Name: Ruis
Letter: R

Rune Character: ᚠ
Name: Feoh/Fehu
Letter: F

Feng Shui Sectors: northeast, southeast, south, west, health, negative areas

Goddesses: all forms of the Great Mother Goddess; Audhumla, Boann, Cailleach Beara, Danu, Hel/Hela, Venus

Gods: Frey, Pryderi, Vulcan

Other Beings/Characters: dryads, elves, faeries, Hylde-moer/Hylde-vinde

Other Names for Tree: elderberry, guardian tree, Lady Elder, pipe tree, faery tree (Isle of Man), ellhorn (Germany)

Zodiac: Aries, Taurus

Celestial Bodies: Saturn, Venus

Plant: dandelion

Gemstones: bloodstone, jet, red jasper

Wildlife: black horse, pheasant, raven, rook

Colors: bright red, light red

Energy: feminine

Other Associations: Monday; Druidic wisdom; sabbats: Beltane, Litha/summer solstice/Midsummer's Eve; Celtic shrub tree

Spellwork and Ritual: healing, protection and attraction spells; an offering in ritual as well as for cleansing an area before ritual

1. Nathaniel Altman, *Sacred Trees* (San Francisco: Sierra Club Books, 1994), 157.

2. Since the snake was a symbol of the Great Mother Goddess, ridding Ireland of snakes was a euphemism for converting Pagans to Christianity. It would have been ironic for St. Patrick to use an elder staff since the tree itself was associated with the Goddess.

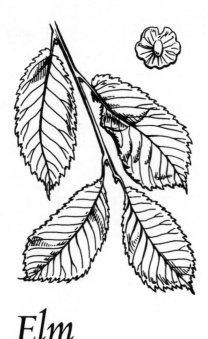

Elm

MEDICINALLY, ELM HAS BEEN USED for skin and kidney problems as well as other internal disorders. The sap from slippery elm contains a soothing substance that has been used to treat burns as well as soften skin. Industrially, elm wood has been prized because it is resistant to splitting and free from knots. All parts, including the sapwood, have been used for carpentry. Even though most elms are ornamental, their strong timber makes them valuable, and their tough, fibrous inner bark can be twisted into rope.

In Europe during the Middle Ages and the Renaissance, elm was used for furniture, chests, and coffins, as well as keels and bilge planks on ships. Part of the chariot found in King Tutankhamun's tomb was made of elm.

One reason that elm became associated with the Goddess was because of its common V-shaped twin trunks and graceful chalice shape. The elm has been described as having "Gothic-arched sylvan splendor."[1] It is also associated with burial mounds and considered a symbolic doorway to eternal life. It has been called "dark and brooding," which may be connected to its attribute of empathy. This tree is said to be very sensitive to damage inflicted on other elms.

Like the chestnut tree, the American elm has fallen victim to a fungus and full-grown trees are difficult to find. If you have one, consider it a blessing from the Great Mother.

A tribe of Celts in Gaul was known as the Lemovices or "people of the elm." Derived from Gaelic *leamh* or *leamhan*, the elm tree, the name of the parish of Laughil (*Leamhchoill*) means "elm wood" and the town Lavagh (*Leamhach*) means "a place producing elms." Lorum (*Leamh-dhruim*), which means "elm ridge," and Lislevane (*Lios-leamhain*), which means "elm fort," are other place names in Ireland that take their names from the elm.

Dreaming of an elm tree indicates hope coming to fruition. If you dream that you are under an elm, pleasant social activities are ahead for you.

Latin Name: *Ulmus procera* (English or common elm), *U. americana* (American elm), *U. rubra* (Slippery elm), *U. glabra* (wych elm); *U. alata* (winged elm)

Seasonal Details: inconspicuous brown-orange flowers, March–May; flat, winged oval fruits April–May; five-veined, oval, pointed leaves that turn yellow or purplish in autumn

Powers/Attributes: birth, compassion, empathy, endurance, grounding, healing, intuition, love, protection, rebirth, stability, wisdom

Elements: air, earth, water

Ogham Character: +
  Name: Ailm
  Letter: A

Rune Character: X
  Name: Gyfu/Gebo
  Letter: G

Rune Character: ᛗ
  Name: Man/Mannaz
  Letter: M

Feng Shui Sectors: center, north, northeast, southwest, west, longevity, negative areas

Goddesses: Cerridwen, Danu, Gaia, Hel/Holle, Ran

Gods: Dionysus, Loki, Odin

Other Beings/Characters: elves, faeries

Other Names for Tree: sweet elm, Elven

Zodiac: Capricorn

Celestial Bodies: Mercury, Saturn

Gemstone: moss agate

Wildlife: deer, lapwing, rabbits, ruffled grouse

Colors: blue, greenish-brown

Energy: feminine

Bach Flower Remedy: when you are overwhelmed by responsibility

Other Associations: inner spiritual progress when dealing with the darker side of self; dates: January 12–24 and July 15–25; sabbat: Yule/winter solstice; Celtic peasant/common tree

Spellwork and Ritual: use in dark moon and initiation rituals; spells to attract love; grounding after ritual; seeking comfort

---

1. Cullina, *Native Trees, Shrubs and Vines*, 248.

Fir

FIR TREES ARE EVERGREENS OF the genus *Abies* and native only in the northern hemisphere. Silver fir is native to the uplands of central and southern Europe and Germany's Black Forest. Balsam fir is usually found in North American uplands as well as swampy areas. The balsam is popular as a Christmas tree because of its pungent fragrance.

Fraser firs only grow at elevations above 4500 feet in the southern Appalachian Mountains. It was named for John Fraser (1750–1811), a botanist from Scotland who explored the Appalachians in the late eigh-teenth century. The Fraser is sometimes called the southern balsam fir because of their many similarities. It is also occasion-ally referred to as the "she balsam" when it grows with the red spruce, which is referred to as the "he balsam."

Fir cones are responsive to sun and rain by opening and closing, respectively.

In Scandinavian folktales, fir was asso-ciated with the spirit of the forest. It was also believed to have a strong connection with the person on whose land it grew. Any catastrophe that befell the tree was a bad omen for the landowner.

Fir has been called "the birth tree" and used for protection spells for mothers and babies by burning a few needles during childbirth.

It is one of the nine sacred woods for a sabbat fire, in which it represents friendship. As an evergreen, fir symbolized the Great Mother Goddess because it seemed immortal—it did not appear to die each year, as did other trees and plants. Adorning evergreens during winter may have been done simply with symbols of life and springtime as a way to manifest intentions for abundance and good crops in the year ahead. Various cultures adapted and evolved this into the present-day Christmas tree.

Native Americans used many parts of the fir tree for medicine, as did Europeans. It was used to treat cuts, burns, colds, and coughs, and was also used as a laxative.

A way to tell a fir tree from a spruce is to remember the saying "Firs are friendly; spruces are not." Firs are soft to the touch, whereas spruce needles have tiny points that scratch.

Latin Name: *Abies amabilis* (silver fir/European fir), *A. balsamea* (balsam fir), *A. concolor* (white fir, also called Rocky Mountain white fir), *A. fraseri* (Fraser fir)

Seasonal Details: female cones stand upright on the upper crown branches and male cones (on the same trees) on the underside of the lower crown branches, May–June; flat needles

Powers/Attributes: birth, cleverness, far-sightedness, protection, prosperity, rebirth, transformation, vitality

Element: air

Ogham Character: +
    Name: Ailm
    Letter: A

Feng Shui Sectors: northeast, north, west, southeast, life, longevity, negative areas

Goddesses: Audhumla, Artemis, Diana, Frigg, Idun, Inanna, Isis, Persephone, Sif

Gods: Adonis, Attis, Bacchus, Dionysus, Osiris, Pan

Other Beings/Characters: dwarves, elves, faeries

Other Names for Tree: fir pine, the birth tree; red fir (silver/European fir)

Zodiac: Aries

Celestial Bodies: Mars, Saturn

Gemstones: green amber, jade

Wildlife: sparrow

Other Trees: hemlock, yew

Color: green

Energy: masculine

Other Associations: the underworld; Thursday; dates: January 2–11, July 5–14 and December 22; sabbats: Beltane, Yule/winter solstice; Celtic chieftain/noble tree (sources disagree whether this was fir or pine)

Spellwork and Ritual: attracting prosperity; inner workings and change; divination work for clarity of vision; protection spells

Gooseberry

Gooseberry, a deciduous woody shrub, is at home in rocky or swampy woodland areas and clearings. It is popular for jams, sauces, and dressings for stuffed fowl. Yellow gooseberries are used to make a sparkling wine. Kiwifruit was formerly called Chinese gooseberry. In Scotland it is know as *grozet*, from the Gaelic word *grosied*. Common names included "hairy grape" and "goosegogs." In Germany, it is called *Jansbeere*, which means John's berry, and was named for the feast of St. John, which took place at about the time gooseberries ripened.

The nickname "currant gooseberry" comes from it being a close relative of the currant. Both are low-growing shrubs; however, the currant does not have thorns. Currants were cultivated since the 1500s in Europe and gooseberries since the 1700s.

Gooseberries have been used to produce a sweet, strong, winelike ale since medieval times. The brewer, Tibbie Shiels, who lived in the Scottish borders region, became well-known for her Green Grozet. Also in Scotland, a type of bogeyman called "Awd Goggie" was said to guard the gooseberries until they were ripe. Children were told to stay clear of the bushes to avoid being kidnapped by him.

Gooseberries have been used to treat stomach and liver problems and inflammation. During outbreaks of the plague in Europe, some doctors recommended eating gooseberries to break the fever. The Indian gooseberry is mentioned in seventh century Ayurvedic medical manuscripts for a range of uses. As a source of vitamin C, it is prescribed to restore vitality. It was also used in traditional recipes for enriching hair growth.

The Egyptian goddess Bastet is frequently described as having gooseberry-green eyes. Hindu legends mention water tasting sweeter after eating gooseberries. In England, a chaperone was called a "gooseberry" because it was a standard ploy to pretend to pick gooseberries while keeping an eye on the young people. "Old Gooseberry" is an alternate name for the devil.

Dreaming of gooseberries means an important event is coming. Gathering them in your dream means that good business prospects are in store; however, eating them indicates disappointment will come.

Latin Name: *Ribes hirtellum* (American or smooth gooseberry), *R. grossularia* (European gooseberry), *R. cynosbati* (pasture gooseberry)

Seasonal Details: greenish pink flowers single or in pairs, April–July; ball-shaped fruit in a variety of translucent colors: green/white, yellow, reds, pinks to almost black June–September; thorns at base of leaf stalks

Powers/Attributes: challenges, gains, success

Element: water

Ogham Character: ᚗ
  Name: Ifin/Iphin
  Letters: IO

Feng Shui Sectors: east, south

Goddesses: Bastet, Morrigan

Gods: Cernunnos, Krishna, Shiva, Vishnu

Other Names for Tree: *grozet*, dogberry, hairystem gooseberry, currant gooseberry

Celestial Body: Venus

Wildlife: butterflies

Energy: feminine

Other Associations: anticipation; comfort; sabbat: Samhain; Celtic bramble tree

Spellwork and Ritual: spells to bring success during challenges and to get through difficult times

Gorse

GORSE IS ONE OF THE needle-bearing, non-cone-bearing evergreens—heather and broom are others. Gorse is sometimes burned for its ashes, which make a good alkali fertilizer. Afterwards, the plants are allowed to grow back and the new shoots used to graze cattle. In nineteenth-century England, bakers frequently used it to fuel their ovens. Gardeners used it as a hedge plant and sowed small pieces of gorse along with their peas to keep pests away.

Because of its bright yellow flowers, gorse has been associated with the sun. As it begins to bloom around the time of the spring equinox, its yellow flowers seem to welcome and amplify the strengthening sunlight. Gorse's densely packed, prickly branches can be used as brooms to symbolically clear away winter. The day before the equinox is sometimes called the Day of Gorse. It is used at Lughnasadh to honor Lugh, whose decline accelerates in August.

Folklore from various countries indicates that it was effective against faery mischief. As it was used on Walpurgis night, April 30/Beltane Eve (see the entry on blackthorn for more on Walpurgis), it became associated with warding off evil, especially that perpetrated by witches. The sweeping away of winter at the spring equinox was equated to sweeping away evil influences. It's still customary to throw some gorse onto a Beltane fire.

The Danes brewed a type of beer or wine from the flowers. Gorse has also been employed as a remedy for depression. It is used for animal feed—ground up for meal as well as burned down for horses and sheep to graze. Gorse flowers have been used for dye.

Gorse attracts large numbers of bees because it is one of the earliest flowers in the spring. Since the Neolithic period (9000–7000 BCE), bees have been associated with the Great Mother Goddess as provider of nourishment and fertility. This, along with being an evergreen, has given gorse a connection with the Goddess.

The name comes from the Anglo-Saxon word gorst, a variant of georst, meaning a heath, which describes the rocky and barren area where it frequently grows. In Ireland, the name of Lisboy means "yellow fort," which is believed to be derived from all the gorse in the area.

Dreaming of gorse means that good fortune is on the way. Picking the flowers in your dream indicates prosperity. However, if other people have the flowers, it means unhappiness.

Latin Name: *Ulex europaeus*

Seasonal Details: bright yellow fragrant flowers May–September, and then on and off during the year; evergreen with sharp, spinelike leaves

Powers/Attributes: divination, fertility, hope, prosperity, protection

Element: fire

Celtic Calendar Dates: seasonal tree for spring

Ogham Character: ╫
  Name: Ohn/Onn
  Letter: O

Feng Shui Sectors: north, southeast, west, longevity, abundance, negative areas

Goddesses: Áine, Arianrhod, Grainne

Gods: Bel, Dagda, Frey, Lugh, Jupiter, Thor

Other Names for Tree: furze, broom, goss

Zodiac: Aries

Celestial Bodies: Mars, Sun

Plant: heather

Wildlife: bees, cormorant, hare, harrier hawk

Colors: gold, yellow

Energy: masculine

Bach Flower Remedy: hopelessness and despair

Other Associations: root chakra; the underworld; sabbats: Beltane, Lugnasadh, Ostara/vernal equinox; Celtic bramble tree

Spellwork and Ritual: attracting money; connecting with the Divine; protection against negativity; breaking a spell; welcoming spring and sweeping away the staleness of winter

Hackberry

THIS TREE'S NAME COMES FROM the Scottish *hagberry*, which means "marsh berry." The wood from this tree is heavy but soft, and has commercial value for practical, utilitarian items such as pallets and barrel staves rather than objects of beauty. It is used for veneer because of the resemblance to ash and elm. Native Americans used the leaves and branches to dye wool brown.

The fruit, sometimes called sugarberries, is used for food flavorings, jelly, and wine. The making of hackberry wine may date back to the Neolithic settlement of Catal Hüyük in Turkey, as it was one of the trees cultivated by the inhabitants.

This rugged tree has the ability to withstand drought (although it prefers moist areas), heat, and wind. Hackberry also has a high tolerance to alkaline soil. As it matures, the trunk tends to take on a "corky" appearance. It has been used as a shade tree substitute for elms (with which it is related) after Dutch elm disease diminished their numbers.

The town of Hackberry, Texas, was named for the grove of trees on the Little

Wichita River that had attracted pioneers to settle there.

Hackberry is most easily identified by its commonly occurring "witches' brooms," knotted balls of twigs that are caused by mite infestations of leaf buds. It is frequently a host tree for mistletoe.

Latin Name: *Celtis occidentalis* (American or common hackberry), *C. australis* (Mediterranean hackberry), *C. laevigata* (sugarberry), *C. pallida* (desert hackberry)

Seasonal Details: small, greenish-white male and female flowers that blend in with the leaves, April–May; sweet, orange-red to dark purple fruit (ruddy brown is the most common color) October–November and longer

Powers/Attributes: adaptability, creativity, resiliency in ability to grieve

Elements: fire, water

Feng Shui Sector: west

Other Names for Tree: nettle-tree, woodland walnut, bastard elm

Wildlife: cedar waxwing, quail, squirrels

Other Trees: maple, sycamore

Energy: feminine

Other Associations: dates: August 14–23 and February 9–18; sabbat: Mabon/autumn equinox

Spellwork and Ritual: healing rituals to allow grief to run its course; rituals during times of transition; rituals for inspiration in creative projects

Hawthorn

MEDICINAL USE OF HAWTHORN DATES back to ancient Greece. Because it was a symbol of hope and happiness, brides and their bridesmaids frequently wore hawthorn blossoms. Its leaves and fruit have been used medicinally in other countries to treat hypertension and heart problems. The Romans used hawthorn sprigs as a charm to protect children while they slept. May blossom wine is made from hawthorn flowers.

The name hawthorn comes from the Anglo-Saxon word, *haegthorn*, hedge thorn, and the Old Saxon word for hedge, *haw*. Its fruit is still called "haws." For centuries, hawthorn has been a popular part of England's hedgerows. By the Middle Ages it was called "May" because it blooms in that month. Garlands of it were hung around doorways to celebrate Beltane. Collecting dew from the flowers and sprinkling it on the face was said to ensure lasting beauty.

Hawthorn can be found near holy wells and will usually have offerings left around it on the ground as well as ribbons in its branches. This tree is also found at crossroads, which is appropriate for its association with Brigid (the Celtic goddess who presides over holy wells and crossroads). Known also as a wishing tree, it is not unusual to see strips of cloth hanging on hawthorns that are not near wells or springs. A strip of cloth (the color is usually symbolic of what is wished for) is tied on the tree while making a wish. It is also said to mark the threshold of the otherworld. For this reason it was used in funeral pyres to assist departing spirits.

Along with ash and oak, hawthorn was considered part of the triad of powerful faery trees. They represent the three realms (underworld, middleworld, upperworld), as well as the maiden, mother, and crone aspects of the Goddess. All three are frequently used for Maypoles. Hawthorn is one of the nine sacred woods for a sabbat fire in which it represents purity.

Hawthorn was celebrated in springtime but it was considered unlucky at other times of the year. While the early Christian church could not wean people away from their May festivities, hawthorn's connection with faeries was enough for priests to use against the tree's popularity. It seems to have been an easy task to manipulate the idea of faery pranks into evil misdeeds. May was also a time to celebrate the sexual union of Goddess and God, and sexuality in general—another reason for Christian priests to frown.

Negativity was also attributed to hawthorn because it was believed to have been used for the "crown of thorns" placed on Jesus's head. Ironically, some Christians believed that the burning bush that confronted Moses was a type of hawthorn. According to legend, the staff Joseph of Arimathea plunged into the ground at Glastonbury turned into a hawthorn tree that was said to have flowered at Christmas. The Puritans cut the tree down.

Derived from the Gaelic *sceach* for whitethorn bush, Skahanagh, Ireland, means "a place full of whitethorns." Both Tullynaskeagh and Knochnaskagh mean "hill of whitethorns."

Dreaming of hawthorn means harmony among friends. White hawthorn flowers in a dream indicate considerable money, and pink hawthorn flowers mean happiness.

(continued on next page)

Latin Name: *Crataegus monogyna* (common hawthorn, England), *C. douglasii* (black hawthorn), *C. pruinosa* (frosted hawthorn)

Seasonal Details: white or pink flowers, May–June; red fruit in clusters in the autumn that may remain through the winter; thorns

Powers/Attributes: ancestry, cleansing, defensive protection, family, fertility, growth, happiness, lift depression, love, luck, marriage, patience, prosperity, protection, purity, reconciliation, wisdom

Elements: air, fire

Celtic Calendar Dates: May 13– June 9

Ogham Character: ⊥
  Name: Huath
  Letter: H

Rune Character: ᛟ
  Name: Odal/Odil
  Letter: O

Rune Character: ᚦ
  Name: Thorn
  Letters: Th

Rune Character: ᚹ
  Name: Wunjo/Wyn
  Letter: W

Feng Shui Sectors: northeast, east, southeast, southwest, west, negative areas

Goddesses: Audhumla, Brigid, Danu, Frigg

Gods: Belenus, Dagda, Prometheus, Thor, Zeus

Other Beings/Characters: Blodeuwedd, elves, faeries, Olwen

Other Names for Tree: May, Maybush, quickthorn, whitethorn, haw bush

Zodiac: Aquarius, Aries

Celestial Body: Mars

Plant: wood sorrel

Gemstones: amethyst, tanzanite, topaz

Wildlife: blackbird, owl, purple martin

Other Trees: apple, ash, hazel, oak

Colors: purple, violet

Energy: masculine

Other Associations: the chalice; Sunday; sabbat: Beltane; Celtic peasant/common tree

Spellwork and Ritual: cleansing an area before ritual; protection spells; attracting love; communication with those who have passed beyond the veil; entering the faery realm

Hazel

THE ATTRIBUTE "CREATIVITY" CAN BE seen in the tree itself, which is known for its unusual branches that grow in curious shapes, especially the variety known as "corkscrew hazel." Its association with the heart chakra comes from the legend that the hazel stood at the heart of the faery realm. When hazel is found growing with apple and hawthorn, it is said that these mark the boundary of a magical place.

Hazel was considered a tree of wisdom by the Celts. Hazelnuts are believed to impart wisdom to whoever eats them and are particularly helpful if eaten before divination. In ancient legend, nine (a sacred number as three times three) hazel trees grew around the Well of Wisdom (also sometimes referred to as the Pool of Life) and their hazelnuts fed the Salmon of Knowledge. Throughout the British Isles, hazel trees can usually be found growing near holy wells. Hazel/*Coll* is the ninth character of the Ogham and the ninth month in the tree calendar. String nine hazelnuts together and consecrate them at Samhain. This can be hung in the house as a protection amulet.

Hazel's importance in Ireland began with pre-Celtic people who arrived there during the Mesolithic Period (8000–4000 BCE). They found hazelnuts to be one of the most import nonmeat food sources. In fact, hazelnuts are highly nutritious—weight for weight with eggs, they have 50 percent more protein, seven times more fat, and five times more carbohydrates, as well as containing vitamin C.

Hazel branches used for divining rods were said to be particularly potent if cut on Midsummer's Eve. Wands of hazel were believed to carry power, and the early Christian bishops of Ireland seemed to put faith in this belief by having staffs of hazel.

Divination power with hazelnuts was said to be at its peak on Samhain. (Hazelnuts are one of the last things to be harvested in the autumn.) People would toss hazelnuts into a fire and watch for colors and listen for noises in response to their questions.

Hazel has a dark side in that its wisdom and power can be used for negative purposes as told in legends of Fionn Mac Cumhail. In using hazel for divination and introspection, one must be honest with oneself and true of heart to avoid negative results. Picking unripe hazelnuts was considered unlucky. Another legend mentions the warrior Mac Roth going to meet Cu Chulainn with a single-edged sword in one hand and a "peeled hazel-wand" in the other. Unfortunately, the *Táin Bó Cuailnge* does not offer details on the use of the hazel wand.

The name of Callowhill or *Collchoill* in Ireland means "hazel wood," and the name of Collon, "a place of hazels." The name of present-day Dromcolliher is a corruption of *Druim-coll-choille*, which means "the ridge of hazels."

Hazel is one of the nine sacred woods for a sabbat fire in which it represents wisdom.

If you dream of hazelnuts you will have financial gain. If you dream that you are eating them, you will have abundant means. It can also mean that you will marry into wealth. Dreaming of the tree itself indicates difficulties in love.

Latin Name: *Corylus avellana* (common hazel, England), *C. americana* (common American hazelnut), *C. cornuta* (beaked hazelnut)

Seasonal Details: yellowish male catkins and red female flowers, April–May; nuts in ragged-edged husks, July–September

Powers/Attributes: creativity, divination, fertility, healing, inspiration, introspection, knowledge, luck, marriage, protection, reconciliation, wisdom

Elements: air, water

Celtic Calendar Dates: August 5–September 1

Ogham Character: ||||
   Name: Coll
   Letters: C, K

Feng Shui Sectors: north, northeast, southwest, west, health, negative areas

Goddesses: Aphrodite, Arianrhod, Artemis, Danu, Diana, Venus

Gods: Manannan Mac Lir, Mercury, Ogma, Thor

Other Beings/Characters: faeries, Milesians

Other Name for Tree: American filbert

Zodiac: Gemini, Libra, Virgo

Celestial Bodies: Mercury, Sun

Plant: vervain

Gemstones: amethyst, lapis lazuli, blue sapphire

Wildlife: crane, salmon

Other Trees: apple, hawthorn

Color: dark blue

Energy: feminine

Other Associations: knowledge of secrets; heart chakra; east; Connla's Well (Ireland); dates: March 22–31 and September 24–October 3; sabbats: Beltane, Samhain; Celtic chieftain/noble tree

Spellwork and Ritual: dark moon rituals; seeking knowledge (eat hazelnuts before shamanic journeying); divination, especially for love and dowsing

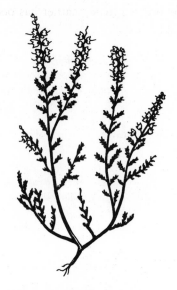

Heather

HEATHER IS A HARDY EVERGREEN shrub that grows in low, dense clusters, and is the main component vegetation of a heath. Common heather can be found from the Arctic Circle to North Africa. The *Erica* genus can be found in southern Africa and Asia. Its branches were used as a source for green and yellow dye.

The Latin name *Erica* comes from the Greek, *ereiko*, which means "to break." This is believed to come from either the medicinal use to dissolve gallstones or the fact that its branches are easily broken. The name *Calluna* comes from the Greek *kallunein*, which means "to cleanse." This may have been derived from the medicinal use to deal with internal disorders as well as the use of its twigs to make brooms (and thus, clean one's home). According to British herbalist John Parkinson, who published his research in 1640, heather could be used for soothing insect stings as well as for treating kidney stones.

St. Dabeoc's heath was named for the fifth or sixth century Welsh monk who traveled to Ireland and established a monastery on Lough Derg in Donegal. He is also known as St. Beoc.

In the highlands of Great Britain where trees are scarce, heather was used as a fuel for fires, as well as for bedding and thatching.

In Scotland where white heather is regarded as a charm for protection and good luck, it is a custom to include it in a bridal bouquet. Heather is believed to be the source of the word "heathen," which is how the Romans viewed the native people of the Scottish highlands.

An ale brewed from heather has been produced since the time of the Picts (circa 325 BCE) and is still in production. A similar drink called heather mead was sometimes referred to as the "water of life." While it was known of in other lands, only the Picts knew how to brew this particular drink.

Honey produced from heather is a component of some Drambuie.

Latin Name: *Calluna vulgaris* (common heather), *Phyllodoce breweri* (mountain heather), *Erica vagans* (Cornish heather), *E. cinerea* (Scotch heather), *Daboecia cantabrica* (St. Dabeoc's heath)

Seasonal Details: small clustered flowers, March–April, July–September, or November–April, depending on variety; colors: white, purples, and oranges

Powers/Attributes: changes/transitions, healing (spiritual and physical), knowledge, luck, passion, protection, reflection, spirituality

Element: water

Ogham Character: ⍚
 Name: Ur
 Letters: U, W

Feng Shui Sectors: north, northeast, southeast, southwest, negative areas

Goddesses: Arianrhod, Isis, Uroica, Venus

Celestial Body: Venus

Wildlife: bees, red grouse

Other Tree: mistletoe

Color: white

Energy: feminine

Bach Flower Remedy: self-centeredness and self-concern

Other Names for this Tree: Irish heath (St. Dabeoc's heath)

Other Associations: admiration; loneliness; earthly realm; west; philosophy; dates: December 16th and January 1st; sabbat: Litha/summer solstice; Celtic bramble tree

Spellwork and Ritual: manifesting dreams and wishes; contacting spirits

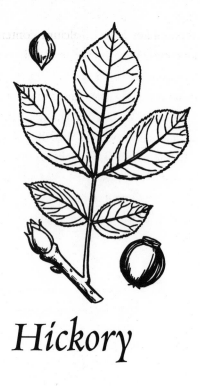

Hickory

A MEMBER OF THE WALNUT family, hickory produces strong and flexible wood that has a wide range of uses in sports equipment, cabinetry, furniture, hammers, brooms, and other tools. The best of the hickory wood comes from the shagbark species. Its durable, shock-resistant timber was used by early American settlers from Europe for wagons and wagon wheels. The wood is considered an excellent fuel; one cord of it has approximately the heating capacity as a ton of coal.

Hickory's aromatic wood produces oily smoke and high heat that has been popular for curing meat because it imparts a special flavor. Nuts of the shagbark hickory are edible and have commercial value. Medicinally, young shoots were used to treat convulsions.

In notes written in 1612, colonial English historian William Strachey mentioned a Native American myth about hickory smoke being used to help departing spirits of the dead find their way. Hickory nuts seemed to have been used in trade among various Native American people as tribes outside the growth range of hickory trees had names for the nuts and trees in their own languages.

Andrew Jackson, seventh president of the United States, was called "Old Hickory," which evolved from the nickname "Old Hero." His men said he was "tough as a hickory stick" because of the strict discipline he used marching them several hundred miles out of the Battle of New Orleans during the War of 1812.

The shagbark hickory gets its name from its bark that separates into long strips and gives it a shaggy appearance. Hickories are considered "soil improvers" because their leaves have a high calcium content that nourishes the soil. They tend to have a long taproot.

The name *Carya* comes from the Greek word for nut. Pignuts are an important part of many woodland animals' diets; however, they are bitter, which makes them less attractive for humans. Thus, the name pignut came about because Colonial Americans considered them only fit for pig feed.

Latin Name: *Carya orata* (shagbark hickory), *C. glabra* (pignut hickory), *C. ovalis* (red or sweet pignut hickory), *C. texana* (black hickory)

Seasonal Details: male flowers in branched catkins, female flowers in short spikes in May; nuts September–November; toothed, long-pointed leaves that turn golden in the fall

Powers/Attributes: abundance, balance, discipline, flexibility, generosity, protection, strength, transformation, unification

Elements: earth, fire

Feng Shui Sectors: center, north, northeast, east, southeast, northwest, abundance, negative areas

Gods: Apollo, Lugh

Other Beings/Characters: archangel Radrael

Zodiac: Gemini, Virgo

Celestial Bodies: Jupiter, Mercury, Sun

Gemstones: citrine, yellow topaz

Wildlife: peacock, phoenix

Other Tree: pecan, oak

Color: yellow

Energy: masculine

Other Association: solar plexus chakra; sabbat: Mabon/autumn equinox

Spellwork and Ritual: spells of protection (especially in legal matters); charms and rituals when moving into a new home; rituals that celebrate abundance

Holly

IN WINTER WHEN MOST PLANTS have faded and seem dead, holly is bright and vital, promising ongoing life. Holly was associated with the Mother Goddess and the red berries were said to represent her life-giving blood as well as her powers of transformation from death to rebirth.

There is a mix of beliefs, possibly from earlier goddess-worshiping times, that were not completely changed or adapted. Holly was thought to be so powerful that it was paired with oak as one of the two most powerful trees. Holly was referred to as the Holly King. While the year is divided by months and seasons, it is also split in two (light half and dark half) with oak and holly each reigning over a half. Holly is the guardian of the waning year and begins his reign as the Wheel of the Year turns just after the summer solstice and we head toward shorter days and darkness.

At winter solstice they switch—the old king dies and the young one, oak personifying the New Year, takes over symbolizing the succession of father to son, and the passage from death to rebirth. Holly and oak also symbolize two aspects of the

God: youth and sage. The Christian church juxtaposing the birthdays of Jesus (winter solstice) and John the Baptist (summer solstice) also splits the year between two sacred beings. The ancient Pagan myth of the holly and oak kings is echoed in the Arthurian legend of Gawain (oak) and the Green Knight (holly).

In the *Táin Bó Cuailnge* legends, the warrior Nadcranntail faces Cu Chulainn armed with nine spears of charred and sharpened holly. None found their mark that day. However, at a later time Cu Chulainn was wounded in the leg and foot by a piece of split holly which he used to slay Ferbaeth who had challenged him.

The ancient Romans believed that holly flowers could turn water to ice. Throughout many European countries it was planted near homes for protection against witchcraft and lightning. In Roman legend, the god Saturn's deadly club was made of holly. Sprigs of holly were used to decorate Roman homes during the festival of Saturnalia, which fell in mid-December and had its dual, light/dark sides like the holly/oak kings switching places.[1]

Holly is considered the male counterpart to female ivy. Even though the Yule festival greens are traditionally burned at Imbolg (symbolically breaking the bonds of winter) a small sprig of holly is kept for luck throughout the year. Refer to the entry on ivy for more of this.

Holly berries were used for divination to predict the winter weather. A profusion of berries meant that it would be a hard winter because the Goddess was providing for the birds with a good crop of berries. A small number of berries meant that the weather would be mild enough for birds to find food elsewhere. It is one of the nine sacred woods for a sabbat fire, in which it represents justice.

Holly has been used medicinally to fight high fevers and to stem jaundice, and so its healing is more in the realm of prevention than cure.

Derived from the Gaelic *cuillionn* for holly, the name of Cloncullen in Ireland means "holly meadow"; Cullen (*Cuillionn*) means "holly land"; Cullenagh, "a place producing holly"; and Kilcullen (*Cill-cuillinn*), "the church of the holly."

Dreaming of holly means that you need to beware of the things that trouble you. Picking holly in your dream means that you will have a long life.

(continued on next page)

Latin Name: *Ilex aquifolium* (English holly), *I. opaca* (American holly), *I. verticillata* (winterberry holly)

Seasonal Details: small white flowers May–June (American) and June–August (winterberry); only female trees produce berries in the autumn, which stay on the tree through the winter; distinctive prickly leaves

Powers/Attributes: courage, death, divinity, guidance, healing, intelligence, luck, protection, rebirth, unity

Elements: air, earth, fire

Celtic Calendar Dates: July 8–August 4

Ogham Character: ᚈ
Name: Tinne
Letter: T

Rune Character: ᛗ
Name: Man/Mannaz
Letter: M

Feng Shui Sectors: north, negative areas

Goddesses: Danu, Gaia, Holle

Gods: Ares, Dagda, Frey, Lugh, Saturn, Tyr

Other Beings/Characters: archangel Gabriel, angels, elves, faeries, unicorns

Other Names for Tree: mountain holly, Christ's thorn

Zodiac: Aries

Celestial Bodies: Earth, Mars

Plant: meadowsweet

Gemstones: carnelian, fire agate, ruby

Wildlife: cardinal, starling

Other Trees: oak, ivy

Colors: dark red, gray green

Energy: masculine

Bach Flower Remedy: hatred, envy, and jealousy

Other Associations: hearth and home; east; date: December 17; sabbats: Yule/winter solstice, Litha/summer solstice; Celtic chieftain/noble tree

Spellwork and Ritual: attracting good luck; dream work, especially divination through dreams; protection spells

1. Ferguson, *The Magickal Year*, 44.

Honeysuckle

UNLIKE MOST OTHER FLOWERS, THE honeysuckle flower scent is stronger at night as it relies on moths for pollination. Essential oil made from honeysuckle is used for incense and massage. In aromatherapy, honeysuckle is applied to situations where prosperity or psychic awareness is sought.

Medicinally it has been used for coughs, asthma, and inflammation. Some varieties are a natural antibiotic and have been used to treat infections. A poultice of honeysuckle relieves skin rashes, especially those caused by poison oak. As a source of salicylic acid, honeysuckle was once used in the making of aspirin.

Honeysuckle is a climbing plant that wraps around anything it encounters, and is popularly used to provide privacy. It is hardy and does well in the garden as well as in the wild, which has caused problems. Some varieties imported into the United States have become invasive pests, especially for pine trees. While splotches of bright color can look festive in an evergreen, these aggressive climbers can eventually choke a tree to death.

Latin Name: *Lonicera dioica* (wild or mountain honeysuckle), *L. xylosteum* (European fly honeysuckle), *L. sempervirens* (trumpet honeysuckle); *L. periclymenum* (woodbine honeysuckle)

Seasonal Details: mountain honeysuckle: spicy fragrant flowers, reddish purple and white, May–July; small orange berries, July–September; trumpet honeysuckle: long reddish vase-like flower, April–September; red berries, August–October

Powers/Attributes: clarity, confidence, creativity, fidelity, financial success, healing, love, psychic abilities and awareness, rebirth

Element: earth

Ogham Character: ᚕ
Name: Éabhadh
Letters: EA, CH, K

Ogham Character: ᚒ
Name: Uilleann
Letters: UI, PE

Feng Shui Sector: southwest

Goddesses: Cerridwen, Gaia, Morrigan, Venus

Other Names for Tree: woodbine, goat's leaf

Zodiac: Aries, Cancer, Leo

Celestial Bodies: Mars, Mercury

Gemstone: Coral

Wildlife: bees, hummingbirds, lapwing, moths

Colors: indigo, lavender, white

Energy: feminine

Bach Flower Remedy: living in the past

Other Associations: tarot Wheel of Fortune; Saturday and Monday; northeast; sabbats: Beltane, Ostara; Celtic shrub tree

Spellwork and Ritual: spells for prosperity and wealth; banishing someone who is clinging or extracting yourself from a situation where you feel constricted; rituals for self-work and when searching for your purpose; enhancing psychic abilities in divination and while journeying

Hornbeam

HORNBEAM PRODUCES A VERY HARD wood that is mainly used for tools. It has also been used for the strip of wood on the outside of Rolls Royce doors.

The name hornbeam comes from its characteristic hardness, which was likened to animal horn, a very hard material. "Beam" in its name evolved from the German word for tree, *baum*. Because of its hardness, it is also called "ironwood." Hornbeam's nickname yoke-elm comes from its European relatives, the wood of which was used for oxen yokes. The American hornbeam is sometimes called water or blue beech because it is often mistaken for a beech tree.

Hornbeam hedges were popular in knot gardens of the fifteenth through seventeenth centuries. The maze at Hampton Court Palace was created by King William III's gardeners in the late seventeenth century. Not far from where I lived in England, a hornbeam maze has been re-created in the gardens at Woburn Abbey (ancestral home of the Duke of Bedford). The hornbeam is tolerant of a variety of soils and does well in urban environments.

Hildegard von Bingen considered the hornbeam to be a tree that protected people from "aerial spirits and diabolic illusions." She suggested that if one were to sleep in a forest it was best to do so underneath a hornbeam.

Latin Name: *Carpinus caroliniana* (American hornbeam), *C. betulus* (English hornbeam), *Ostrya virginiana* (American hophornbeam)

Seasonal Details: long male catkins, shorter female catkins (on the same tree) protected by bracts[1] April–May; the bracts also protect a small nut August–October; Hophornbeam: bracts hang like clusters of hops that turn color in autumn but stay on the tree into winter

Powers/Attributes: lifting/removing the unwanted, prosperity, protection, spiritual love, strength/stamina

Element: water

Rune Character: ᚠ
  Name: Feoh/Fehu
  Letter: F

Feng Shui Sectors: southeast, southwest, negative areas

Other Names for Tree: yoke-elm, ironwood, blue beech, water beech (American hornbeam)

Zodiac: Taurus

Celestial Body: Saturn

Plant: ginger

Gemstones: aventurine, opal, smoky quartz

Wildlife: cottontail rabbit, deer

Other Trees: ash, maple

Color: green

Energy: feminine

Bach Flower Remedy: against feelings of exhaustion and tiredness from effort

Other Association: unsettled changes; dates: June 4–13, December 2–11

Spellwork and Ritual: use in rituals that mark life transitions; banishing spells

---

1. A bract is somewhat leaf-like and petal-like but lightly woody.

Ivy

IN ANCIENT GREECE, PEOPLE WORE a circlet of ivy leaves on their heads at drinking festivals, especially those honoring Dionysus. A story tells of Cissos, a young woman who died of exhaustion after dancing at a festival. Dionysus turned her corpse into an ivy vine so she could continue to live. This folktale was the basis for the belief that ivy could prevent drunkenness and that it would thrive when planted on the grave of a woman who had died for love. A variety of beliefs follow this theme. One is that a sprig of ivy under your pillow will make you dream of your true love.

Ivy is associated with the Goddess because it grows in a spiral, which is one of her symbols. Use ivy on your altar to symbolize your spiritual journey through the Wheel of the Year: in winter we follow the spiral of energy down and within, and in the spring we follow it back up into the light for our own symbolic rebirth.

Medicinally ivy has been used for toothaches, as an astringent, and as an aid to bring on menstruation. It also calms the nerves. Ivy ale was an intoxicating drink brewed in medieval England.

It was the custom in England into Victorian times for girls and boys, ivy girls and holly boys, to compete for treats at Yule.[1] This symbolized the struggle for balance between the light and dark times of the year. Light and dark, female and male energies are essential and best when in balance. A sheaf of grain brought in at harvest time was tied with a strand of ivy and called the Ivy Girl. It was presented to the farmer who was the last to get his harvest in—this was not an honor.

In English and Irish folktales, on December 26 when the wren was hunted by the robin (see birch for more details), the wren tries to hide by taking shelter in ivy. Other versions of the story say that he hid in furze/gorse. Derived from the Gaelic word *eidhneán* for ivy, the name of Clonenagh (*Cluain-eidhnech*) in Ireland means "the meadow of ivy." Even though this name dates to before the sixth century, there is a great deal of ivy in and around the town today.

In ancient Rome, ivy was associated with the god Saturn because his symbol, the gold crested wren, made its nest in ivy. Along with holly, ivy was used as decoration for the Saturnalia festival.

Dreaming of ivy can foretell of a broken engagement. If ivy is growing on a tree in your dream, you may have grief. If it is growing on a house, you will have wealth. If it is growing on a friend's house it means that they will have good health. If ivy is a potted plant in your dream you will have happiness.

Latin Name: *Hedera helix* (English ivy)

Seasonal Details: evergreen; yellow-green flowers in October that produce black berries

Powers/Attributes: fertility, fidelity, good luck, growth, healing, love, protection, resurrection, transformation, vitality

Elements: air, earth, water

Celtic Calendar Dates: September 30–October 27

Ogham Character: ╫
Name: Gort
Letter: G

Ogham Character: ◇
Name: Oir
Letters: OI, TH

Feng Shui Sectors: northeast, east, southwest, life, negative areas

Goddesses: Arianrhod, Danu, Hel/Holle, Persephone, Rhea

Gods: Bacchus, Cernunnos, Dionysus, Frey, Hermes, Loki, Ogma, Osiris, Pan, Saturn

Other Being/Character: faeries

Other Name for Tree: true ivy

Zodiac: Gemini

Celestial Body: Saturn

Plant: woody nightshade

Gemstones: Alexandrite, chrysoberyl, opal

Wildlife: butterfly, lark, mute swan, swallow

Other Trees: holly, vine

Colors: blue, light brown

Energy: feminine

Other Associations: poetry; search for self; mazes and labyrinths; south; date: December 17; sabbat: Yule/winter solstice; Celtic bramble tree

Spellwork and Ritual: celebrating and honoring the balance of light and dark, life and death; protection spells against negativity; spiritual journeys that take you inward as well as bring you out

1. Ferguson, *The Magickal Year*, 70.

Juniper

A COMMON COMPONENT OF TRADITIONAL foods in Southern Germany and Central Europe, juniper berries are well known for their use as flavoring in stews and roasts as well as gin. Medicinally, the berries and twigs have been used in remedies for colds, aches and pains, hemorrhaging, and scurvy. Juniper is still used as an antiseptic for urinary problems.

Oil from the leaves is used in perfumes, soaps, and cosmetics. In India, the leaves are burned as incense. Even though the wood is durable and fine-grained, it is not generally used as a commercial product. However, the thick exposed roots of Rocky Mountain juniper are being used to create unusual and artistic furniture. Those who work with this wood usually scavenge for dying junipers rather than kill living ones.

At one time it was believed that burning juniper during childbirth would protect a baby from being taken by faeries. This concept may have come from a story connected with the infant Jesus during the flight from Egypt, when Juniper was burned for protection against leprosy, the plague and other illnesses. In contrast, there was also the belief that a person who cut down a juniper would die within a year.

Juniper was planted in front of a house as protection against witches who were (for some inexplicable reason) expected to count all the needles on the tree before they could pass through the doorway. Apparently the theory was that the witch would lose count, get bored, or simply not bother. Germanic folktales tell of a spirit of the juniper who aided in recovering stolen goods. In connection with this, planting a juniper beside one's front door would prevent thieves from plundering the house.

It has been suggested that *Juniperus*, the Latin name for the plant, could have a Celtic origin—possibly from a misidentification with the yew with its Gaelic/Irish root words of *iubhar* and *eochaill*.

Dreaming of a juniper tree means that someone may speak badly of you. Eating juniper berries means an important event is about to happen.

Latin Name: *Juniperus communis* (common or dwarf juniper), *J. scopulorum* (Rocky Mountain juniper)

Seasonal Details: round blue-black berries that take about two years to mature; berries frequently have a dusting of white powder; scale-like leaves that grow in whorl patterns

Powers/Attributes: cleansing, healing, love, protection

Elements: earth, fire

Rune Character: ⚡
  Name: Sigel/Sig
  Letter: S

Feng Shui Sectors: southwest, health, negative areas

Goddesses: Audhumla, Hel/Holle, Morrigan, Ran

Gods: Baldar, Loki, Tyr

Other Being/Character: dwarves

Celestial Body: Sun

Gemstone: green sapphire

Wildlife: cedar waxwing, geese, white tail deer

Color: light green

Energy: masculine

Other Association: second chakra; winter

Spellwork and Ritual: attracting a lover using dried berries on a string as an amulet; good luck in childbirth; attraction spells; dispelling negativity

Laurel

THE MOST FAMOUS LEGEND INVOLVING a laurel tree is the one from ancient Greece about Daphne and how she avoided the attentions of Apollo by being turned into a laurel. Undaunted, Apollo adopted it as his sacred tree. Laurel was a symbol of victory, and athletes were crowned with laurel wreaths, replacing the use of olive wreaths. It was also a symbol of merit and accomplishment, which is still apparent in the words poet laureate and baccalaureate (*baca lauri* means "laurel berry"). Because of the many curative powers of the tree, Aesculapius, the Greek god of medicine, was associated with it.

Laurel became a symbol of resurrection to Christians because of the plant's ability to be revived after a long drought. In later centuries, the sudden drooping or withering of its leaves was a sign that difficulties (especially a royal death) would soon occur. The sounds made by laurel branches placed on a fire were used for divination: a crackling noise was a good sign while silence meant that one should tread carefully for a while. A dying laurel tree on one's property was considered a bad omen.

In addition to its properties of divination, it was believed to provide protection against witches and lightning. In sixteenth-century England, a sprig of laurel was carried for protection against a multitude of mishaps, especially getting hit by lightning.

In addition to food flavoring, bay laurel has been used to treat stomachaches and rheumatism as well as bruises, sprains and earaches. It is used in cosmetics, perfumes and in both alcoholic and soft drinks. The berries are also used for flavoring but not as commonly as the leaves. The wood is occasionally used for inlay. Outdoors the bay laurel finds use in hedges and for topiary sculpture. In cooler climates it can be grown in pots indoors. Mountain laurel tends to grow at the edge of forests, at streams and openings such as trails.

In mountain laurels' name, *Kalmia* is in honor of the Finnish botanist Peter Kalm, who was the first to study the genus. *Latifolia* means "wide leaf." It was introduced into Europe from North America in 1726. Kalm noted the nearly fatal effects that the leaves had on local lambs, giving rise to the nickname "lambkill." Deer and horses can also be affected but usually avoid eating it.

Dreaming of a laurel tree indicates pleasant times ahead. If you dream that you are given laurel, you may be given money. Holding a laurel branch means that you will advance in life.

Latin Name: *Laurus nobilis* (bay laurel), *Kalmia latifolia* (mountain laurel)

Seasonal Details: both are evergreens; bay laurel: small white or yellowish inconspicuous flowers in spring followed by blue-black berries; mountain laurel: pink buds in the autumn, white and light pink star-shaped flowers in clusters, June–July; oval, leathery leaves

Powers/Attributes: divination, expanded awareness, healing, poetic inspiration, prophetic dreams, protection, purification, psychic abilities, strength, wisdom

Elements: air, fire

Rune Character: ⚡
   Name: Sigel/Sig
   Letter: S

Feng Shui Sectors: center, south, northeast, negative areas

Goddess: Ceres

Gods: Aesculapius, Apollo, Balder, Kernunnos

Other Being/Character: Daphne

Other Names for Tree: bay tree, sweet bay (bay laurel), calico bush (mountain laurel), lambkill (mountain laurel)

Zodiac: Gemini, Leo

Celestial Body: Sun

Energy: masculine

Other Association: poetry

Spellwork and Ritual: divination rituals; spells and charms to get creative (especially poetic) juices flowing; aids dream prophecy when placed under a pillow

Linden

LINDEN BECAME POPULAR AFTER THE fourteenth century on the Continent and in England for carving and other work that did not require strength. Many of the carvings in St. Paul's Cathedral (London) and Windsor Castle are of linden wood. The tree's fibrous bark has been used for rope, mats and baskets. Honey from the flowers is considered some of the best flavored in the world, and in France, *Tilleul* is a tea made from them.

Like blackthorn, gorse, and heather, linden attracts large numbers of bees, which has given it an association with the Great Mother Goddess (fertility and provider aspects). In Greece and Poland linden was a symbol of divine power and love.

In Greek myth, Philyra, the mother of the centaur Cheiron, was transformed into a linden tree. In eastern and central Europe, linden trees were an integral part of the culture and usually marked a place of importance such as a town center, a spring, well, or castle. In more recent times, lindens were used as shade trees to line city streets. However, the name of Berlin's street, *Unter Den Linden*, could refer to walking under the trees or to an old phrase "under linden" which meant under someone's protection. Germanic tribes frequently used linden wood for battle shields.

Like blackthorn and gorse, linden is also associated with Walpurgis, but more so for a connection with St. Walburga than with the activities of clearing away evil spirits. The chapel in Bavaria where it is believed the saint lived is said to have been "linden-tree shaped" and surrounded by lindens. St. Walburga became widely famous for her posthumous healings accomplished through the oil that is said to have oozed from her gravestone. Local Bavarian folktales about her also connect her with trees: She is said to have flown on a broom (bristles forward), and to have taken tree branches into her rooms and decorated them with ribbons, creating the forerunner of the Maypole according to Christian legend.

Linden combined with lavender in a sachet and tucked under your pillow will help you sleep. Dreaming of a linden tree means that you will receive good news, but if you cut down a linden in your dream, your love life will be in danger.

Latin Name: *Tilia europaea* (European linden), *T. americana* (American linden), *T. heterophylla* (white linden)

Seasonal Details: tiny greenish-yellow fragrant flowers in June–July; pea-like fruits August–October; heart-shaped, fine-toothed leaves

Powers/Attributes: attraction, immortality, love, luck, peace, prophecy, protection

Element: air

Rune Character: ᛅ
   Name: As/Asa
   Letter: A

Feng Shui Sectors: center, southwest, longevity, negative areas

Goddesses: Arianrhod, Eostre, Freya, Frigg, Lada, Nehalennia, Philyra, Venus, Zemyna

Gods: Odin, Tyr

Other Names for Tree: lime tree, basswood, bee tree, white wood

Zodiac: Gemini, Sagittarius

Celestial Bodies: Jupiter, Sun

Gemstone: tree agate

Wildlife: turtle dove

Other Trees: blackthorn, gorse, heather

Color: white

Energy: feminine

Other Associations: dates: March 11–20 and September 13–22; sabbats: Beltane, Litha/summer solstice, Ostara/vernal equinox

Spellwork and Ritual: attracting love; balancing energy; neutralizing negativity

Locust

THE HONEY LOCUST IS NATIVE to North America and has been naturalized into Central and Southern Europe. Its durable wood is used for railroad ties, fencing, and agricultural tools. The black locust produces one of the hardest woods and, because it does not easily rot, it has been used extensively in shipbuilding, general construction, and fencing. The bark has a wavy texture and has been described as "Rorschach-like," an attribute that made one locust tree the focus of miraculous apparitions in August 1999 when locals near Colt Park, Hartford, Connecticut, claimed to see a vision of the Virgin Mary.

The locust has been described as a sinister tree because of the thorns that can grow six inches and longer on its trunk. Native Americans used the thorns for spear points and animal traps. Shoots, bark, and leaves of the black locust are poisonous, which may have added to its dark reputation. The black locust has been known as a place to bury "evil things" because it has been associated with the Dark Mother aspect of the Goddess. As one who protects, she neutralizes harmful and negative energy.

Locust pods hold approximately twenty seeds, which are surrounded by a sugary pulp that has been used for making beer. While the seeds can be eaten raw or cooked, the pods are used for animal feed as well as ethanol production. Locust trees have been planted for hedges and windbreaks.

The locust tree mentioned in the Bible and other ancient sources is the carob tree, a native of the Mediterranean area and the Middle East. Food made from its pods was called St. John's bread because this was the only thing he ate during his time in the wilderness. It is believed that carob seeds were the unit of measure for gemstone weight that became known as the carat.

The locust can be a challenge to work with, but persistence and honesty go a long way with this tree.

Dreaming of locust trees means that happiness may be short lived. Dreaming of picking locust pods means that you have a good loyal friend. Dreaming of eating locust honey indicates a change in environment.

Latin Name: *Gleditsia triacanthos* (honey locust), *Robinia pseudoacacia* (black locust), *Ceratonia siliqua* (carob)

Seasonal Details: honey locust: feathery leaves; sweet-pea shaped reddish flowers on both male and female trees, May–July; long, flat and twisted pods, September–February; thorns on trunk; black locust: white fragrant flowers in pendulous clusters, May–June; flat pods, September–April

Powers/Attributes: balance, friendship, platonic love, perseverance, protection, secret love, strength

Elements: earth, water

Feng Shui Sectors: center, east, southwest, negative areas

Goddesses: Cerridwen, Hecate, Morrigan, Sekhmet

Other Names for Tree: sweet locust, honeyshuck

Zodiac: Aries

Gemstone: amber

Wildlife: finch, rabbit, squirrel

Energy: feminine

Other Associations: sabbats: Mabon/autumn equinox, Samhain

Spellwork and Ritual: protection and strength (call on the locust in dark moon rituals); rattles for autumn rituals (use dried seed pods); seeking the calm center within (use leaves); protection spells (use thorns)

Magnolia

THE MAGNOLIA WAS NAMED FOR Pierre Magnol (1638–1715) who was head of the botanical gardens in Montpellier, France. This distinctive, tropical-looking ornamental tree was cultivated in China for its buds, which were used to flavor food and medicines. Tea made from the bark of the cucumber magnolia was used in place of quinine to treat malaria. Wood from the cucumber magnolia is used for interiors, cabinets, and ornamental boxes.

There are approximately eighty species worldwide, eight of which are native to North America. Although it is a tree that epitomizes the American South, magnolia adorns lawns and graces avenues from eastern Massachusetts to Florida and west to eastern Texas. In its northern reaches it is deciduous but in the South it's an evergreen.

If you live in the southeastern United States, use this tree to find and evoke the beauty of sultry summers as well as your forefathers and mothers who lived in this lush garden.

Latin Name: *Magnolia grandiflora* (southern magnolia), *M. virginiana* (sweetbay magnolia), *M. acuminata* (cucumber magnolia), *M. macrophylla* (bigleaf magnolia)

Seasonal Details: large creamy white or yellowish blossoms, May–July; conelike fruit in heavy long pods with bright red seeds, September–October; southern and sweetbay magnolias are evergreen in the southern United States; cucumber magnolia flowers are green or green/yellow, May–June; fruits are cucumberlike but turn dark red, August–October

Powers/Attributes: clarity, dreams, love, protection, self-awareness, truth

Element: water

Goddesses: Aphrodite, Venus

Feng Shui Sectors: northeast, southwest, negative areas

Other Names for Tree: swamp-bay, Virginia magnolia (sweetbay), bullbay (southern magnolia), whitebay

Celestial Bodies: Venus, Saturn

Other Trees: holly, maple

Energy: feminine

Other Associations: sabbats: Mabon/autumn equinox, Samhain

Spellwork and Ritual: clarity in divination especially when seeking self truth; attraction and love spells; dreamwork and dream divination

Maple

MAPLE IS A VALUABLE HARDWOOD that has been popular for furniture and carvings because of its beautiful grain. Even its roots were valuable for carving small objects, and the wood of old maples was used for mahogany inlay. Fiddled maple's erratic grain provides intricate and attractive patterns, and the nickname "bird's eye" maple comes from the eye-like patterns produced by the knots.

Striped maple is named for the pattern of its bark and is called "whistlewood" because its outer bark is easy to peel off and was the source for wooden whistles.

It has been widely used for other musical instruments as well as violin cases. The nickname "moosewood" comes from its popularity with moose that seem to find the young shoots a delectable treat. In France the flexible young shoots were used as horse whips.

Colonial settlers used the unprocessed sap as a tonic for coughs and to treat liver and kidney problems. Highly prized maple syrup is produced by sugar maples in New England. One tree can produce between five and sixty gallons of sap annually with ten to twenty gallons the average.[1] Before leaves appear in early spring, the trees are tapped, which fortunately does not damage the tree. Sunny days and cold nights with a northwest wind tend to increase the flow of sap. Sensitive to climatic conditions, the flow decreases or stops with a southwest wind or an approaching storm. The sugar season lasts from five to six weeks and the sap that flows after that is used for molasses and vinegar. The canyon maple in the western United States has a sweet sap that is also made into syrup. In hopes of tapping into the syrup market, the sugar maple was introduced into Britain in 1735; however, there and in Europe it was mainly useful as a hedgerow tree.

As the year draws to a close, it is the maple that provides a brilliant blaze of color that can rival spring's vibrant palette.

Latin Name: *Acer campestre* (European field maple), *A. saccharum* (sugar maple), *A. rubrum* (red maple), *A. pseudoplatanus* (sycamore maple), *A. pensylvanicum* (striped maple)

Seasonal Details: petalless green/yellow flowers in long clusters, April–June; winged seeds called "keys" appear in spring and drop off, June–September; red maple: flowers are red and in short clusters, March–May; reddish seeds, May–July

Powers/Attributes: abundance, balance, communication, creativity, divination, grounding, longevity, love, money, positive energy, transformation, wisdom

Elements: air, earth

Rune Character: ᛗ
  Name: Man/Mannaz
  Letter: M

Feng Shui Sectors: center, north, northeast, southeast, southwest, west, abundance, longevity, negative areas

Goddesses: Athena, Rhiannon, Venus

Other Beings/Characters: archangels Chamael (red maple) and Jophael; faeries

Other Names for Tree: moosewood and whistlewood (striped maple), hedge maple (European field maple), bird's eye (sugar maple)

Zodiac: Cancer, Libra, Virgo

Celestial Body: Jupiter

Wildlife: deer, horned owl, moose, rabbit

Color: orange-red

Energy: masculine

Other Associations: dates: April 11–20 and October 14–23; sabbats: Ostara/spring equinox, Mabon/autumn equinox

Spellwork and Ritual: spells to attract love; working with the faery realm; appreciating the beauty of the season in late winter/early spring; excellent for wands

---

1. *The Encyclopedia American International* (Danbury, CT: Grolier, 2001), s.v. "Maple Syrup."

Mesquite

MESQUITE IS MOST WIDELY KNOWN as a fire-wood to flavor barbecued meat, but its use by humans dates back to prehistoric times. It originated in Central and South America and is now found in the Southwestern United States, South Africa, Australia, India, and Iran.

The pods have been used for food for over a thousand years and are still used for flour, gruel, jelly, and wine, as well as fodder for livestock. Toasted seeds are sometimes added to coffee. The flowers produce a rich nectar which attracts bees and yields a superior honey. Gum from the tree is used in confectionery. Medicinally, mesquite has been used to treat colds, flu, sore throats, inflammation, diarrhea, and dysentery.

The wood from this tree is becoming increasingly popular for furniture, flooring, lamps, fireplace mantels, and wall carvings—especially Christian crosses. Woodcrafters who work with mesquite claim that its properties, beautiful colors, and swirling grain can rival oak, cherry, and walnut. In the American Southwest, mesquite has become a symbol of the region and is the focus of annual events by the growing number of enthusiasts. Formed by lumber mills, furniture makers and woodcrafters in 1992, the Texas Mesquite Association promotes the use of this wood.

While many may extol the virtues of mesquite, others perceive it as an albatross around the neck. In the arid areas of the Southwest, this fast-growing tree is a strong competitor against cultivated crops in the struggle for water resources. Ironically, in 2002 the town of Mesquite, Nevada received federal funds to eradicate the invasive tamarisk trees that were draining the groundwater supply.[1]

Mesquite is mentioned in the Aztec creation myth: During the second sun—the second time the universe was created (we are presently in the fifth sun)—Quetzalcoatl in his role as god of winds created the world and fed people by the fruit of the mesquite tree.

Native Americans, particularly the Paiutes and the Shoshones, used fire-hardened pieces of mesquite wood as arrow tips for duck hunting, and gum from the tree for creating designs on pottery.[2]

In the late 1800s when Wickenburg, Arizona was a mining town, the citizens did not have time to build a jail so instead they chained prisoners to a conveniently located mesquite tree. This 200-year-old tree is now a tourist attraction for the town.

Latin Name: *Prosopis glandulosa* (honey mesquite), *P. juliflora* (common mesquite)

Seasonal Details: greenish-yellow spiky flowers that appear in April, June–July, and then intermittently until autumn; fruit is a thin pod that turns brown when ripe; thorny

Powers/Attributes: persistence, protection, purification, strength through healing, success

Elements: air, fire, water

Feng Shui Sectors: negative areas

Gods: Ixtlilton, Quetzalcoatl

Other Names for Tree: mizquitl (Aztec), southwest thorn

Celestial Bodies: Moon, Saturn

Wildlife: bees, coyote

Energy: feminine

Other Association: compassion; opening to receive; root chakra

Spellwork and Ritual: spells to bring success; situations where it is essential to "hang in there"; increasing the power of healing herbs; magical fires

---

1. Associated Press, "Mesquite to Get Help with Weeding Out Troublesome Tree," *Las Vegas Sun*, December 26, 2002.

2. Edith Van Allen Murphy, *Indian Uses of Native Plants* (Ukiah, CA: Medocino County Historical Society, 1987), 52, 56.

Mimosa

With fern-like leaves and delicate flowers, one would not expect the mimosa to be an aggressive competitor on many gardeners' "least wanted" list. It is highly competitive with native plants in open spaces along forest edges and is a common sight along many U.S. interstate highways.

While the mimosa can grow in a variety of conditions and is regarded as a problem to some, others love its exotic appearance and cultivate it as an ornamental asset. Mimosa's native range extends from Iran to Japan, but because it can thrive in a variety of soils it makes itself at home in many areas around the globe.

Mimosa was introduced into the United States in 1745 and was chosen by Thomas Jefferson to grace the gardens at his home, Monticello. (Jefferson was said to have been fanatical about his gardens and trees.) While mimosas are usually short-lived and have brittle wood, one lasted twenty-five years at Monticello. Mimosa seeds seem to be hardier than the trees as they can be germinated after fifty years of dormancy.

Medicinally, mimosa is an astringent but it also has been used to treat depression and insomnia. Its flowers have been used for liver problems, as a sedative, and as an ingredient in skin care products.

The leaves are used in Chinese cooking. There is a theory that mimosa bark is an ingredient in the heavily guarded Coca-Cola recipe.

It was given the common name of "mimosa" because of its resemblance to the *Mimosa pudica*. That tree is commonly called the "sensitive plant" because its leaves fold up when touched, whereas the flowers of the mimosa/silk tree fold up at night. The name "silk tree" describes its flowers, which look like silky threads rather than petals.

Latin Name: *Albizia julibrissin* (silk tree)

Seasonal Details: fernlike leaves; feathery fragrant pink flowers, June–August; flat pods develop in August–September and remain on tree into the winter

Powers/Attributes: happiness, love, peace, perseverance, protection, purification, sensitivity

Elements: air, water

Feng Shui Sectors: center, southwest, negative areas

Other Being/Character: archangel Hanriel

Other Names for Tree: silky acacia, powder puff tree, happiness tree

Zodiac: Cancer, Capricorn, Virgo

Celestial Body: Saturn

Wildlife: butterflies, hummingbirds

Colors: pink, purple, red

Energy: feminine

Other Associations: copper; January full moon

Spellwork and Ritual: love charms; rituals to lift worries; prophetic dreams (use in sachet under pillow); purifying ritual space; self-work for raising awareness

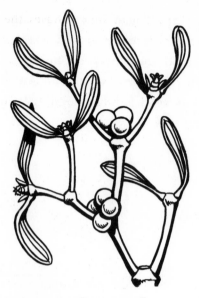

Mistletoe

MISTLETOE IS INEXORABLY LINKED WITH the oak tree. It is a parasitic evergreen that grows on the branches of deciduous trees—frequently on apple, poplar, and willow, but rarely on oak, which is why it was considered a precious commodity. The Celts of Gaul believed that anything that grew on an oak was a gift from the God. When mistletoe was found on the sacred oak, it was believed to carry the life essence of the God. Because it frequently outlived its host tree, mistletoe was also a symbol of survival and immortality.

Mistletoe's white juicy berries, plentiful at Yule (the full moon of December is referred to as the oak moon), represented the seed of the God/Green Man and the quickening spirit of nature. The red berry of the holly (also prevalent at Yule), represented the life blood of the Goddess—together they ensured the continuity of life. As evergreens, they both symbolized the immortality of the Goddess and God.

Mistletoe's association with fertility remains to this day with our custom of kissing under a sprig of it at Yule. In the past, it was believed that sweethearts who kissed under it were destined to marry but only if the mistletoe was burned on Twelfth Night.

Mistletoe was regarded as particularly magical because it occupied the heavenly realm, always growing atop trees. Because its seeds were dropped by birds or blown on the wind, mistletoe seemed to suddenly appear out of nowhere.

There is no mention of mistletoe in Irish legend because it was not introduced into that island until the late eighteenth/early nineteenth century. In addition, according to Celtic scholar Peter Berresford Ellis, Pliny's description of the elaborate procedures for mistletoe gathering may have been mistakenly attributed to Celtic Druids instead of the Germanic tribes near Gaul.[1]

There is also controversy whether or not the vegetation found in a Bronze Age burial site near Scarborough in Yorkshire, England, was mistletoe.

Mistletoe gathered at the summer solstice was used as a household amulet and hung above a doorway to ward off mischievous spirits. In Virgil's *The Aeneid* (19 BCE) the hero Aeneas gained access and safe conduct through the world of the dead because he carried a sprig of mistle-toe. According to Robert Graves, the cutting of mistletoe from an oak symbolized the emasculation of the old king.[2] The summer solstice occurs just before the end of the oak king's reign, after which the holly king comes to the throne.

Medicinally, mistletoe was used as a sedative by the Celts of Gaul, the ancient Romans, and into the eighteenth century by the Swedes. It was used as a fertility aid, an antidote to poisoning, and a treatment for epilepsy.

Mistletoe's nickname "golden bough" is derived from the color of its berries and branches, which take on a rich golden hue as they age and whither.[3] Its name in English comes from its Old Norse name, *Mistelteinn*. The suffix, *teinn*, designates a sacred tree.

Dreaming of mistletoe means that you will have good fortune. If you pick it in your dream, you will receive unexpected money. If you are given mistletoe, you will find happiness, and if you give it to someone else, you will have good luck.

(continued on next page)

Latin Name: *Viscum album* (European mistletoe), *Phoradendron flavescens* (American mistletoe), *Loranthus bengwensis* and *L. micranthus* (African mistletoe)

Seasonal Details: small white flowers, May–June (European), October–November (American); whitish berries November–December

Powers/Attributes: birth/rebirth, fertility, health, hidden sources, immortality, love, protection, secrets

Element: air

Celtic Calendar Dates: December 23, The Nameless Day

Rune Character: ⚡
  Name: Sigel/Sig
  Letter: S

Feng Shui Sectors: north, southwest, west, health, negative areas

Goddesses: Arianrhod, Freya, Venus

Gods: Apollo, Aesculapius, Balder, Jove, Odin

Other Being/Character: Aeneas

Other Names for Tree: golden bough, all heal

Celestial Body: Sun

Gemstone: black pearl

Other Tree: oak

Energy: masculine

Other Associations: survival; sabbats: Yule/winter solstice, Litha/summer solstice

Spellwork and Ritual: winter and summer solstice rituals; symbolically for fertility spells; spells and rituals of change and transformation; celebrating the God and male energy/the Green Man; rituals for balance of male/female energy

1. Ellis, *The Druids*, 61–62.

2. Graves, *The White Goddess*, 65.

3. Ferguson, *The Magickal Year*, 70.

Myrtle

IN MEDIEVAL EUROPE, MYRTLE WAS revered for its healing properties. It is connected with love and lovers because it has been associated with Venus, the Roman goddess of love. Venus is frequently depicted wearing a sprig of myrtle. In some legends, she is said to have risen from the sea wearing a crown of myrtle leaves. Myrtle trees were planted on the grounds around her temples and she was sometimes known as Myrtilla.

In some versions of the Greek story of Daphne and Apollo, it is a myrtle tree rather than a laurel into which Daphne transforms, which may be the basis for the belief that it protects against enchantments.

The name "myrtle" comes from the Greek word meaning "perfume." The common myrtle was cultivated by the Romans and its leaves used as a spice. In later centuries they were used as a substitute for bay leaves. The wood is still used for outdoor grilling because of the spicy flavor it gives to meat. Leaves sprinkled over charcoals also provide a rich flavor.

Bog myrtle is strongly aromatic and found in wet moorland, heath, bogs, and fens throughout England. The leaves of bog myrtle were once used instead of mothballs, and sometimes as a substitute for hops in brewing.

Myrtle wood has a wide range of colors from light gold to black depending on the minerals present in the soil. It is famous for the variety of grain patterns—burls, flames, and tiger stripes.

In Victorian England, myrtle flowers were included with the bride's bouquet for good luck and fidelity in the marriage. The custom in Wales is for the bride to give each of her bridesmaids a sprig of myrtle.

Throughout the Bible, myrtle is a symbol of divine generosity.

Dreaming of myrtle means that your desires will come to fruition. If the tree is in bloom in your dream, you will have the pleasures you desire. Picking myrtle means that you will have luck and prosperity.

Latin Name: *Myrtus communis* (common myrtle), *Myrica gale* (bog myrtle), *Lagerstroemia indica* (crepe myrtle)

Seasonal Details: small white sweet-smelling flowers, July–August; black berries in autumn; bog myrtle: lance-shaped, grey-green toothed leaves; golden-brown catkins, March–May; small, nutlike fruits each have two wings; crepe myrtle: white, pink, red, purple, or lavender flowers, July to autumn; leaves turn orange, red, and yellow in autumn

Powers/Attributes: fertility, healing, love, luck, money, peace, youth

Element: water

Feng Shui Sectors: center, southeast, southwest, west, negative areas

Goddesses: Aphrodite, Artemis, Ashtoreth, Astarte, Hathor, Venus

Other Being/Character: archangel Mareael

Zodiac: Taurus

Celestial Body: Moon, Venus

Energy: feminine

Other Name for Tree: sweet gale (bog myrtle)

Other Association: marriage; sabbats: Ostara/spring equinox, Litha/summer solstice; Celtic bramble tree (bog-myrtle)

Spellwork and Ritual: attracting prosperity; love spells and love divination; rituals of healing

Oak

In ancient Greece, the oak was a symbol of the strength and might of Zeus. The oracle of Zeus was an oak grove in Dodona, Greece, where priests would provide an interpretation of the sounds of rustling leaves. The oak was known as the Mother Tree to the Greeks who had a creation myth in which the first man was created from oak branches.

A German folk story tells of children being born from oak trees. The Romans had a similar story that went on to say that acorns were the first food. Peter Berresford Ellis provides a beautiful interpretation of a Celtic creation myth about the Children of Danu coming from the sacred oak father, Bíle.[1] According to Jean Markale, the Celts viewed the oak as a "representation of divinity."

In England, circa 1660, the oak became a symbol of the monarch Charles II after he hid in an oak tree to escape opposition soldiers. People exhibited their support of the exiled king by wearing a sprig of oak leaves.

The Lithuanians, Estonians, Slavs, and other people in almost every country where the oak grows regarded it as sacred.

It is one of the longest living trees and considered by the Celts to be one of the kings of trees.

Yuletide is when the Oak King takes over from the Holly King. (See the entry for Holly.) Oak is the traditional wood for the Yule log as well as a rare host for the mystical mistletoe. Mistletoe and holly sprigs are usually tied to the oak log to dress it for the occasion. A piece of the Yule log is kept from one year to the next so that as one year ends and the new begins, there is symbolic continuity of life. A piece of the Yule log also functioned as a protective amulet for the home. In the temple of Vesta in the Roman Forum, from which people took fire to restart their hearths at certain times of the year, the eternal flame was fuelled exclusively with oak wood.

Since the oak and Yule log symbolized the Green Man, the God, and the spirit of vegetation, the ashes from the fire were scattered outside to fertilize the fields and bring abundance in the following year. This is similar to the Hindu belief that the ashes are the seed of the fire god Agni.

To the Romans, oak along with birch and yew represented the three pillars of wisdom. Along with ash and hawthorn, it was considered part of the triad of powerful faery trees. To the Celts, the oak symbolized the Dagda, the oldest, most encom-passing of the Gods. Sacred oak groves were places of worship and learning. Each tribe had its own oak *crann beatha*, Tree of Life, that functioned as the community's talisman. The Oak of Munga was one of the five great trees of Ireland.

Many places in Ireland are based on *dairoch*, the Gaelic word for oak and its many derivations. The town Adare in County Limerick comes from *Ath-dara* meaning "ford of the oak tree." Derry or Doire means "an oak grove" or "oak wood," and is incorporated into many place names such as Derrybeg, "little oak wood," Derrydorragh, "dark oakwood," and Derrylough, "the oak wood of the lake." The names of the towns of Aghav-ille (*Achadh-bhile*) and Ballinvella (*Baile-an-bhile*) mean "field of the *bile* (ancient tree)."

Oaks account for approximately half the annual production of hardwood lumber in the United States because it provides some of best building material. As fuel, its hot-burning fire worked well for heating in earlier times. Because it is such a hardy wood, oak has been used for doors and gates that require strength, which enhances the belief that oak provides a doorway to other realms.

Medicinally, astringent tonics made from oak have been used to treat sore throats, fevers, varicose veins, and skin rashes. The tanic acid of oak's bark is used in tanning hides. Burning oak leaves is said to cleanse the atmosphere. The early Romans relied on acorns as a food source, as did the pre-Celtic Mesolithic people of Ireland, who used them second only to the hazelnut.

Carrying an acorn is said to bring luck and ward off illness. Acorns have been used for love divination. Lovers would each drop an acorn in water. Whether they sank, floated or drifted apart foretold how the couple's relationship would proceed—or not.

It is said that the tree's roots mirror its branches and stretch as far below ground as the branches do above.[2] Oak is one of the nine sacred woods for a sabbat fire in which it represents the God. It is traditional for the Litha fire to be oak wood as that is the time of year when oak reaches its zenith of power.

Dreaming of an oak tree, especially resting under one, means that you will have a long life and wealth. Climbing the tree in your dream indicates a bad time is ahead for a relative. Dreaming of fallen oak leaves means the loss of love.

(continued on next page)

Latin Name: *Quercus robur* (English oak), *Q. alba* (white oak), *Q. velutina* (black oak), *Q. palustris* (pin oak), *Q. chrysolepis* (canyon live oak)

Seasonal Details: male flowers in slender cluster of catkins, female flowers are inconspicuous, May–June; acorns ripen in the autumn

Powers/Attributes: ancestry, fertility, healing, health, justice, longevity, loyalty, luck, prosperity, protection, self-confidence, strength, subtlety, success, wisdom, wit

Elements: air, fire

Celtic Calendar Dates: June 10–July 7

Ogham Character: ⚇
Name: Duir
Letter: D

Rune Character: ᛞ
Name: Dag/Dagaz
Letter: D

Rune Character: ᛗ
Name: Ehwaz/Eh
Letter: E

Rune Character: ᛃ
Name: Jera/Jara
Letter: J

Rune Character: ᚱ
Name: Rad
Letter: R

Rune Character: ᚦ
Name: Thorn
Letter(s): Th

Rune Character: ᛏ
Name: Tyr
Letter: T

Feng Shui Sectors: northeast, east, southeast, south, southwest, west, northwest, health, longevity, negative areas

Goddesses: Artemis, Brigid, Cerridwen, Circe, Cybele, Diana, Morrigan, Rhea, Zemyna

Gods: Aegir, Apollo, Balder, Dagda, Cernunnos, Helios, Hercules, Herne, Janus, Jove/Jovyn, Jupiter, Pan, Percunis, Perkunas, Perun, Thor, Tyr, Zeus

Other Beings/Characters: archangels Gabriel and Metrael, elves, faeries, King Arthur

Zodiac: Gemini, Leo, Sagittarius, Virgo

Celestial Bodies: Jupiter, Sun

Plant: coltsfoot

Gemstone: amber

Wildlife: oriole, white horse, wren

Other Trees: holly, mistletoe

Color: gold

Energy: masculine

Bach Flower Remedy: keeps one who plods through things from pushing past the point of exhaustion

Other Associations: dates: May 29, March 21; Thursday; the cauldron; crown chakra (acorn); sabbats: Beltane, Yule/winter solstice, Litha/summer solstice; Celtic chieftain/noble tree

Spellwork and Ritual: oak leaves in the home help clear away negative energy; carry an acorn for good luck; use oak when you need to build inner strength; in ritual or on the altar, oak represents the God

1. Ellis, *The Chronicles of the Celts*, 21. The name Bíle was also used to indicate a large old tree that was considered sacred—not necessarily an oak.

2. Graves, *The White Goddess*, 176.

Olive

Olive is a slow-growing tree that does not produce a crop unit it is approximately eight years old. From eight to thirty-five years, it is very productive and after 150 years it begins to slow down. After 200 years, young shoots at the base of the trunk take over and create a new tree. This gave rise to its association with immortality.

The highly valued olive tree was domesticated in the Mediterranean area approximately six thousand years ago. Phoenician amphorae dating to 500 BCE were found to contain olive oil.[1] The Egyptians employed olive oil in the mum-mification process, but it was the ancient Greeks who integrated the use of the olive with everyday life. Olive oil found func-tion for cooking, lighting, and personal body care. Winners of Olympic competi-tions were prestigiously crowned with woven sprays of olive branches. At the Panathenaic games, winners received large jars of olive oil. Athletes used this valuable oil in their daily training regimen for lubrication and to moisturize the skin.[2]

The olive tree has frequently played a part in mythology. One legend tells of Athena striking the ground with her spear to bring forth the olive tree as a gift to humans. The Bible mentions an olive branch that a dove brings to Noah, signifying hope and signs of new/renewed life. The club that Hercules used was made of olive wood. In Homer's *Odyssey*, Ulysses's spear of olive wood brings down the Cyclops.

Today the Mediterranean diet is widely regarded as the healthiest because of its use of olive oil. Medicinally, olive leaves and fruit have been used to cure headaches, fevers, malaria, sore throats, and rashes. It was also used to ensure fertility. As a "healer," it seems appropriate that the United Nations has incorporated it into its logo and symbol of peace.

The name of the American olive *osmanthus* comes from the Greek words *osme*, meaning "fragrance" and *anthos*, "flowers."

Dreaming of an olive tree means that you will have great happiness. Planting one in your dream indicates an upcoming marriage. Picking an olive branch brings happiness and prosperity. Eating olives indicates a happy domestic life.

Latin Name: *Olea europaea sativa* (cultivated olive tree), *O. europaea sylvestris* (wild olive tree), *Osmanthus americanus* (American olive)

Seasonal Details: feather-shaped evergreen leaves that are replaced every two to three years; small cream-colored flowers in groups, April–June; one olive is produced per twenty flowers; fruit may be green, copper, or blackish-purple; wild olive is thorny

Powers/Attributes: abundance, balance, fertility, fidelity, fruitfulness, harmony, healing, hope, longevity, marriage, peace, potency, prosperity, rebirth, reconciliation, security, success, victory

Elements: air, earth, fire, water

Feng Shui Sector: center, north, southeast, south, southwest, west, abundance, longevity

Goddesses: Amaterasu, Athena, Minerva, Pele

Gods: Apollo, Hercules, Horus, Ra, Zeus

Other Beings/Characters: archangels Michael and Raphael, unicorns

Zodiac: Aquarius, Aries, Leo

Celestial Bodies: Mercury, Moon, Sun

Gemstone: lapis lazuli

Wildlife: dove

Other Tree: ash

Energy: masculine

Bach Flower Remedy: exhaustion after mental or physical effort

Other Associations: immortality; date: September 23

Spellwork and Ritual: strengthening fidelity in a relationship; reaching a calm, peaceful state of mind; rituals for healing and charms for health; elemental balance

---

1. William J. Broad, "Deep-Sea Clues to an Ancient Culture," *The New York Times*, October 12, 1998.

2. Nigel Spivey, *The Ancient Olympics* (Oxford: Oxford University Press, 2004), 125–128.

Palm

NATIVE TO NORTH AFRICA, DATE palm branches were used in Egyptian winter solstice celebrations. It appeared on Carthaginian coins, Egyptian monuments, and its leaves were carried in Greek and Roman pageants. Ancient depictions of the goddess Diana show her merged with a palm tree with abundant dates as multiple breasts. In the Bible, the palm is the Tree of Life in the Garden of Eden, and its leaves symbolize peace. Its fruit was called "the bread of the desert." The timber was occasionally used for roofing.

The date palm is named for the Phoenicians (*phoenix*) as they are credited with dispersing this tree in the Middle East. *Dactylus* comes from the Greek *dactylos*, meaning "date." Elbugat was a Syrian festival that used dates to honor Tammuz.

The coconut palm is a versatile tree that originated in Southeast Asia. Its nut is highly prized for "milk and meat." Charcoal is made from the coconut shell while brushes and rope are produced from the husks. The trunk is used for lumber. Its name comes from the Spanish *cocos*, meaning "monkey" or "eerie face," and *nucifera*, Latin meaning "nut-bearing."

Fan palms are native to the mountains of Southeast Asia and can withstand extended periods of cold weather. They do not grow in hot tropical areas, but do well in the southern United States and on the West Coast up to Vancouver. Native Americans used the berries for food and the seeds for grinding into flour.

Dragon's blood was used medicinally by the Romans and Greeks for respiratory and gastrointestinal problems. Its unripe fruit was the source of coloring for tinctures, toothpaste, plasters, and varnish.

Dragon's blood is popularly used in essential oils, incense, and ink. Eighteenth century Italian violinmakers used the resin to tint their varnish. This plant was formerly classified as *Calamus draco*.

Dreaming of a palm tree means that you will have success. Multiple palm trees indicate a high position for you. If you see your friends under a palm tree in your dream, you will overcome difficulties.

Latin Name: *Phoenix dactylifera* (date palm), *Trachycarpus fortunei* (fan palm), *Sabal palmetto* (cabbage palm), *Cocos nucifed* (coconut palm), *Butia capitata* (jelly palm), *Daemonorops draco* (dragon's blood)

Seasonal Details: date palm: twenty–thirty leaves clustered in a loose crown shaft; small white flowers; fruits are oblong and dark-orange when ripe; it often takes ten–fifteen years for the date palm to bear fruit; fan palm: yellow-green to green leaves are about three feet wide; cabbage palm: leaves emerge directly from the trunk and can grow up to twelve feet long; creamy-white flowers in mid-summer; small round black fruit in late fall; coconut: blooms take about ten months to mature into fruit; dragon's blood: long slender leaves with prickly bristles; round, pointed berries about the size of a cherry

Powers/Attributes: abundance, fertility, potency, protection, strength

Element: air, fire

Feng Shui Sectors: southeast, west, abundance, negative areas

Goddesses: Artemis, Ashtoreth, Diana, Ishtar, Isis, Tamar

Gods: Apollo, Damuzi, Tammuz

Other Beings/Characters: archangel Ithuriel, phoenix

Other Name for Tree: windmill palm (fan palm); blume (dragon's blood)

Zodiac: Leo, Sagittarius

Celestial Bodies: Mars, Moon, Sun

Energy: masculine

Other Associations: love; protection; sabbat: Yule/winter solstice

Spellwork and Ritual: attracting abundance; increasing inner strength; fertility rituals; love spells; protection against negative energy

Pine

SCOTCH PINE IS THE ONLY pine that is native to Britain; white pine was introduced in 1705. Besides the oak, pines are the most wide-ranging and successful trees in North America. White pine is prized by carpenters because it is easy to work and takes a good finish. Pine is one of the most important timber trees in the world for a wide range of commercial uses.

In addition to lumber, they also yield turpentine, tar, and pitch. Pine rosin has been especially important for violinists and other musicians to "wax" their bows. The rosin is also used for some soaps, varnishes, and sealing wax. In Germany and Sweden, resin is removed from pine needles and the loosened fibers used to make a "wool" for stuffing mattresses and cushions. This pine needle wool has also been used for blankets.

Pinyon pine nuts are edible and have been ground to make flour. Pine oil is used as an antiseptic and has been used to treat respiratory problems, bladder and kidney ailments. White pine found use in treating colds and coughs. Native Americans employed pine gum to treat boils.

The ancient Romans had a practice similar to present-day Christmas tree decorating. On the night before a major holiday, such as Saturnalia, a pine tree from a sacred grove would be cut down by priests and taken into the temple and decorated. To the Romans, pine symbolized the powers of male fertility.

On New Year's Eve in the Alsace region of France, a pine tree was decorated and the girls of the village would dance around it *a la* Maypole fashion.

If you dream of using pine wood you will have happiness. Buying pine furniture in your dream means that you will find happiness in love. Dreaming of tall straight pine trees means that you will receive good news.

Latin Name: *Pinus sylvestris* (Scotch pine), *P. strobus* (white pine), *P. resinosa* (red pine), *P. virginiana* (scrub pine), *P. aristata* (bristlecone pine)

Seasonal Details: cone-bearing evergreen with slender needles in clusters; male cones produce pollen; female cones mature in about two years

Powers/Attributes: abundance, emotions, fertility, good fortune, healing, health, immortality, love, prosperity, protection, purification, regeneration

Elements: air, fire

Ogham Character: +
Name: Ailm
Letter: A

Ogham Character: ▦
Name: Amhancholl
Letters: AE, X, XI

Rune Character: ⟨
Name: Ken
Letter: K

Feng Shui Sectors: southeast, southwest, west, north, abundance, health, longevity, negative areas

Goddesses: Aphrodite, Artemis, Astarte, Cybele, Diana, Ishtar, Isis, Venus

Gods: Attis, Bacchus, Dionysus, Hermod, Mithra, Pan, Vulcan

Other Beings/Characters: archangels Ambriel and Phanael, dwarves, elves, faeries, pitys

Other Names for Tree: the sweetest of woods, balm of Gilead

Zodiac: Cancer, Capricorn

Celestial Bodies: Jupiter, Mars

Gemstones: black opal, onyx

Wildlife: crow, jackdaw, raven

Color: black

Energy: feminine, masculine

Bach Flower Remedy: guilt

Other Associations: dates: February 28–29 and August 24–September 2; Celtic chieftain/noble tree (sources disagree whether this was pine or fir)

Spellwork and Ritual: attracting prosperity; purifying ritual areas and new homes; helping you "stay the course" during difficult times; meditation with it to alleviate dark moods

Reed

REED DOES NOT SEEM LIKE a prestigious enough plant to be considered a tree, but to the early people of the British Isles it was extremely important for warm, dry homes. Nowadays, a thatched roof is a luxury of country charm but "thatch" used to be cheap and plentiful. It was a perfect insulator to keep homes warm in winter and cool in summer. Thatch is excellent for keeping out rain, sleet, and snow, as well as insects and vermin. Depending on the type of reed, a thatched roof can last anywhere from fifteen to seventy-five years. Norfolk Reed is considered the best.

In addition to thatching for the roof, peasants in the Middle Ages used reeds for the walls of their homes. The timber framework was filled in with "wattle and daub," woven reeds that were covered in a plaster usually made by mixing mud, dung, and straw. The dirt floors were usually covered with reeds, straw, and grasses to minimize the dust and occasional animal dung—one room of the peasants' two-room cottages was usually shelter for livestock. In addition to a floor covering, reed and especially the sweetly aromatic sedge served as a room deodorizer.

In Ceylon and India, the powdered root of sedge was used as an insecticide against fleas, and perhaps the grass itself on the floor served as a way to combat these pests. When a crop of reeds was cut, the old soiled ones were removed from the floor and a new layer put in place. Reeds were an all-purpose plant for the peasantry—soaked in fat, reeds served as a cheap alternative to candles.

The word *phragmites* in reed's name comes from the Greek *phragma*, which means "hedge." The word *calamus* in sedge's name comes from the Greek *calamos*, meaning "reed." The word *acorus* comes from the Greek *acoron*, which was their name for sedge grass. This is believed to been derived from the word *coreon*, meaning cornea or pupil of the eye, because the plant was used to treat eye problems. Derived from the Gaelic *luachra* for rushes, the town name Ardlougher (*Ard-luachra*) in Ireland means "rushy height," and the name of the town Cloonlougher means "meadow of the rushes."

Reed is a long grass that grows in coastal marshes, estuaries and fresh water. It is native to the British Isles, and sedge grass was introduced around 1596.

A number of plants vie for attention as the pipes used for the Greek god Pan's musical instrument—reed is one of them. However, Pan is associated with woodlands, not wetlands where reeds thrive, thus reed may not fit the story. There has also been speculation that the Pied Piper of Hamelin played his magical tune on a reed flute. Today reed is used for woodwind instruments. Other uses included arrow shafts and writing pens.

In addition to an eye treatment, sedge has been used as a tonic for stomach ailments and to lower fever. The essential oil was used as an inhalant to ease bronchitis.

Dreaming of reeds means that not all friends are true. Handling reeds in your dream indicates that you may be deceived in business.

Latin Name: *Phragmites communis* (common reed), *Acorus calamus* (sedge)

Seasonal Details: aerial stems, April–May; flowers, late July and on; the reed is harvested in November

Powers/Attributes: growth, harmony, healing, loyalty, protection, unity, will

Element: air, earth, water

Celtic Calendar Dates: October 28–November 24

Ogham Character: #
  Name: Ngetal
  Letters: Ng

Feng Shui Sectors: center, east, southwest, negative areas

Goddesses: Coventina, Morrigan, Rhiannon

Gods: Manannan Mac Lir, Poseidon, Pwyll

Other Being/Character: Cu Chulainn

Other Names for Tree: Norfolk reed (common reed); sweet flag or myrtle grass (sedge)

Zodiac: Pisces

Celestial Bodies: Mars, Pluto

Plant: watermint

Gemstones: jasper, aquamarine, green chrysoprase

Wildlife: kingfisher, geese, owl

Color: pale green

Energy: feminine and masculine

Other Associations: direction of purpose; south; Celtic bramble tree (sources disagree whether this was reed or broom); La Fal (the stone of destiny); sabbat: Samhain

Spellwork and Ritual: expanded awareness; journeys to other realms; soul retrieval; rituals to bring harmony to your life; protection of home; balancing your energy

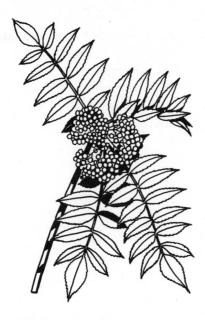

Rowan

THE FIRST PART OF ROWAN'S Latin name (its genus) means "go fowling" and comes from the practice of hunters using the berries to attract birds. Songbirds in particular are attracted to the berries, giving rowan its association with music, poetry, and the goddess Brigid. Twigs of rowan were commonly used for rune sticks. Its common name, rowan, comes from the Gaelic *rudha-an*, meaning "the red one."

In England during the fifteenth and sixteenth centuries, rowan had a negative reputation because it was linked with witchcraft, most likely because the berries carry a pentagram design at their base. During this period, herbalists avoided using it for fear of being labeled a witch.

Medicinally, rowan berry tea is still used to treat diarrhea. The berries are also high in vitamin C and have been used to fight colds and other diseases. The berries are used for jellies, jams, and wine. At one time it was believed that eating rowan berries would extend one's life.

Because of the rowan's hardiness, country folk in England either had one on their land or hung branches on their house and barns for protection. One belief related to protection was that wearing a sprig of rowan would prevent faeries from kidnapping you. Other tales tell of this tree being brought from the faery realm. Still others advised to plant it near the front door of a house to protect the occupants from evil spirits. According to Jean Markale, rowan was used by the Celts when reciting magical incantations. Since it had an association with Thor, it was planted near homes and stables to protect them from the Norse god's lightning.[1]

In the lore of the Celtic salmon of wisdom, it is sometimes rowan berries rather than hazelnuts that these fish feed upon. Rowan berries are said to have given the salmon their red spots.

Early settlers brought rowan to North America. Rowan has been called mountain ash because its leaves and bark are similar to the ash, but it is more closely related to hawthorn and apple trees. The word "mountain" is also descriptive of rowan because it does well in upland areas.

Rowan is one of the nine sacred woods for a sabbat fire in which it represents life.

Latin Name: *Sorbus americana* (American mountain ash), *S. aucuparia* (European mountain ash/rowan)

Seasonal Details: clusters of white flowers, May–June; red/orange berries, August–March

Powers/Attributes: blessings, centering, dedication, expression, fertility, grounding, healing, imagination, insight, luck, music, poetry, protection, quickening, strength

Elements: earth, fire

Celtic Calendar Dates: January 21–February 17

Ogham Character: ╥
  Name: Luis
  Letter: L

Rune Character: ᚾ
  Name: Nyd
  Letter: N

Feng Shui Sectors: center, north, northwest, west, negative areas

Goddesses: Aphrodite, Brigantia, Brigid, Cerridwen, Hecate

Gods: Dagda, Herne, Pan, Thor, Vulcan

Other Beings/Characters: elves, dragons, Fionn

Other Names for Tree: quickbeam, witch wood, sorb apple

Zodiac: Capricorn

Celestial Bodies: Moon, Saturn, Sun, Uranus

Plant: snowdrop

Gemstones: diamond, peridot, smoky quartz

Wildlife: duck, quail

Colors: gray, red

Energy: feminine

Other Associations: counteracts negative energy; dates: April 1–10 and October 4–13; sabbats: Beltane, Imbolg, Lughnasadh; Celtic peasant/common tree

Spellwork and Ritual: protection during ritual and astral travel to other realms; a powerful ally in divination; contacting elementals; enhancing psychic abilities; healing spells and rituals

---

1. Markale, *Merlin*, 117.

Spindle Tree

Spindle tree is native to Europe and western Asia where it grows in woods and scrubland areas. In England it was commonly used in hedgerows. In America, the tree's tolerance for salty air has made it a popular ornamental tree in coastal areas.

Medicinally, the European varieties have been used as a laxative; however, a small amount may be toxic and dangerous if not used properly. The word *euonymus* in its name is associated with the goddess Euronyme, the mother of the Furies. Some have speculated that spindle tree's effective purgative properties may be the reason for this connection. The herbal remedy "wahoo bark" is made from the American spindle tree root bark and is used for constipation and gallbladder problems. Most animals will not eat anything from the tree.

The wood of this tree has been popular for making lace spindles, knitting needles, skewers, and birdcages because of its hardness. Artists have found it a good material for carving as well as for charcoal made from it for drawing. Red and yellow dye from the spindle tree has been used for decorating fabric. An oil from the tree has been used in soap making and as an ingredient in cosmetics.

The spindle and the act of spinning are powerful female symbols. Various goddesses are credited with teaching humans this craft, which was vitally important for survival and comfort. Spinning was one form of woman's work that was highly prized; prior to the Industrial Revolution cloth was a valuable commodity. In addition to keeping her family clothed, an industrious woman could also provide for them by spinning enough to sell or trade. While "spinster" has come to have a nega-tive connotation for an unmarried woman, the woman who could spin well would not be trapped as anyone's dependent.

The spindle was the tool of the Fates, daughters of the goddess Necessity, who fashioned the destiny of humans. In Norse Pagan tradition, the spindle is a symbol of magic. Another name for the constellation Orion was "Freya's Spindle."

Spinning is associated with Athena because she was credited with being the inventor not only of womanly arts, but of all arts.

Latin Name: *Euonymus europaeus* (European spindle), *E. japonicus* (Japanese spindle), *E. alata* (burning bush / winged spin-dle), *E. atropurpureus* (eastern wahoo / American spindle)

Seasonal Details: small, yellow-green, four-petalled flowers in June; reddish-pink fruits in late summer; colorful autumn foliage; wahoo: dark purple flowers and purple-tinged leaves; *japonicus* is an evergreen

Powers / Attributes: attaining quests, cleansing, divination, honor, inspiration, spiritual work

Element: water

Ogham Character: ◈
Name: Oir
Letters: OI, TH

Feng Shui Sectors: north, north-east, east

Goddess: Athena, Frigg / Freya, Minerva, the Fates

Other Beings / Characters: Frau Holda

Other Names for Tree: spindle-berry, peg wood

Celestial Body: Orion

Energy: feminine

Other Associations: comfort; feminine power; seeking true self; community spirit; poetry; southeast; sabbat: Imbolg; Celtic shrub tree (sources dis-agree whether this was a shrub or peasant / common tree)

Spellwork and Ritual: cleansing rituals to heal old emotional wounds; spinning and weaving spells that bring people together; confronting shadow self or when facing difficulties; divination

Spruce

THE SYMMETRICALLY SHAPED SPRUCE IS the quintessential Christmas tree in Europe and the United States. There are approximately forty-five species of spruce that are native to Europe, Asia, and North America. It is an important timber tree for general-purpose construction for both indoor and outdoor use. During the era of sailing ships, black spruce was favored for masts. Violin makers such as Stradivari, Amati, and Bergonzi valued spruce wood for its excellent resonance. In Bavaria, Germany, only spruce and birch were used for Maypoles.

Spruce's resins are an important component of turpentine as well as ointments and liniments for muscle pain. It has also been used for rheumatism, gout, and cough medicine, as well as skin care products.

Spruce appears in legends from Europe and North America. In a Cherokee creation myth, spruce is among the trees that passed an endurance test and were given the power to remain green all year.

Black spruce was so named because from a distance the bark has a charred look. The Blue Mountains in Virginia were named after the bluish haze created by refracted light caused by naturally occurring spruce resin droplets in the air.

Norway spruce is sometimes called "red fir" because of its reddish bark as well as the confusion between spruce and fir trees. White spruce has the nickname "skunk" or "cat" spruce because of the odor that is emitted from crushed needles.

The wood of the white spruce is light and soft and has been used mainly for pulpwood, furniture, boxes, and crates.

Spruce beer is made by fermenting molasses and malt with the sap of a spruce. This brew originated in the sixteenth century to prevent scurvy.

Latin Name: *Picea abies* and *P. excelsa* (Norway spruce), *P. mariana* (black spruce), *P. glauca* (white spruce), *P. pungens* (blue spruce), *P. rubens* (red spruce)

Seasonal Details: yellow-brown (male) flowers in groups and purplish upright (female) flowers are produced on the same tree but different branches; cones mature September–November: female cones are reddish and male cones are small like catkins; needles are short, stiff, and sharp

Powers/Attributes: enlightenment, grounding, healing, hope, intuition, protection, well-being, versatility

Elements: earth, water

Rune Character: ᛗ
   Name: Dag/Dagaz
   Letter: D

Feng Shui Sectors: center, north, south, negative areas

Goddesses: Cerridwen, Cybele, Danu, Zemyna

Gods: Attis, Poseidon

Other Beings/Characters: archangel Gadreal, woodland spirits

Other Names for Tree: red fir (Norway spruce), alpine spruce (Norway spruce), German or Bavarian (Norway spruce), skunk spruce (white spruce) cat spruce (white spruce)

Wildlife: mallard duck, grouse

Zodiac: Cancer, Capricorn

Color: green

Energy: feminine

Other Associations: north; sixth chakra; sabbat: Imbolg

Spellwork and Ritual: spells for healing and protection; working with earth elementals and animals; dreamwork

Sycamore

THE FAST-GROWING SYCAMORE BELONGS TO one of the oldest groups of trees, *Platanaceae*, which have been around for more than 100 million years. It can tolerate a wide range of climates and can be found most often along streams and bottomlands. Sycamore wood is coarse grained, very hard and resistant to decay, which has made it popular for flooring, furniture, butcher blocks, and other specialty uses. A number of sycamore plantations were established in the 1960s and '70s to meet the demand for its wood.

Through misidentification as sycamore fig, the Tree of Life in ancient Egypt (*Ficus sycomorus* which is not related), sycamore has maintained its association with Egyptian deities. Hathor was believed to live in a sycamore by the side of a stream (tree and sacred water), and was called the "Lady of the Sycamore."

In India, the Trees of the Sun and of the Moon were possibly plane trees, a relative of the American sycamore. These fabled trees were said to have given prophecy to Alexander the Great and Marco Polo. An Oriental plane tree was considered so beautiful by King Xerxes of Persia (519–465 BCE) that he had gold ornaments hung from it and posted guards to keep watch over it. The king is said to have worn a gold amulet with an image of the tree. Another Oriental plane tree of Kashmir was mentioned by twelfth century travelers.

The name "ghost tree" came about because of the sycamore's pale mottled bark that gives it a ghostly appearance especially on foggy winter mornings. The tree's twigs grow in a zigzag pattern from one bud to the next, which also adds to its unusual appearance.

The American sycamore has the largest leaves of any native tree in America and the largest circumference with some measuring up to forty-nine feet. It is a favored shade tree, especially in cities, because of its resistance to pollution as well as the amount of pollutants it can remove from the air. Sycamores can live for five hundred to six hundred years. At around two hundred to three hundred years, it is fairly common for the trunks to become hollow, which in past centuries has made them convenient shelters for travelers caught in sudden bad weather. New trees will grow from the stumps if the original trees are cut down when they reach ten feet in height.

Latin Name: *Platanus occidentalis* (American sycamore), *P. acerifolia* (London plane tree), *P. orientalis* (Oriental plane tree)

Seasonal Details: small green flower clusters, April–June; seed balls on individual stems turn brown in autumn before breaking open, February–March; Old World species have more than one seed ball per stem; distinctive yellowish underbark; large maple-like leaves

Powers/Attributes: abundance, communication, immortality, love, perseverance, protection/shelter, purification, rebirth, vitality

Elements: air, water

Feng Shui Sectors: southeast, southwest, abundance, life, negative areas

Goddesses: Bhavani, Hathor, Isis, Nut

God: Osiris

Other Being/Character: Ani Hyuntikwalski

Other Names for Tree: buttonwood, ghost tree, great maple

Celestial Bodies: Jupiter, Venus

Wildlife: goldfinch

Color: pink

Energy: feminine

Other Associations: harmony; winter; summer; sabbat: Imbolg

Spellwork and Ritual: vision work as an aid to open and receive; rituals when you seek shelter and comfort from the world

Vine/Bramble

LEGEND SAYS THAT THE TUATHA De Danann brought vine with them to Ireland and that it is not native to the British Isles. The nature of Celtic interlacing design work would seem to indicate their interest in the plant, and most likely imported it to the isles when the Celts migrated from the Continent. While vines do not fit our present-day idea of trees, the Celts classified any plant with woody stems as trees. *Muine* is an Irish word meaning thicket, especially of thorny plants, and so while vine has come to include an association with the grapevine, realistically it also refers to brambles/blackberry vines that populated the hedgerows. Wine was, and still is, produced from blackberries.

There was a prohibition in the British Isles against picking and eating blackberries on or after October 10 due the folk belief that the devil spit on them, making them poisonous. According to Julia Jones and Barbara Deer, this came about because prior to the calendar change in 1752, October 10 was known as St. Michael's Day, and it was St. Michael who physically threw the devil out of heaven and into a blackberry bush.[1] The fact is, blackberries are generally past their peak at this time of year.

Like ivy, vine grows in a spiral, which is a symbol of the Mother Goddess. It is one of the sacred woods for a sabbat fire in which it represents joy. The full moon of September is called the wine moon in some traditions and rituals include wine made from blackberries. Imbolg is Brigid's sabbat and blackberry wine or juice is used in ritual.

The name of the town Ballymoney in Ireland means "the town of muine/shubbery," and the name Tinnascart means "house of the thicket." The word "bramble" comes from "brambel" or "brymbyl," which means prickly.

Since the bramble vine and holy wells were associated with Brigid, a cure for burns (she is also a fire goddess) was to dress the wound with nine bramble leaves (nine is a multiple of the magic number three) dipped in spring water. This has to be done three times to make it work.

The blackberry fruit is used for jams and teas. Its dried leaves are also made into tea. The roots produce an orange die. The ancient Greeks used blackberries as a remedy for gout, and in England the leaves were used to treat burns. Blackberries were also employed at various times to treat insect bites, loose teeth, and sore throats. The bark and root are still used for their astringent properties.

In Neolithic Europe, vine was a symbol of vital life-force energy.

Dreaming of blackberries or grapes on the vine symbolizes abundance. A vine of green leaves means that you will soon have success. Harvesting fruit from vines means that you will have a good income. Walking through a vineyard in your dream indicates prosperity.

(continued on next page)

Latin Name: *Rubus allegheniensis* (common blackberry), *R. villosus* (American blackberry), *Vitis aestivalis* (summer grape), *V. labrusca* (fox grape), *V. riparia* (riverbank grape)

Seasonal Details: blackberry: white flowers, May–July; black fruit, July–September; grape: greenish-white flowers, May–July; black or green fruit, August–October (purple or amber, fox grape; blue-black with whitish powder, riverbank grape); leaves paired with tendrils that provide support

Powers/Attributes: fertility, happiness, intellect, intuition, wealth

Element: water

Celtic Calendar Dates: September 2–29

Ogham Character: ᚋ
Name: Muin
Letter: M

Rune Character: ᚦ
Name: Thorn
Letters: Th

Rune Character: ᚹ
Name: Wunjo/Wyn
Letter: P

Feng Shui Sectors: southeast, west

Goddesses: Branwen, Brigid, Danu, Freya, Hathor

Gods: Bacchus, Dagda, Dionysus, Llyr, Osiris, Poseidon

Other Beings/Characters: faeries, Guinevere, Maenads

Other Names for Tree: bramble, brombeere, brambleberry

Zodiac: Scorpio, Taurus

Celestial Bodies: Moon, Venus

Plant: valerian

Gemstones: blue beryl, emerald

Wildlife: eagle, titmouse, white swan

Other Tree: ivy

Color: dark blue

Energy: feminine

Bach Flower Remedy: dominance and inflexibility

Other Associations: comfort; south; sabbats: Beltane, Imbolg, Lughnasadh, Mabon/autumn equinox; Celtic bramble tree

Spellwork and Ritual: rituals of celebration and for grounding; working with the faery realm; reaching deeper levels of consciousness

1. Julia Jones and Barbara Deer, *The National Trust Calendar of Garden Lore* (London: Dorlling Kindersley Ltd., 1989), 107.

Walnut

THE WALNUT WAS INTRODUCED INTO England from its native Iran by the Romans. As an offering to the Roman goddess of fruit trees, the Romans would bury a coin beneath a walnut tree. Archaeologists have found that black walnuts were a popular food with Roman people. The word *Juglan* in its name means Jove's/ Jupiter's acorn. In addition to its edible nuts, walnut oil is used in cooking.

Painters and cabinetmakers have also found the oil useful for wood finishes. Walnut wood has been used extensively for furniture since the fourteenth century in England and on the Continent. During the Renaissance in Italy and France it was the predominant wood for furniture. Wood from the black walnut is one of the most expensive in the world. Because of its resistance to decay it was widely used for waterwheels before the Industrial Revolution. Dye made from the nut husks has been used to color cloth, wood, and hair.

Black walnut leaves produce a herbicide that prevents a number of other plants from growing too close. In the competition for resources, this herbicide also inhibits walnut seedlings from growing too close to their parent trees.

Wood from the butternut is lighter in color and softer. It is easily worked and polished, and is used for interiors, cabinets, and musical instrument cases. Early American colonists used the half-ripened fruits for a yellow-brown dye. It gets its name from the practice of boiling the nuts to collect the oil that rose to the top, which was used in place of butter. Syrup was made from the boiled down sap.

Latin Name: *Juglans nigra* (black walnut), *J. cinerea* (butternut)

Seasonal Details: inconspicuous yellow-green catkins, April–June; spherical nuts (black walnut), oblong (butternut), October–November

Powers/Attributes: change, fertility, healing, inspiration, intentions, new perspectives, protection, wealth

Elements: air, fire

Feng Shui Sectors: north, northeast, southeast, west, negative areas

Goddesses: Aphrodite, Artemis, Astarte, Carmenta, Carya, Diana, Pomona, Rhea

Gods: Apollo, Jupiter, Thor, Vishnu, Zeus

Other Beings/Characters: archangel Remiel, elves

Other Name for Tree: white walnut (butternut)

Zodiac: Gemini, Leo, Virgo

Celestial Bodies: Jupiter, Sun

Gemstones: turquoise, blue topaz, sardonyx

Wildlife: eagle

Color: light blue

Energy: masculine

Back Flower Remedy: protection from change and unwanted influences

Other Associations: crown chakra; dates: April 21–30 and October 24–November 11

Spellwork and Ritual: rituals and meditations that deal with life transitions; rituals of initiation; manifesting intention into the physical realm; weather magic

Willow

WILLOW HAS BEEN USED AS a symbol of forsaken love. By wearing a sprig of willow one could subtly share one's heartache with others (or at least gain sympathy). It has a long association with dispelling sadness and darkness. Roman burial sites were planted with willows, and in Victorian England and America the willow was a popular motif for gravestones. It seems obvious that it was popular because of the "weeping" drape of branches; however, sitting under or near a willow tree helps to calm one's energy.

Beliefs swing like a pendulum—at one time it was thought that to take willow catkins indoors would bring bad luck. Medicinally, willow has been used to treat fevers and headaches. It has also been used as an aphrodisiac, sedative, and general tonic.

It is an important tree for maintaining healthy riverbanks by circumventing erosion. Willow is connected with the moon and moon goddesses because it is a tree that loves water and all waters are controlled by Luna.

Willow can teach you to go with the flow of life and be flexible. I have found willow a wonderful wood for wands. Once you befriend this tree it is very generous and will provide you with many wands and other gifts. Willow dryads tend to be curious.

Willow is one of the nine sacred woods for a sabbat fire in which it represents death. In the traditional witches' besom broom, willow is used to secure birch twigs to an ash handle.

Native Americans used willow to create fine baskets for food storage as well as for transporting babies. Sieves of willow were used to catch fish. Thin willow twigs were used to lash teepee poles together, and to create woven backrests for comfortable sitting.

Dreaming of willow means that a rival may take your love. Weaving baskets of willow in your dream means that you will receive money.

Latin Name: *Salix babylonica* (weeping willow), *S. alba* (white willow), *S. nigra* (black willow), *S. discolor* (pussy willow), *S. fragilis* (crack willow), *S. lucida* (shining willow), *S. cinerea* (European gray willow)

Seasonal Details: downy male catkins, April–June; long narrow leaves

Powers/Attributes: birth, connections, enchantment, fertility, flexibility, healing, intuition (and trusting it), knowledge, protection, relationships, wishes

Elements: fire, water

Celtic Calendar Dates: April 15–May 12

Ogham Character: ᚎ
  Name: Saille
  Letter: S

Rune Character: ᛚ
  Name: Lagu
  Letter: L

Feng Shui Sectors: northeast, east, southwest, west, northwest, negative areas

Goddesses: Artemis, Athena, Audhumla, Brigid, Ceres, Cerridwen, Circe, Danu, Diana, Hecate, Hel/Holle, Hera, Ishtar, Luna, Morrigan, Persephone

Gods: Arawen, Belenus, Loki, Mercury, Orpheus, Poseidon, Zeus

Other Beings/Characters: archangel Zadkiel, faeries, Gwion/Taliesin, Morgan le Fay

Other Name for Tree: tree of enchantment

Zodiac: Capricorn, Pisces

Celestial Bodies: Moon, Venus

Plant: primrose

Gemstones: opal, pearl, moonstone

Wildlife: deer, hare, hawk, snowy owl

Color: gray

Energy: feminine

Bach Flower Remedy: self-pity and resentment

Other Associations: death; dates: March 1–10 and September 3–12; sabbats: Beltane, Samhain; Celtic peasant/common tree

Spellwork and Ritual: love spells and divination; rituals for raising moon energy; contact with faeries and earth elementals; aid for learning to trust your intuition

Witch Hazel

WITCH HAZEL IS BEST KNOWN for the distilled astringent extract made from its bark, leaves, and twigs. It is used in general skincare as well as to treat bruises and fevers, insect bites, and varicose veins, and has been confirmed as an antioxidant and protective against radiation. A tea made from the leaves is used to treat sore throats and colds. The nutty seeds, which are said to have a flavor similar to pistachio nuts, were a source of food for Native Americans.

The word *hamamelis* in its name means that it bears flowers and fruit at the same time. Hamamelis has also been interpreted as meaning that it resembles the apple tree. The word "witch" comes from the Old English word "wice" or "wych," and meant a plant that had pliant branches. It is derived from the same Indo-European root word as the Middle English "wiker" (wicker). This was also applied to magical people who were believed to "bend" things to their will. The name "hazel" has been given to the witch hazel because its leaves are very similar to the hazelnut tree.

In England and Colonial America, forked branches were used for dowsing as well as love divination. This tree is associated with Samhain because the common variety blooms at that time of year. Perhaps its power and magic comes from its ability to bloom when most other plants are at rest during the winter.

Witch hazel was given the name snapping alder because of the loud sound the fruit pods make when they snap open to release seeds, which can be propelled twenty feet from the tree.

Latin Name: *Hamamelis virginiana* (common witch hazel), *H. mollis* (Chinese witch hazel), *H. vernalis* (spring witch hazel)

Seasonal Details: spidery yellow flowers, September–November or December–February; pods, August–October; spring witch hazel flowers, January–April

Powers/Attributes: healing, inspiration, protection, strength of will

Elements: earth, fire, water

Ogham Character: ᚌ
 Name: Amhancholl
 Letters: AE, X, XI

Feng Shui Sectors: southwest, west, health, negative areas

Other Names for Tree: winterbloom, snapping alder, spotted alder

Zodiac: Libra

Celestial Bodies: Saturn, Sun

Wildlife: deer, rabbit

Energy: masculine

Other Associations: chastity; courage; Druidic wisdom; northwest; winter; sabbat: Samhain

Spellwork and Ritual: banishing and purging; love divination; protection spells and rituals

Yew

SMALL IN APPEARANCE TO FIR, yew is one of the "seasonal trees" on the tree calendar and finishes the dark of the year on the eve of winter solstice. Fir begins the spring season the day after the solstice. Because it stands at the end of the year in the darkest time, it is associated with death and the Goddess as crone. It is also associated with the Goddess because it is an evergreen that does not seem to die each year, thus symbolizing immortality.

The Greeks and Romans used yew wood for bows, which began its association with death. The Latin, *taxus*, in its name comes from the ancient Greek word meaning "bow." In addition, the Celts frequently used yew wood for spears and shields. In later times yews were planted at burial sites because it was believed that they stood as a gateway to the otherworld. Grave goods from the late fifth century BCE in Germany included jewelry with depictions of yew foliage and berries.

According to Jean Markale, Druids used yew wood for their magic wands.[1] Shakespeare also connected it with magic as the witches in *Macbeth* use yew in casting their spells. Derived from Gaelic for yew, *eburo* or *iubhar* was the basis for the name of the people known as the Eburovices who lived in the Rhine/Main area of Germany. In Ireland, the town name of Ballinure means "the town of the yew tree," and Crockanure (*Cnoc-an-iúbhair*) means "the hill of the yew." The name of the town Aghadoe (*Achadh-dá-eó*) means "the field of two yew trees."

To the Romans, yew along with birch and oak symbolized the three pillars of wisdom. Symbolizing wisdom, stability, and sovereignty to the Celts, yew was one of the five great trees of Ireland—the Tree of Ross. Because it rarely grows in the woods with other trees, it was considered mysterious and special.

In addition to items of warfare, yew's hard wood has been used for bowls, shuttles, pegs, religious objects, and reliquary boxes. It has had limited use in cabinetry. Yew trees were popular for topiary in Elizabethan England and is still practiced in places like Clipsham Hall (Leicestershire) with its Yew Avenue. Although the leaves, seeds, and bark are poisonous to humans, the skin of the berries has been used as a laxative as well as a cardiac stimulant.

Dreaming of yew means that an aged relative may die. If you dream that you are sitting under a yew you may have a short life. However, admiring a yew in your dream means that you will have a long life.

Latin Name: *Taxus canadensis* (American yew); *T. baccata* (English yew)

Seasonal Details: evergreen with flat needles; red berries on female plants through the winter

Powers/Attributes: ancestry, change, communication with the dead, death, divinity, flexibility, immortality, longevity, rebirth, strength

Elements: air, fire, water

Ogham Character: ⏟
   Name: Iodho
   Letters: I, J, Y

Rune Character: ᚺ
   Name: Hagal
   Letter: H

Rune Character: ᛇ
   Name: Eoh/Eihwaz
   Letters: E, EI

Rune Character: ᛉ
   Name: Elihaz
   Letter: Z

Feng Shui Sectors: north, northeast, east, longevity, negative areas

Goddesses: Badb, Banba, Cailleach Beara, Hecate, Hel/Holle

Gods: Dagda, Hermes, Loki, Lugh, Odin

Other Beings/Characters: Gwion/Taliesin, Medb

Zodiac: Capricorn

Celestial Bodies: Jupiter, Mars, Saturn

Gemstones: emerald, yellow jasper

Wildlife: deer, eagle, hummingbird

Color: dark green

Energy: feminine and masculine

Other Associations: accessing the otherworld; west; date: December 20; sabbats: Ostara/spring equinox, Samhain, Yule/winter solstice; Celtic chieftain/noble tree

Spellwork and Ritual: heightening psychic abilities; aiding in drawing close to ancestors at Samhain; spells to provide physical and emotional strength during difficult times; protection

1. Markale, *Merlin*, 117.

APPENDICES

When summer lies upon the world,
　　　and in a noon of gold,
　　　Beneath the roof of sleeping leaves
　　　the dreams of trees unfold.

J. R. R. TOLKIEN
The Lord of the Rings

Trees by Date

THE FOLLOWING CALENDAR LISTS ASSOCIATED trees for each day of the year and the sabbats. This reference is based upon the dates for each month, and is applicable to any calendar year.

JANUARY		1 Apple Birch Heather	2 Birch Fir	3 Birch Fir	4 Birch Fir	5 Birch Fir
6 Birch Fir	7 Birch Fir	8 Birch Fir	9 Birch Fir	10 Birch Fir	11 Birch Fir	12 Birch Elm
13 Birch Elm	14 Birch Elm	15 Birch Elm	16 Birch Elm	17 Birch Elm	18 Birch Elm	19 Birch Elm
20 Birch Elm	21 Elm Rowan	22 Elm Rowan	23 Elm Rowan	24 Elm Rowan	25 Cypress Rowan	26 Cypress Rowan
27 Cypress Rowan	28 Cypress Rowan	29 Cypress Rowan	30 Cypress Rowan	31 Cypress Rowan		

FEBRUARY		1 Cypress Rowan	2 Cedar Cypress Rowan	3 Cedar Cypress Rowan	4 Aspen Cedar Rowan	5 Aspen Cedar Rowan
6 Aspen Cedar Rowan	7 Aspen Cedar Rowan	8 Aspen Cedar Rowan	9 Cedar Hackberry Rowan	10 Cedar Hackberry Rowan	11 Cedar Hackberry Rowan	12 Cedar Hackberry Rowan
13 Cedar Hackberry Rowan	14 Cedar Hackberry Rowan	15 Cedar Hackberry Rowan	16 Cedar Hackberry Rowan	17 Cedar Hackberry Rowan	18 Ash Cedar Hackberry	19 Ash
20 Ash	21 Ash	22 Ash	23 Ash	24 Ash	25 Ash	26 Ash
27 Ash	28 Ash Pine	29 Ash Pine	**Imbolg:** *Blackthorn, Cedar, Ivy, Rowan, Spruce, Vine/Bramble*			

MARCH		1 Willow	2 Willow	3 Willow	4 Willow	5 Willow
6 Willow	7 Willow	8 Willow	9 Willow	10 Willow	11 Linden	12 Linden
13 Linden	14 Linden	15 Linden	16 Linden	17 Linden	18 Alder Linden	19 Alder Linden
20 Alder Linden	21 Alder Oak	22 Alder Hazel	23 Alder Hazel	24 Alder Hazel	25 Alder Hazel	26 Alder Hazel
27 Alder Hazel	28 Alder Hazel	29 Alder Hazel	30 Alder Hazel	31 Alder Hazel	Ostara: *Ash, Birch, Gorse, Honeysuckle, Linden, Maple, Myrtle, Sycamore, Yew*	

APRIL		1 Alder Ash Aspen Rowan	2 Alder Ash Aspen Rowan	3 Alder Ash Aspen Rowan	4 Alder Ash Aspen Rowan	5 Alder Ash Aspen Rowan
6 Alder Ash Aspen Rowan	7 Alder Ash Aspen Rowan	8 Alder Ash Aspen Rowan	9 Alder Ash Aspen Rowan	10 Alder Ash Aspen	11 Alder Ash Aspen	12 Alder Ash Aspen
13 Alder Ash Aspen	14 Alder Ash Aspen	15 Ash Willow	16 Ash Willow	17 Ash Willow	18 Willow	19 Willow
20 Willow	21 Walnut Willow	22 Walnut Willow	23 Walnut Willow	24 Walnut Willow	25 Walnut Willow	26 Walnut Willow
27 Walnut Willow	28 Walnut Willow	29 Walnut Willow	30 Blackthorn Gorse, Linden Walnut Willow			

MAY		**1** Willow	**2** Willow	**3** Willow	**4** Willow	**5** Willow
6 Willow	**7** Willow	**8** Willow	**9** Willow	**10** Willow	**11** Willow	**12** Willow
13 Hawthorn	**14** Hawthorn	**15** Chestnut Hawthorn	**16** Chestnut Hawthorn	**17** Chestnut Hawthorn	**18** Chestnut Hawthorn	**19** Chestnut Hawthorn
20 Chestnut Hawthorn	**21** Chestnut Hawthorn	**22** Chestnut Hawthorn	**23** Chestnut Hawthorn	**24** Chestnut Hawthorn	**25** Ash Hawthorn	**26** Ash Hawthorn
27 Ash Hawthorn	**28** Ash Hawthorn	**29** Ash Hawthorn Oak	**30** Ash Hawthorn	**31** Ash Hawthorn	**Beltane:** *Apple / Crabapple, Ash, Birch, Elder, Fir, Gorse, Hawthorn, Hazel, Honey-suckle, Linden, Oak, Rowan, Vine / Bramble, Willow*	

JUNE		**1** Ash Hawthorn	**2** Ash Hawthorn	**3** Ash Hawthorn	**4** Ash Hawthorn Hornbeam	**5** Ash Hawthorn Hornbeam
6 Ash Hawthorn Hornbeam	**7** Hawthorn Hornbeam	**8** Hawthorn Hornbeam	**9** Hawthorn Hornbeam	**10** Oak Hornbeam	**11** Oak Hornbeam	**12** Oak Hornbeam
13 Oak Hornbeam	**14** Oak	**15** Oak	**16** Oak	**17** Oak	**18** Oak	**19** Oak
20 Oak	**21** Oak	**22** Oak	**23** Oak Birch	**24** Apple / Crabapple Oak	**25** Apple / Crabapple Oak	**26** Apple / Crabapple Oak
27 Apple / Crabapple Oak	**28** Apple / Crabapple Oak	**29** Apple / Crabapple Oak	**30** Apple / Crabapple Oak	**Litha:** *Elder, Heather, Holly, Linden, Mistletoe, Myrtle, Oak*		

JULY		1 Apple/ Crabapple Oak	2 Apple/ Crabapple Oak	3 Apple/ Crabapple Oak	4 Apple/ Crabapple Oak	5 Fir Oak
6 Fir Oak	7 Fir Oak	8 Fir Holly	9 Fir Holly	10 Fir Holly	11 Fir Holly	12 Fir Holly
13 Fir Holly	14 Fir Holly	15 Elm Holly	16 Elm Holly	17 Elm Holly	18 Elm Holly	19 Elm Holly
20 Elm Holly	21 Elm Holly	22 Elm Holly	23 Elm Holly	24 Elm Holly	25 Elm Holly	26 Cypress Holly
27 Cypress Holly	28 Cypress Holly	29 Cypress Holly	30 Cypress Holly	31 Cypress Holly		

AUGUST		1 Cypress Holly	2 Cypress Holly	3 Cypress Holly	4 Cypress Holly	5 Aspen Hazel
6 Aspen Hazel	7 Aspen Hazel	8 Aspen Hazel	9 Aspen Hazel	10 Aspen Hazel	11 Aspen Hazel Maple	12 Aspen Hazel Maple
13 Aspen Hazel Maple	14 Cedar Hackberry Holly Maple	15 Cedar Hackberry Holly Maple	16 Cedar Hackberry Holly Maple	17 Cedar Hackberry Holly Maple	18 Cedar Hackberry Holly Maple	19 Cedar Hackberry Holly Maple
20 Cedar Hackberry Holly Maple	21 Cedar Hackberry Holly	22 Cedar Hackberry Holly	23 Cedar Hackberry Holly	24 Hazel Pine	25 Hazel Pine	26 Hazel Pine
27 Hazel Pine	28 Hazel Pine	29 Hazel Pine	30 Hazel Pine	31 Hazel	**Lughnasadh:** *Apple/ Crabapple, Gorse, Oak, Rowan, Vine*	

SEPTEMBER

	1	2	3	4	5
	Hazel Pine	Pine Vine/Bramble	Vine/Bramble Willow	Vine/Bramble Willow	Vine/Bramble Willow
6 Vine/Bramble Willow	**7** Vine/Bramble Willow	**8** Vine/Bramble Willow	**9** Vine/Bramble Willow	**10** Vine/Bramble Willow	**11** Vine/Bramble Willow	**12** Vine/Bramble Willow
13 Linden Vine/Bramble	**14** Linden Vine/Bramble	**15** Linden Vine/Bramble	**16** Linden Vine/Bramble	**17** Linden Vine/Bramble	**18** Linden Vine/Bramble	**19** Linden Vine/Bramble
20 Linden Vine/Bramble	**21** Linden Vine/Bramble	**22** Linden Vine/Bramble	**23** Olive Vine/Bramble	**24** Hazel Vine/Bramble	**25** Hazel Vine/Bramble	**26** Hazel Vine/Bramble
27 Hazel Vine/Bramble	**28** Hazel Vine/Bramble	**29** Hazel Vine/Bramble	**30** Hazel Ivy	**Mabon:** *Aspen, Hackberry, Hickory, Locust, Magnolia, Maple, Vine/Bramble*		

OCTOBER

	1	2	3	4	5
	Hazel Ivy	Hazel Ivy	Hazel Ivy	Ivy Rowan	Ivy Rowan
6 Ivy Rowan	**7** Ivy Rowan	**8** Ivy Rowan	**9** Ivy Rowan	**10** Ivy Rowan	**11** Ivy Rowan	**12** Ivy Rowan
13 Ivy Rowan	**14** Ivy Maple	**15** Ivy Maple	**16** Ivy Maple	**17** Ivy Maple	**18** Ivy Maple	**19** Ivy Maple
20 Ivy Maple	**21** Ivy Maple	**22** Ivy Maple	**23** Ivy Maple	**24** Ivy Walnut	**25** Ivy Walnut	**26** Ivy Walnut
27 Ivy Walnut	**28** Reed Walnut	**29** Reed Walnut	**30** Reed Walnut	**31** Reed	**Samhain:** *Apple/Crabapple, Beech, Blackthorn, Gooseberry, Hazel, Locust, Reed, Willow, Witch Hazel, Yew*	

NOVEMBER		1 Reed Walnut	2 Reed Walnut	3 Reed Walnut	4 Reed Walnut	5 Reed Walnut
6 Reed Walnut	7 Reed Walnut	8 Reed Walnut	9 Reed Walnut	10 Reed Walnut	11 Reed Walnut	12 Chestnut Reed
13 Chestnut Reed	14 Chestnut Reed	15 Chestnut Reed	16 Chestnut Reed	17 Chestnut Reed	18 Chestnut Reed	19 Chestnut Reed
20 Chestnut Reed	21 Chestnut Reed	22 Ash Reed	23 Ash Reed	24 Ash Reed	25 Ash Elder	26 Ash Elder
27 Ash Elder	28 Ash Elder	29 Ash Elder	30 Ash Elder			

DECEMBER		1 Ash Elder	2 Elder Hornbeam	3 Elder Hornbeam	4 Elder Hornbeam	5 Elder Hornbeam
6 Elder Hornbeam	7 Elder Hornbeam	8 Elder Hornbeam	9 Elder Hornbeam	10 Elder Hornbeam	11 Elder Hornbeam	12 Elder
13 Elder	14 Elder	15 Elder	16 Elder Heather	17 Elder Ivy Holly	18 Elder	19 Elder
20 Elder Yew	21 Elder	22 Beech Elder Fir	23 Apple/ Crabapple Mistletoe	24 Birch Apple/ Crabapple	25 Birch Apple/ Crabapple	26 Birch Apple/ Crabapple
27 Birch Apple/ Crabapple	28 Birch Apple/ Crabapple	29 Birch Apple/ Crabapple	30 Birch Apple/ Crabapple	31 Birch Apple/ Crabapple	**Yule:** *Chestnut, Elm, Fir, Holly, Ivy, Mistletoe, Oak, Palm, Yew*	

Tools

FOLLOWING ARE A FEW BASIC instructions on how to create tools and other items mentioned in this book. Bringing things from nature into the home conveys that energy into our personal environments. As in the cycle of life, some things—especially leaves and flowers—do not last long. However, there are ways to preserve them so that they may continue to nourish our spirits.

Tools that we make ourselves are imbued with the intentions that we hold in our minds and function with powerful purpose. Whether or not you create your own Ogham or tree calendar, the tools you develop will carry your belief. Being personal tools, wands are all the more special when crafted with loving care by our own hands.

Leaves

The easiest way to identify a tree is by its leaves, which contain a great deal of their energy and embody the turning cycle of the Wheel of the Year.

Gather the most colorful fallen autumn leaves and allow them to dry. They will curl into fascinating shapes. Place them along with acorns, other nuts, or husks (the husk of the beechnut is rather interesting) on your altar or in various places around your home. These serve as a reminder of transition and change as the earth prepares for a winter's rest and we prepare for our personal journey through the dark of the year. Using leaves from a tree with which you are currently working deepens your experience and energy connection with that tree.

You may want to gather other autumn leaves to press. You don't need a flower press or any special equipment, and this can be done with leaves at any time of year. As in flower pressing, the object is to remove moisture and maintain shape. Place the leaves between two layers of paper towels and then position a large book or two on top of them to keep them flat. Autumn leaves only require a couple of days. Fresh green leaves will take longer to dry out.

Colorful autumn leaves can be just as attractive as dried flowers, and a combination of pressed and curled leaves can be used to make a wreath or table arrangement. If you have patience, gather and preserve leaves for a year to create a seasonal, Wheel of the Year wreath for your altar. This can be done quickly with items from a craft store, but when you are working with tree energy, you learn that wisdom and things of importance take time. You accumulate emotions and experiences when you invest time and work with a particular tree (or several trees). The items you gather over time can be reminders of that. If you created your own tree calendar, a wreath of this nature can serve to deepen your association with it.

Like the season, autumn leaves seem to have a fleeting moment of glory before they become brittle and crumble. Even in this state, they can be used in ritual and spellwork because they can be mixed with other tree leaves or herbs and burned in your cauldron.

If you want them to keep their shape and color, preserve them when you first bring them home. There are floral sprays available at craft and art stores that can be applied to keep them pliable. Another way to keep leaves fresh is to place their stems in a cup of glycerin just as you would cut flowers in water.

When I was a child, we used to "wax" the leaves we had collected by gently ironing them between two pieces of waxed paper. Set the iron to "wool" and be careful not to press too hard because the leaves are easily damaged. When cool, the paper can be trimmed to the shape of the leaf or cut into an oval, circle, or any shape that appeals to you. Use this method on especially colorful leaves and then hang them in a window or any place where they can be lit from behind. These are nice to keep in the house from Samhain to Yule to reflect on this time of change.

If you are keeping a journal of your work with trees, you may want to add some pictures by incorporating leaf rubbings. This can be done with fresh or dried leaves, although you will need to be particularly gentle with the dried ones. Position the leaf underneath the page where you want its image and then carefully rub the side of a pencil point or crayon over the area above the leaf. The details will be captured and like each leaf, each picture will be unique.

This technique can also be used to create a visual representation of your tree calendar. Create separate pictures for each of your tree months—or whatever time frame you use—and place them on your altar to help you reflect on its meaning.

If you like to create unique altar cloths, you can incorporate tree leaves and flowers by the pounding method. This transfers the image and colors directly to the cloth. We did this at a women's retreat I attended to create a banner that would commemorate the event.

This method requires fresh leaves and flowers, a sturdy flat surface, a small board, and a hammer. If you are working on a good table, you may want to place a layer of cardboard on the table to protect it before you start. The board only needs to be slightly larger than the leaves or flowers. Place the board on the cardboard and then place a leaf or flower, or arrange a few of them together. Lay the cloth on top of the arrangement and be careful to avoid moving anything out of position. Hold the cloth in place with one hand, and using the hammer, tap the cloth repeatedly until images of the leaves and/or flowers bleed through.

Continue tapping until the colors and image reach the desired intensity. You may want to experiment with a few scraps of material to get a feel for this before launching into an altar cloth project. Details can be added to the images by drawing with a laundry marker. There is a wide array of fabric paints available at craft stores that you can use to supplement the pounded images with text, symbols, or your own Ogham.

Experiment to find what appeals to you and brings more personal contact with tree energy into the everyday and magical aspects of your life.

Ogham Staves, Fews, and Cards

Staves (sticks) are the "classic" Ogham objects. These can be bought or made, and can be as elaborate or simple as you choose. Making your own tools imbues them with your energy as well as the tree you "know," which personalizes and makes them more powerful. The stave is a small stick or twig approximately six inches long. A set will have one for each Ogham character. You can work with the original twenty feadha, all twenty-five, or your own.

Before collecting twigs for your staves, you may want to send out the intention that you seek fallen branches. Prepare a candle (preferably brown) by scratching the full Ogham or your own Ogham on one side of it. Remember to start at the bottom. The night before you go out to collect branches, light the candle and sit in front of it. Think of where you will go, and ask the trees for their help. I've found that trees will offer gifts, and I always find more than what I'm looking for. All of my wands have come to me this way.

Collect twigs of about the same thickness. The length won't matter because you can cut them to size—sometimes cutting several staves from one branch. Remove any small side twigs and then let the wood season or dry out before working with it. This may take a couple of months depending on your local climatic conditions.

Some people prefer that the full set be from the same type of wood, others prefer each stave to be from the type of wood the Ogham character represents. This can be difficult if you don't live in an area where all the types of wood grow, especially if you are using the original Ogham. Working with vine and reed to make staves can present their own problems—finding a vine that is straight and thick enough is a challenge. The important thing is the intent used when creating them.

Once you have collected enough twigs and the wood has had time to season, lay them out on a table. Whether or not the bark should be removed is a personal preference and there is no right or wrong way. If you strip the bark off, you can leave the wood in its natural color or use a little lemon oil to bring out a rich patina. Hold each stick in turn and decide which one will be used for which character. As you work with each one, focus your mind on the tree that it is to represent. Chant the name of the tree, the Ogham character, and the letter to "fix" that tree energy to that particular stave.

Cut one end, which will be the bottom, to create a straight edge. Cut the other end on a diagonal. The flat surface of the diagonal cut is where you will carve or paint the Ogham character. Marking an object imparts symbolic power. You may want to use a color associated with the tree and Ogham letter. The character can also be burned into the wood if you have the tool and ability to do so. (There's a tool called a woodburner or pyrography tool that is available in arts and crafts or woodworkers' supply stores. Either a cone or flat tip would work well.) When not in use, tie the sticks into a bundle with a piece of yarn or ribbon and wrap them in a soft cloth.

Like Ogham staves, fews can be bought or made. Fews are usually a couple of inches long (no longer than your index finger), and can be squared or flat pieces of wood. Small wooden tiles can also be used. Check your local hardware store for square dowels that can be cut to the appropriate length. In a pinch, if you cannot find what you want, Popsicle sticks can be used.

As with the staves, take time to decide which piece will represent which tree. With flat sticks or tiles, the Ogham characters can be painted, carved, or burned on both sides. When squared pieces of wood are used, the Ogham can be written along the edge as they were on the ancient stones. Be sure to distinguish the starting point of the stem line so you will know which way to orient the Ogham character. If space allows and you are so inclined, decorate them with symbols. Since fews are small, they are usually kept in a pouch.

There are several forms of Ogham cards on the market, but they are usually not available separately from kits and books. These are easy to make using 3 x 5 index cards, which can be cut in half if you prefer smaller cards. Like the staves and fews, the cards can be as simple or decorative as you like. You can put the Ogham character, name, and letter on one side, and the tree name in English along with its attributes on the other.

Alternatively, you can put all this information on one side of the card and glue a picture of the tree on the other to create a colorful deck. Be creative—make the cards personal and meaningful to you. As with the staves and fews, when you are not using the cards, wrap them in a soft cloth, or put them in a pouch or a box. However you store them, you will want to keep them easily accessible for frequent workings.

As with other ritual or magic tools, consecrate your staves, fews, or cards before using them. If you are accustomed to casting a circle before such workings, do so. Light the brown candle on which you inscribed the Ogham. To consecrate your staves, fews, or cards, pass them through the smoke of incense or burning herbs such as sage, mugwort, or lavender. If using herbs, you might also want to crumble a dried leaf into the mix. As you do this you may want to call on Ogma, Danu, and the Dagda (or however you address the Divine) to bless your tools and their purpose.

Wands and Walking Sticks

For many years I had not used a wand in ritual or even given it a thought until one presented itself to me. Knowing that it is important to be open to receive information during magic work as well as everyday life, I didn't ignore the image that popped into my mind when I noticed a fallen tree branch. It was as if I were looking at one picture superimposed over another: the branch with the wand inside.

I picked up the branch and continued my walk, getting a feel for the future wand in my hand. There were no leaves attached to the branch and only a few tiny side twigs. When I returned home, I wasn't quite sure what to do with it. I knew very little about wand making at that point, but I had a feeling this one would "tell" me what I needed to know. It did, and so my first wand emerged into this world.

Wands can be natural and simple, or as elaborately decorated as you like. I prefer the branches to be gifts from the trees and I collect fallen ones for the wand making workshops I teach. However, if you feel the need to make a wand and you cannot find a branch of the proper size, cut one from a tree. Seek its permission first by spending time with it. Touch its trunk and let it know your intentions. Be sure to leave an offering.

When making a wand, consider the type of wood. Match the tree's attributes to the purpose of your wand, or if you are particularly attracted to a certain tree, use it. In addition, you may want to collect or cut a branch during a certain phase of the moon or at a specific time of year. This is an entirely personal matter. As with the Ogham sticks, you may want to do a ritual or meditation before heading out to the woods (or wherever) to send forth your intention and ask for blessings and guidance.

The length of a wand varies according to one's practice. Some say it should measure from the elbow to the tip of the middle finger, others say shorter. Work with whatever fits your background, training, and personal preference. If a longer or shorter wand seems appropriate to you, that's the length you should use. You will rarely find a branch of the exact length, so look for one that is longer and thicker than you envision your finished wand to be. If you think of your wand as being perfectly straight, look for that sort of branch. Or if you prefer, look for one with a slight curve at one end, which can provide a comfortable handle. If you are collecting fallen branches, take several that seem right. When you get home, cut them slightly longer than you intend the finished wand to be, and then heft them one by one. Check how each one feels in your hand and make your selection. If you plan to remove the bark and do some carving, you will want to choose one that is slightly fatter. Set it aside for a couple of months to allow the wood to season or dry out. If it is a damp or wet time of year, the process may take longer. If you live in a dry climate, the time will be shorter.

While the wood is seasoning, take time to plan what you will do. You may want to carve or paint sacred symbols and runes or use the Ogham to inscribe your name or whatever is appropriate for your practice. Inscriptions can also be burned into the wood. Decide if you will leave the bark on or remove it. If you leave the bark on, any inscriptions or symbols that you carve will reveal a light inner bark and contrast with the darker outer bark. If you remove the bark, decide whether or not to stain the wood.

Some people like to wrap ribbon, yarn, or strips of leather at one end to create a handle. Alternatively, you can carve it to create a handle, as well as hollow one end and then put something inside. Crystals or other objects can be attached if you feel these will enhance your own energy as it passes through the wand.

Most of the work can be done with an X-acto knife; however, a few basic—and I mean very basic—woodworking tools can be useful. Most arts and crafts stores carry an inexpensive four or five-piece set. There are two tools that I found most useful from this type of set: one has a V-shaped blade, and the other has a narrow, slightly curved blade. The former is good for inscriptions, especially the Ogham; the latter is good for scooping out the tip for a crystal as well as hollowing the handle. Refer to the list at the end of this section for the things you will need.

Spread out newspapers on a table or other flat work surface. Begin by removing small side twigs and then the bark (if you decided to do this). Use a straight-edged woodworking tool or an X-acto knife. Gently work from one end to the other, removing the top layer or outer bark. Be careful not to make gouges. The inner bark is usually much smoother and pleasant to touch. As you work, you may want to chant, or recite poetry or a spell to begin your magical association with the wand.

If you plan to differentiate the handle from the shaft, decide where the handle ends. Generally, this should be a little longer than your hand is wide. You can make this differentiation by simply staining them separate colors or different shades of the same color. You can carve a groove to mark where the handle ends, whittle the shaft to make it more narrow, or do both to make it very distinguishable. Cut the bottom of the handle end straight across. The shaft can also be tapered, but if you are going to use a crystal be sure not to taper it too much.

Once you decide on the type of crystal, place the tip of your wand on a piece of paper and draw a circle around it. Take this along with you when you go to buy or find your crystal and remember that the stone needs to fit well within the circle. If possible, look for a crystal point that is relatively flat on one end.

To fit the crystal to the wand, begin to carve out the tip with the X-acto or straight edge and then switch to the narrow, slightly curved woodworking tool. This can be tedious because you will need to constantly check the fit of the crystal. Chanting can be multi-purpose in that it can keep part of your brain engaged as you begin your magical association with the wand. Once you get the crystal to fit snugly, stop carving, remove the crystal and set it aside. Setting the crystal in place should be done last, especially if you are going to stain or paint the wand. When you come to that final step, use a little bit of jewel glue to secure the crystal in place.

After you've whittled the shaft and handle, use sandpaper to smooth the surface. Also sand down the remnants of side twigs. After carving symbols or words into the wand, lightly sand the area to give it a smooth finish.

If you are going to place anything within the handle, you will need to hollow it out. Begin with the X-acto and then use the narrow, slightly curved woodworking tool. If you are good with power tools, you could use a drill to bore into the handle. I am not adept with such tools, nor did I want to damage the wand (or my hands), so I used the drill bit and manually twisted it into the handle. If your wand is slightly curved, be careful not to drill a hole through the side of the wood. Once you place whatever you want inside the handle, use wood filler to seal it. Stain or paint the wand, attach the crystal, and you are ready to consecrate it.

Basic items needed for wand making:

- X-acto knife or small straight-edge blade

- V-shaped woodworking tool

- Narrow, slightly curved woodworking tool

- Sandpaper

- Jewel glue (if you are attaching a crystal)

- Water-based wood stain and sealer or stenciling paint

- Stainable wood filler

If you spend any amount of time in the woods, you know the value of a walking stick. It is worth the time and effort to use these same methods for creating your own special and magical walking stick. The main difference, of course, is that a walking stick is much larger.

When looking for a stick, be sure to get out to the woods as soon as you can after a storm to search for fallen branches. Look for one (or several and make your final choice later) that is longer and thicker than you envision your finished stick. Since the bark will be removed, the branch sanded and possibly carved, you don't want to end up with a stick that is too thin.

As with a wand, allow the wood to dry out before you begin working with it. Once you remove the bark you may have a lot of sanding to do. Start with a coarse sandpaper, especially if there are knotholes and stubs of removed twigs. Even though this can be a lengthy process, I find that doing the sanding by hand gives me time to get to know the wood and the particular branch. It is also a good way to slow down and get into the rhythm of the tree energy. In modern life we tend to expect immediate results and just want to "get the job done." Ignore these impulses and listen for the whispers from the woods to guide you.

Making a walking stick may be a longer project than you originally anticipated, but why rush? Put time and loving care into it. Use your work time as time for meditation or an inward journey. Make your work time a special part of a day or weekend that you set aside to think about your spiritual journey. Make it a sacred act to work on your walking stick (and wand for that matter). Enjoy the work and live the magic.

Associated Goddesses, Gods, and Others

FOLLOWING IS A LIST OF goddesses, gods, and other beings and characters mentioned in part 2. This is not intended to be a comprehensive guide to the plethora of their aspects; however, knowing the lands of their origins and correspondences to other gods and goddesses will give you enough information to pursue more details if you are interested.

Goddesses

Áine—Celtic (Ireland), goddess of healing, fertility, love, and prosperity; known as the celebrated banshee of Munster; associated with Danu and the Morrigan

Amaterasu—Japanese, sun goddess

Aphrodite—Greek, goddess of love, beauty, and sexual delight

Ardvi—Persian, heavenly goddess known as the Mother of the Stars

Arianrhod—Celtic (Welsh), goddess of beauty, fertility, and reincarnation

Arinna—Anatolia, sun goddess

Artemis—Roman, goddess of all wild things, protector of women; counterpart to Greek Diana

Ashtoreth—Hebrew, goddess of fertility; variation of Astarte and Ishtar

Astarte—Semitic/Phoenician, goddess of love and fertility

Astraea—Greek, goddess of justice

Athena—Greek, goddess of wisdom and war

Audhumla—Norse, primal goddess who appeared as a cow

Badb—Celtic (Ireland), goddess of enlightenment, wisdom, and life; sister to Morrigan

Banba—Celtic (Ireland), one of the triple goddesses who represent the spirit of Ireland

Bastet/Bast—Egyptian, protective goddess; depicted with the head of a cat; daughter of Ra

Bertha—Norse, goddess of spinning

Bhavani—Kashmiri, goddess of shrines

Boann—Celtic (Ireland), goddess of bounty and fertility, and the spirit of the River Boyne

Branwen—Celtic (Wales), goddess of love and beauty; daughter of Llyr and sister to Bran and Manawydan

Brigantia—Celtic (England), goddess of rivers and water; possibly linked with or a variation on Brigid

Brigid—Celtic (Ireland), goddess of holy wells, crossroads, metal crafts, healing, poetry; daughter of the Dagda, became Christianized as St. Brigette

Cailleach Beara—Celtic (Ireland), goddess of sovereignty, crone aspect of the Great Goddess

Calypso—Greek, goddess of light

Carmenta—Roman, goddess of prophecy; one of the Camenae, variation of the Muses

Carya—Greek, goddess with the gift of prophecy who turned into a walnut tree

Ceres—Roman, goddess of agriculture, especially grain; counterpart to Demeter

Cerridwen/Kerridwen—Celtic (Wales), goddess of death, initiation and magic; also call Dark Mother; also spelled Ceridwen or Keridwen

Circe—Greek, goddess of darkness and wisdom

Coventina—Celtic (England), mother goddess associated with water and springs

Cybele—Roman, goddess of fertility/Mother Earth; lover of Attis

Danu/Dana—Pan-Celtic, Great Mother Goddess, supreme divinity

Demeter—Greek, goddess of agriculture, especially grain

Devaki—Hindu, mother goddess

Devi—Hindu, universal goddess

Diana—Greek, goddess of the moon, goddess of the hunt, sister to Apollo

Disir—Norse, guardian goddesses of men who appear in dreams of warning

Domna—Celtic (Ireland), goddess of sacred stones

Eostre—Norse, goddess of spring, rebirth and fertility; also known as Ostara, Eos and Aurora

Epona—Celtic (Gaul), goddess associated with horses, their power and speed; also associated with fertility and dreams

Fand—Celtic (Ireland), goddess of love and desire; wife of Manannan Mac Lir; lover of Cu Culhainn

Fates—Greek, daughters of the mother goddess, Necessity, who shaped the destiny of people

Felicitas—Roman, goddess of good luck and joy

Ferona—Roman, goddess of fertility and woodlands

Fides—Roman, goddess of faithfulness

Fortuna—Roman, goddess of luck and prosperity

Freya—Norse, goddess of love, fertility, sensuality and sex

Frigg—Norse, goddess of love, fertility, marriage, motherhood; also goddess of spinning who knew the fate of all people

Gaia—Greek (but of older origin), earth goddess; Great Mother Goddess

Grainne—Celtic (Ireland), goddess of the sun; faery queen of Leinster; sister of Áine

Hathor—Egyptian, goddess of love, music, and beauty; she was known as the "Eye of Ra"

Hebe—Greek, goddess of youth; wife of Hercules

Hecate—Greek (but of older origin), goddess of witchcraft, and birth and death; also known as the Dark Mother

Hel/Holle—Norse, goddess of death and the underworld; she was known by both names as well as Frau Holda in Germany; the Christian "Hell" was named after her

Hera—Greek, goddess of marriage and women in general; Queen of Heaven; wife of Zeus

Hestia—Greek, goddess of hearth and home

Hina—Hawaiian, goddess of the moon

Iduna—Norse, goddess of eternal youth

Ilmater—Finnish, goddess of water; also a mother goddess

Inanna—Sumerian, goddess of heaven and earth; her consort was Dumuzi; variation of Ishtar

Ishtar—Babylonian, mother goddess; her consort was Tammuz; variation of Inanna

Isis—Egyptian, goddess of love, nurturing, and magic; wife of Osiris

Izanami—Japanese, mother goddess of Shinto legends

Juno—Roman, queen of the gods; sister and wife of Jupiter

Kali—Hindu, dark goddess of destruction

Kore—Roman, goddess of the underworld who guided the dead to rest; daughter of Ceres; counterpart to Greek Persephone

Kwan Yin—Asian, goddess of compassion

Lada—Slavic, goddess of love, beauty, and springtime

Luna—Roman, goddess of the moon, cycles, and life

Ma'at—Egyptian, goddess of truth, balance, and order

Macha—Celtic (Ireland), war goddess; mother of life and death

Maia—Roman, goddess of growth and springtime; daughter of Atlas

Medeine—Lithuanian, goddess of woodlands

Minerva—Greek, goddess of wisdom and inspiration

Morrigan—Celtic (Ireland), goddess of fertility, battle, and strife; she is both an individual and triple goddess

Muses—Greek, goddesses who preside over and inspire the arts

Nanna—Norse, goddess of flowers

Nehalennia—Netherlands, goddess of abundance and protection to seafarers

Nemesis—Greek, goddess of vengeance and retribution

Nephthys—Egyptian, goddess of death who ruled the unseen world

Nut—Egyptian, mother of the sun, moon, and heavens

Pales—Roman, goddess of shepherds

Parvati—Hindu, goddess of love; one aspect of the goddess Devi; wife of Shiva

Pele—Hawaiian, goddess of fire, volcanoes, and passion

Persephone—Greek, goddess of the underworld who guided the dead to rest; daughter of Demeter

Philyra—Greek, goddess of beauty, healing, and writing; a shape-shifter

Pomona—Roman, goddess of cultivated gardens

Ran—Norse, goddess of sea storms; wife of Aegir

Rhea—Greek, mother of the gods; daughter of Gaia

Rhiannon—Celtic (Wales), goddess of transformation, rebirth, and wisdom

Sekhmet—Egyptian, goddess of strength who wages war against evil

Sif—Norse, goddess of crops, corn, and fertility

Sophia—Greek (possibly of older origin), a very ancient goddess of wisdom

Syn—Norse, goddess of trials; the defender and protector

Tamar—Canaanite, goddess of birth, nourishment, and prophecy; earth goddess

Tiamat—Babylonian, dark goddess of destruction, death, and regeneration

Trivia—Roman, goddess of crossroads and magic

Uroica—Breton, summer goddess of heather and heather wine

Ursala—Slavic, moon goddess

Venus—Roman, goddess of love and beauty

Vesta—Roman, goddess of hearth and home; counterpart to Greek Hestia

Yaya Zakurai—Japan, cherry tree goddess

Zemyna—Lithuanian, earth goddess

Gods

Abellio—Celtic (Gaul), god of apple trees

Adonis—Greek, god of fertility and abundance; lover of Aphrodite

Aegir—Norse, god of shore and ocean

Aengus Mac Og—Celtic (Ireland), god of youth, love, and beauty; son of the Dagda and Boann

Aesculapius—Greek, god of medicine; also spelled Asclepius

Amaethon—Celtic (Wales), god of agriculture

Amen—Egyptian, creation deity; the eternal transformer; Amenet is his consort

Apollo—Greek, god of music, fine arts, and prophecy

Arawen—Celtic (Wales), god of the underworld

Ares/Aries—Greek, god of war

Attis—Roman (imported from Persia), god of vegetation and fertility; son of Cybele

Bacchus—Roman (counterpart to Dionysus), god of wine; son of Jupiter

Balder—Norse, god of light and love

Bel/Belenus—Celtic (Gaul), creation god, sun god, god of fire; variation of Beli/Bíle, Beli Mawr

Beli/Bíle—Celtic (Ireland), creation god associated with the oak tree; consort of Danu; variation of Bel/Belenus, Beli Mawr

Beli Mawr—Celtic (Wales), sun god; variation of Bel/Belenus, Beli/Bíle; the name/word Bíle was also used to designate an ancient tree

Bran—Celtic (Wales), god of inspiration and protection of Bards; also known as Bran the Blessed; son of sea god Llyr and brother of Branwen

Cernunnos—Celtic (Wales), horned god representing the spirit of nature; variation of Kernunnos

Cupid—Roman (counterpart of Eros), god of love

Dagda—Celtic (Ireland), the "all father" god of wisdom, protector of crops; god of plenty; consort of Boann and father of Brigid and Aengus

Dionysus—Greek, god of fertility and wine

Donar/Thunar—Teutonic, god of thunder; variation of Thor

Dumuzi—Sumerian, god of vegetation; consort to Inanna; variation of Tammuz

Eros—Greek, god of love

Frey—Norse, god of sun and rain, the harvest, peace, and war

Gwynn ap Nudd—Celtic (Wales), lord of the underworld/Annwn

Helios—Greek, sun god

Hercules—Roman, greatest mortal hero who was turned into a god by Jupiter; variation of Greek Heracles

Hermes—Greek, god of trade; winged messenger of the gods

Hermod—Norse, messenger of the gods

Herne—Celtic, horned god of the hunt

Horus—Egyptian, sky god; ruler of the day

Ixtlilton—Aztec, god of healing, medicine, and feasting

Janus—Roman, god of beginnings

Jove/Jovyn—Roman, older names of Jupiter

Jupiter—Roman (counterpart of Zeus), god of the gods; defender of the state

Kernunnos—Celtic (Gaul), god of nature, fertility, and plenty; variation of Cernunnos

Krishna—Hindu, the eighth avatar/earthly incarnation of Vishnu.

Kronos—Roman, god of the universe and time; counterpart to Greek Cronos

Lir/Llyr—Celtic (Ireland/Wales respectively), sea god

Loki—Norse, god and trickster

Lugh—Celtic (Ireland), sun god and god of crafts and arts; a Tuatha De Danann

Manannan Mac Lir—Celtic (Ireland/Wales), sea god with powers of magic and storms; son of Lir; variation of the Welsh Manawydan ap Llyr

Mars—Roman, god of war; son of Juno

Mercury—Roman (counterpart of Hermes), god of commerce and speed

Mithra—Persian, god of the sun; later adopted by the Romans

Neptune—Roman, god of the sea and waters

Nuada—Celtic (Ireland), god of harpers, healing, and poetry; king of Tuatha De Danann

Odin—Norse, god of death, poetry, wisdom, and war

Ogma—Celtic (Ireland), god of eloquence and language; devised the Ogham alphabet

Osiris—Egyptian, god of the dead and ruler of the underworld; consort to Isis

Pan—Greek, god of nature and the woods

Percunis—Prussian, thunder god associated with oaks; variation of Thor

Perkunas—Lithuanian, god of thunder and lightning; variation of Thor

Perun—Slavic, god of thunder and oak trees; variation of Thor

Poseidon—Greek, god of earthquakes and floods; lord of the seas

Prometheus—Greek, god of creation and evolution

Proteus—Greek, old sea god and herdsman for Poseidon's seals

Pryderi—Celtic (Wales), son of Pwyll

Pwyll—Celtic (Wales), god of cunning who aided Arawen and was god of the underworld for a year

Quetzalcoatl—Aztec, god of civilization; one of the gods of wind

Ra (Amun-Ra)—Egyptian, god of the sun, power and wealth

Saturn—Roman, god of the harvest

Seth—Egyptian, god of storms and chaos

Shiva—Hindu, god of transformation; husband of Parvati

Silvanus—Roman, god of woodlands and forests

Tammuz—Babylonian, god of vegetation and the harvest; variation of Dumuzi

Thor—Norse, god of thunder, protection, and war

Thoth—Egyptian, god of sacred writing, wisdom, and magic

Tyr—Norse, god of war and justice

Vertumnus—Roman, presides over the change of seasons, known for shape-shifting

Vishnu—Hindu, god who sustains the universe

Vulcan—Roman, god of fire, craft, and metalwork

Woden—Anglo-Saxon/Teutonic, god of the hunt, war, poetry, and learning

Zeus—Greek, god of the gods and men

Zoroaster/Zarathustra—Persian, ancient mystical priest and philosopher

Other Beings and Characters

Aeneas—Greek, hero of Virgil's *The Aeneid*; son of Aphrodite and Anchises, the Trojan

Ani Hyuntikwalski—Cherokee, thunder beings who send fire to earth in a hollow sycamore tree to provide warmth for the world

Blodeuwedd—Celtic (Wales), known as the Lady of Flowers; created for hero Llew Llaw Gyffes who was forbidden to have a human wife

Cu Chulainn—Celtic (Ireland), great hero of Ulster

Cyparissus—Greek, an attendant to Apollo who could not find consolation after accidentally killing his favorite stag

Daphne—Greek, nymph who avoided Apollo's advances by being turned into a laurel tree

Dryads—Greek, female spirits of groves and forests

Eurydice—Greek, a nymph who died of a snake bite and was almost brought back from the underworld by her husband, Orpheus

Fionn—Celtic (Ireland), Fionn Mac Cumhaill, leader of the Fianna, the standing army circa the third century CE

Gwern—Celtic (Wales), son of Branwen and Irish king Matholwch; his name means "alder tree"

Gwion Bach/Taliesin—Celtic (Wales), apprentice of Cerridwen; great poet; some sources consider him a god of magic and shape-shifting

Gwydion—Celtic (Wales), a powerful magician who transformed the trees into warriors in the *Câd Goddeu*, *The Battle of the Trees*

Hamadryads—Greek, nymphs who live and die within one tree

Hylde-moer/Hylde-vinde—Russian, forest spirits that dwell in elder trees; also known as Elder Mother

Kirnis—Lithuanian, guardian spirit of forests

Ljesch—Slavic, divine spirit beings who lived in the tops of birch trees; also known as the genii of the forest

Maenads—Greek, nymphs associated with Dionysus

Medb—Celtic (Ireland), queen of Connacht who made battle with Ulster and the hero warrior Cu Culhainn; Ailill was her consort-king

Milesians—Celtic (Ireland), the last mythic invaders of Ireland who drove the Tuatha De Danann into the hollow hills/sídhe

Olwen—Celtic (Wales), A Celtro-Arthurain heroine

Orpheus—Greek, musician who played and sang so well that wild animals were tamed and rivers stopped to listen; husband to Eurydice

Pitys—Greek, a nymph who was changed into a pine tree

Theseus—Greek, hero who killed the Minotaur

Thunderbird—Native American (multiple tribes), a great eagle that created thunder with the flap of its wings and lightning by a glance of its eye; believed to be the Great Spirit by some tribes

Bibliography

Altman, Nathaniel. *Sacred Trees*. San Francisco: Sierra Club Books, 1994.

Baggott, Andy. *Celtic Wisdom*. London: Piatkus Publishers, Ltd., 1999.

Cahill, Thomas. *How the Irish Saved Civilization: The Untold Story of Ireland's Heroic Role from the Fall of Rome to the Rise of Medieval Europe*. New York: Doubleday, 1995.

Campanelli, Pauline and Dan. *Wheel of the Year: Living the Magical Life*. St. Paul, MN: Llewellyn Publications, 1995.

Carr-Comm, Philip. *In the Grove of the Druids: The Druid Teaching of Ross Nichols*. London: Watkins Publishing, 2002.

Chaline, Eric. *Gods and Goddesses*. New York: HarperEntertainment, 2004.

Codding, Dana. "Tree Ring Research Yields Clues To Pacific Climate Change," *The Ring The University of Victoria's Community Newspaper*, February 18, 2000.

Conway, D. J. *By Oak, Ash & Thorn: Modern Celtic Shamanism*. St. Paul, MN: Llewellyn Publications, 1997.

———. *Celtic Magic*. St. Paul, MN: Llewellyn Publications, 2002.

———. *Norse Magic*. St. Paul, MN: Llewellyn Publications, 1990.

Cotterell, Arthur, and Rachel Storm. *The Ultimate Encyclopedia of Mythology*. New York: Hermes House, 1999.

Cowan, Tom. *Fire in the Head: Shamanism and the Celtic Spirit*. New York: HarperCollins Publishers, 1993.

Cullina, William. *Native Trees, Shrubs and Vines*. New York: Houghton Mifflin, 2002.

Cunningham, Scott. *Encyclopedia of Magical Herbs*. St. Paul, MN: Llewellyn Publications, 1998.

Davies, John. *The Celts: Prehistory to Present Day*. London: Cassell & Co., 2002.

Devereux, Paul. *Shamanism and the Mystery Lines: Ley Lines, Spirit Paths, Shape-shifting & Out-of-Body Travel*. St. Paul, MN: Llewellyn/Quantum, 1993.

Dobelis, Inge N., ed. *Magic & Medicine of Plants*. Pleasantville, NY: The Reader's Digest, 1986.

Dolan, Ronald E., and Robert L. Worden, eds. *Japan: A Country Study*. Washington, DC: Federal Research Division of the Library of Congress, 1992.

Dunwich, Gerina. *The Wicca Book of Days*. New York: Citadel Press, 1995.

Ellis, Peter Berresford. *The Chronicles of the Celts*. New York: Carroll & Graf Publishers, Inc., 1999.

———. *The Druids*. New York: Carroll & Graf Publishers, Inc., 2002.

———. "The Fabrication of 'Celtic' Astrology." *The Astrological Journal* 39, no. 4 (1997).

Fell, H. Barry, ed. "The Ogam Scales of the Book of Ballymote." *The Epigraphic Society Occasional Papers* 22, part II (1993).

———. "Old Irish Rock Inscriptions from West Virginia: Ogam Translated." *The Epigraphic Society Occasional Papers* 11, no. 252 (1983).

Fenyvesi, Charles. *Trees: For Shelter and Shade; For Memory and Magic*. New York: St. Martin's Press, 1992.

Ferguson, Diana. *The Magickal Year: A Pagan Perspective on the Natural World*. London: Labyrinth Publishing, 1996.

Flanagan, Laurence. *Ancient Ireland: Life Before the Celts*. Dublin: Gill & Macmillan Ltd., 2000.

Fontana, David. *The Meditator's Handbook: A Comprehensive Guide to Eastern and Western Meditation Techniques*. Rockport, MA: Element, Inc., 1994.

Fowler, Brenda. *Iceman: Uncovering the Life and Times of a Prehistoric Man Found in an Alpine Glacier*. New York: Random House, 2000.

Gimbutas, Marija. *The Civilization of the Goddess*. New York: HarperCollins Publishers, 1991.

———. *The Language of the Goddess*. New York: HarperCollins Publishing, 1991.

Gore, Belinda. *The Ecstatic Body Postures: An Alternative Reality Workbook*. Rochester, VT: Bear & Company, 1995.

Graves, Robert. *The White Goddess: A Historical Grammar of Poetic Myth*. New York: The Noonday Press, Farrar, Straus and Giroux, 1975.

Green, Miranda J. *The Celtic World*. New York: Penguin, 1995.

———. *The World of the Druids*. New York: Thames and Hudson, Inc., 1997.

Hameroff, Stuart. "Breathrough Study on EEG of Meditation." *Science & Consciousness Review*, June 2005, no. 1.

Harte, Jeremy. *The Green Man*. Andover, Hampshire, England: Pitkin Unichrome, Ltd., 2001.

Hatch, Peter. "Tree Preservation at Monticello." St. Louis, MO: The Society of Municipal Arborists, *City Trees*, 37, no. 2 (March/April 2001).

Heinrich, Bernd. *The Trees in My Forest*. New York: Cliff Street Books, 1997.

Hessayon, D. G. *The Tree & Shrub Expert*. Waltham Cross, England: PBI Publications, 1983.

Holden, Edith. *The Country Diary of an Edwardian Lady: Nature Notes from 1906*. London: Sphere Books, 1977.

Hope, Murray. *Practical Celtic Magic*. London: The Aquarian Press, 1987.

Hulse, David Allen. *The Western Mysteries*. St. Paul, MN: Llewellyn Publications, 2000.

Hutchins, Ross E. *This Is a Tree*. New York: Dodd, Mead & Company, 1964.

Jackson, Kenneth Hurlston. *A Celtic Miscellany: Translations from the Celtic Literatures*. Harmondsworth, England: Penguin Books Ltd., 1982.

Johnsen, Jan, and John C. Fech. *Trees*. Des Moines, IA: Meredith Books, 1999.

Jones, Julia, and Barbara Deer. *The National Trust Calendar of Garden Lore*. London: Dorlling Kindersley Ltd., 1989.

Joyce, P. W. *Irish Place Names*. Belfast: Appletree Press Ltd. (no date given).

Kessler, George D., and Roland E. Schoenike. *Familiar Trees of South Carolina: A Manual for Tree Study*. Clemson, SC: PSA Publishing, Clemson University, 1998.

Kinsella, Thomas, trans. *The Táin Bó Cuailnge*. Oxford: Oxford University Press, 1969.

Knight, Sirona. *Faery Magic: Spell, Potions, and Lore from the Earth Spirits*. Franklin Lakes, NJ: New Page Books, 2003.

Kynes, Sandra. *Gemstone Feng Shui*. St. Paul, MN: Llewellyn Publications, 2002.

———. *A Year of Ritual: Sabbats and Esbats for Solitaries and Covens*. St. Paul, MN: Llewellyn Publications, 2004.

Leeming, David, and Jake Page. *Myths of the Female Divine Goddess*. Oxford: Oxford University Press, 1996.

Macalister, R. A. Stewart. *The Secret Languages of Ireland*. Cambridge: University Press, 1937.

MacIntyre, Tom. "Mind the Trees." *Ireland of the Welcomes Magazine*, vol. 39, no. 1, 1990.

Mackillop, James. *Oxford Dictionary of Celtic Mythology*. Oxford: Oxford University Press, 1998.

MacManus, Seumas. *The Story of the Irish Race*. Old Greenwich, CT: The Devin-Adain Co., 1990.

Marinelli, Janet, ed. *Going Native: Biodiversity in Our Own Backyards*. Brooklyn, NY: Brooklyn Botanic Gardens Publications, 1994.

Markale, Jean. *The Celts: Uncovering the Mythic and Historic Origins of Western Culture*. Rochester, VT: Inner Traditions International, 1993.

———. *Merlin: Priest of Nature*. Rochester, VT: Inner Traditions International, 1995.

Martin, Laura C. *The Folklore of Trees & Shrubs*. Chester, CT: The Globe Pequot Press, 1992.

Matthews, Caitlin and John. *Encyclopedia of Celtic Wisdom: A Celtic Shaman's Sourcebook*. Rockport, MA: Element Books, Inc., 1994.

Mehta, Silva, Mira Mehta, and Shyam Mehta. *Yoga: The Iyengar Way*. New York: Alfred A. Knopf, 1995.

Mercer, Derrick, ed. *Exploring Unspoilt Britain and Northern Ireland*. London: The National Trust Octopus Books, 1989.

Murphey, Edith van Allen. *Indian Uses of Native Plants*. Ukiah, CA: Mendocino County Historical Society, 1987.

The National Arbor Day Foundation, http://www.arborday.org/trees/.

Newberg, Andrew, Eugene G. d'Aquili, and Vince Rause. *Why God Won't Go Away: Brain Science and the Biology of Belief*. New York: Ballantine Books, 2002.

Nowak, David J. "Tree Species Selection, Design and Management to Improve Air Quality." Annual Meeting Proceedings. Washington, DC: American Society of Landscape Architects, 2000.

Ó Broin, Toma. "Lia Fáil: Fact and Fiction in the Tradition." Dublin: Dublin Institute for Advanced Studies, *Celtica*, 21 (1990).

Pepper, Elizabeth. *Celtic Tree Magic*. Newport, RI: The Witches' Almanac Ltd., 1996.

Pepper, Elizabeth, and John Wilcock. *The Witches' Almanac*. Newport, RI: The Witches' Almanac, Ltd., 1986–2003.

Petrides, George A. *A Field Guide to Trees and Shrubs*. Boston, MA: Houghton Mifflin, 1972.

Rolleston, T. W. *Celtic Myths and Legends*. New York: Dover Publications, 1990.

Service, Alastair, and Jean Bradbery. *The Standing Stones of Europe*. London: Weidenfeld & Nicolson, 1996.

Skafte, Dianne. *Listening to the Oracle: The Ancient Art of Finding Guidance in the Signs and Symbols All Around Us*. New York: HarperSanFrancisco, 1997.

Spivey, Nigel. *The Ancient Olympics*. Oxford: Oxford University Press, 2004.

Stephanich, Kisma K. *Faery Wicca: Book One*. St. Paul, MN: Llewellyn Publications, 1996.

Suzuki, David. *The Sacred Balance: A Vision of Humanity's Place in Nature*. Four-part video series. Toronto: Kensington Communications, 2003.

Tsai, Allen. "Where Does the Yin Yang Symbol Come From?," http://www.chinese fortunecalendar.com/yinyang.htm.

Wolfe, Amber. *Elemental Power*. St. Paul, MN: Llewellyn Publications, 2001.

Zim, Herbert S., and Alexander C. Martin. *Trees: A Guide to Familiar American Trees*. New York: Golden Press, 1987.

Zolar. *Zolar's Encyclopedia & Dictionary of Dreams*. New York: Fireside Books, 1992.

Index

To Write to the Author

If you wish to contact the author or would like more information about this book, please write to the author in care of Llewellyn Worldwide and we will forward your request. Both the author and publisher appreciate hearing from you and learning of your enjoyment of this book and how it has helped you. Llewellyn Worldwide cannot guarantee that every letter written to the author can be answered, but all will be forwarded. Please write to:

Sandra Kynes
℅ Llewellyn Worldwide
2143 Wooddale Drive, Dept. 0-7387-0781-3
Woodbury, MN 55125-2989, U.S.A.

Please enclose a self-addressed stamped envelope for reply,
or $1.00 to cover costs. If outside U.S.A., enclose
international postal reply coupon.

Many of Llewellyn's authors have websites with additional information and resources. For more information, please visit our website at:

http://www.llewellyn.com